On the Museum's Ruins

On the Museum's Ruins

Douglas Crimp
with photographs by Louise Lawler

The MIT Press   Cambridge, Massachusetts   London, England

This book was set in Bembo and Univers by DEKR Corp., Woburn, MA, and was printed and bound in the United States of America.

Published with the assistance of the Getty Grant Program.

Library of Congress Cataloging-in-Publication Data

Crimp, Douglas.
    On the museum's ruins / Douglas Crimp ; with photographs by
  Louise Lawler.
        p.   cm.
    Includes bibliographical references and index.
    ISBN 0-262-03209-0
    1. Art museums.   2. Art—Exhibition techniques.   3. Modernism
(Art).   4. Postmodernism.   5. Photography, Artistic.   6. Art and
photography.   7. Avant-garde (Aesthetics)—History—20th century.
I. Lawler, Louise.   II. Title.
N420.C75   1993
709′.04′5—dc20   93-22531
                                                              CIP

Contents

(Right)

La Halte devant l'auberge
de Philips Wouwerman,
dit aussi Wouwermans
Haarlem 1619–1668
Huile sur toile
Inv. 1942–30
Legs Guillaume Favre, Genève 1942

(Left)

Paysage (vers 1607)
de Roelond Jacobsz Savery
Born in Courtroi 1576
Died in Utrecht 1639
Huile sur bois
Inv. CR 144
Legs Gustave Revillod, Genève 1890

Preface and Acknowledgments

With the exception of the introduction, the essays in this book have appeared previously in journals and museum catalogues. The purpose of reprinting them here is twofold: to make their overall project comprehensible and to present them alongside the parallel photographic work of Louise Lawler. One governing idea of these essays is that an artwork's meaning is formed in relation to its institutional framing conditions, and I am here reframing my own critical work—in part, of course, on conventional principles: under the sign of authorship and with a view to thematic coherence. But by conceiving the book as a collaboration with Lawler, I hope to strain those conventions. Lawler's photographs—whether accompanying individual essays or positioned separately—are intended not simply to illustrate my ideas but to expand on and reorient them. Her photographic contributions are of three kinds: photographs made expressly to illustrate my essays, already existing photographs appropriated for my essays, and photographic works made for this project but not connected to particular essays. Illustrations not photographed by Lawler have been selected in consultation with her.

At the time I wrote these essays, I was an editor of the journal *October,* in whose pages a number of the essays appeared for the first time. Many of my positions were formulated within the terms of that journal's general project of bringing current theoretical concerns to bear on contemporary art practices. Several people associated with the journal were especially important to my intellectual development: in the early years, Craig Owens; later, Benjamin Buchloh, Rosalyn Deutsche, and Allan Sekula. Abigail Solomon-Godeau, Linda Nochlin, and Richard Serra and Clara Weyergraf-Serra offered support and sustenance along the way. In preparing this publication, my research assistant Cameron Fitzsimmons helped with photographs, bibliographic details, and preparing the index; the introduction profited from the advice of Michael Warner and that of Rosalyn Deutsche, who has been a constant source of help and friendship. Louise Lawler would like to thank Benjamin Buchloh for his editorial expertise and advice regarding her photographic contributions.

Most of these essays were tried out on academic and art-world listeners, and I am grateful to the many museums, art schools, and universities that invited me to lecture, most particularly the California Institute of the Arts and the Independent Study Program of the Whitney Museum of American Art, whose faculty members and students were especially challenging interlocutors on many occasions.

My initial research on museums was facilitated by a Chester Dale Fellowship from the Center for Advanced Study in the Visual Arts of the National Gallery of Art, a year's work in Berlin was made possible by an Art Critics Fellowship from the National Endowment for the Arts, and the publication of this book was assisted by the Getty Grant Program.

Client Lines

Free-standing, carpet-covered display
wall, auctioneer's podium, sculpture,
crowd control stanchion, pedestal,
small velvet-covered easel

Arranged by Donald Marron, Susan
Brundage, Cheryl Bishop at Paine
Webber, Inc., NYC, 1982

Introduction

Photographs at the End of Modernism

From the parochial perspective of the late-1970s art world, photography appeared as a watershed. Radically reevaluated, photography took up residence in the museum on a par with the visual arts' traditional mediums and according to the very same art-historical tenets. New principles of photographic connoisseurship were devised; the canon of master photographers was vastly expanded; prices on the photography market skyrocketed. Counterposed against this reevaluation were two coincident developments: a materialist history of photography and dissident photographic practices. My own view of these transformations was that, taken together and brought into relation, they could tell us something about postmodernism, a term coming into wide use at just that time.

But my first essay about photography proposed a modernist interpretation. Two years before writing "On the Museum's Ruins," I still wanted to discriminate between a "legitimately" modernist photographic practice and an "illegitimate" presumption that photography is, as a whole, a modernist aesthetic medium. I argued, in "Positive/Negative," that the few existing photographs by Edgar Degas, made around 1895, were about photography itself (the very notion—"photography itself"—would later seem preposterous to me). Degas accomplished this modernist self-reflexivity by making photography's negative-positive process manifest in the photographic print, for example by double printing or by employing the Sebatier-effect—a usually accidental effect of exposing the negative to extraneous light during the developing process, which results in a partial reversal of light and dark.

The final photograph I discussed was, however, a straightforward portrait of Degas's niece Odette. I described the little girl as photogenic, intending a play on the literal meaning of that word, wherein something—such as the lace Fox Talbot used to demonstrate the technique of a photogram in *The Pencil of Nature*—is itself purely positive-negative and therefore a suitable metaphor for the photographic process. The essay concludes,

Degas's photograph of Odette is replete with this kind of metaphor, with its lace backdrop, its patterned wallpaper, its illustrated newspaper. Odette herself wears a lace dress. This is a photograph of the photogenic, everything already resolved into black and white. Even Odette's cute smile is so resolved. She is at that age when children lose their baby teeth, and her smile reveals the gaps where two of her incisors are absent. The preponderance of lace in this photograph is a pun on that smile, for the French word for lace is *dentelle,* a diminutive form of the word *dent,* meaning tooth. So Odette's smile is indeed photogenic; already reduced to presence and absence, positive and negative, black and white, it is a wry metaphor for photography.[1]

I visited my family in Idaho the summer "Positive/Negative" was published, and my grandmother, then in her eighties, asked if she might read it. I couldn't imagine what she would make of it, because, although she was an educated woman, she certainly had no familiarity with modernist art theory or with the Derridian inflection—photography as a kind of Mallarméan writing—with which I attempted to imbue that theory. After she had read the article, she told me that she found it interesting, but that I had made a mistake: "That isn't a lace dress the little girl is wearing," she informed me, "it's eyelet embroidery" (not "little tooth," then, but "little eye").

Such a grandmotherly observation, I thought, thinking especially of my other grandmother, who was so adept at "women's work"—needlepoint, quilting, braiding rugs from old socks whose holes she'd previously darned. I don't remember if she ever made lace or embroidery. But whether lace or embroidery, I reassured myself, what's the difference? What matters is the *theory*. I realize now, though, that my self-defense in the face of my grandmother's correction arose not really because the comment was grandmotherly but because it reminded me of the sort of art historian who, when presented with a theoretical argument, repudiates it by citing trivial empirical mistakes. But my grandmother was not an art historian; her seeing was situated differently. Her recognition of the difference between lace and embroidery, a tooth and an eye, resulted from an expertise uncredited within the disciplinary dispute I imagined. It may be true that it matters little in this case whether lace or embroidery, but it matters much that my grandmother could see what I could not: it demonstrates that what any of us sees depends on our individual histories, our differently constructed subjectivities.

∽

Hanging on the wall behind me is a black-and-white photograph by Louise Lawler. Its subject is at first somewhat difficult to discern. The picture divides two-thirds of the way down; the upper part is mostly dark, but interspersed with lighter areas; the lower third is itself split in half, light above, dark below. The light stripe has a darker rectangle in the center on which one can read, close up, "Edgar DEGAS (1834–1917)/Danseuse au bouquet,/saluant sur la scène, vers 1878/Legs Isaac de Camando 1911." With this information we can more easily "see" the picture. It shows the lower center portion of a pastel by Degas in which we can make out a tutu, a ballerina's legs, a bouquet of flowers, and some reflections on a shiny stage floor. Below that is part of the picture's frame, with its engraved label, and below that the wall on which the picture hangs. The photograph presents a work by Degas, but re-presents it—

reframes it, crops it, and slides down to show its frame and the museum wall.

I've had this photograph since 1982, when, having paid in advance for 100 sheets of Lawler's *Documenta 7* stationery,[2] I asked Lawler if I might have a photograph instead. Knowing of my interest in Degas, she gave me this one. I came to think of the picture as neatly describing the trajectory of my writing, a trajectory that moved beyond discrete works of art to encompass their institutional framing conditions: from artwork to museum. But in thinking that, I missed the photograph's pun on "legs."

About the time I acquired this picture and began overlooking the "legs," Craig Owens published his essay "The Discourse of Others: Feminists and Postmodernism." There he criticized a number of theorists of postmodernism—himself among them—for "skirting" feminist content in readings of work by various women artists; included in his critique were my interpretations of photographs by Cindy Sherman and Sherrie Levine. Here is Owens on Levine:

When Sherrie Levine appropriates—literally takes—Walker Evans's photographs of the rural poor or, perhaps more pertinently, Edward Weston's photographs of his *son* Neil posed as a classical Greek torso, is she simply dramatizing diminished possibilities for creativity in an image-saturated culture, as is often repeated? Or is her refusal of authorship not in fact a refusal of the role of creator as "father" of his work, of the paternal rights assigned to the author by law? (This reading of Levine's strategies is supported by the fact that the images she appropriates are invariably images of the Other: women, nature, children, the poor, the insane. . . .)[3]

I had reason, at a later time, to consider a possible addition to Owens's parenthetical list of "others." For several years I had hanging in my bedroom Levine's series of Weston's photographs of his son Neil. On a number of occasions, a certain kind of visitor to my bedroom would ask, "Who's the kid in the photographs?"—generally with the implication that I was into child pornography. Wanting to counter that implication but unable easily to explain what those photographs meant to me, or at least what I thought they meant to me, I usually told a little white lie, saying only that they were pictures by a famous photographer of his son. I was thereby able to establish a credible reason for having the photos without having to explain postmodernism to someone I figured—given the nature of these encounters—wouldn't be particularly interested anyway.

But then I was forced to recognize that this question was not so naive as I'd assumed. The men in my bedroom were perfectly able to read—in Weston's posing, framing, and lighting the young Neil so as to render his body a classical sculpture—the long-established codes of homoeroticism. And in making the leap from those codes to the codes of kiddie-porn, they were stating no more than what was enacted, in the fall of 1989, as the law governing federal funding of art in the United States. That law—proposed by right-wing senator Jesse Helms in response to certain of Robert Mapplethorpe's photographs—implicitly equated homoeroticism with obscenity and with the sexual exploitation of children.[4]

In "Appropriating Appropriation," written in 1982 and reprinted in this collection, I compare Robert Mapplethorpe's classically posed photographs of nudes to Sherrie Levine's appropriations of Edward Weston's photographs of Neil. I attempt to distinguish between two forms of appropriation: Mapplethorpe's modernist appropriation of style—the classical style of Weston, for example—and Levine's postmodernist appropriation of material, the appropriation of Weston's actual pictures by simply rephotographing them. Mapplethorpe's appropriations, I argue, align him with a tradition of aesthetic mastery, simultaneously referring to that tradition and appearing to renew it, whereas Levine's work interrupts the discourse of mastery through the refusal to reinvent an image. Mapplethorpe's work, I contend, continues the tradition of museum art, whereas Levine's holds that tradition up to scrutiny.

Debates about contemporary art could no longer be the same, however, after the national furor over Mapplethorpe's photographs, initiated by the Corcoran Gallery's cancellation of *Robert Mapplethorpe: The Perfect Moment,* peaking in the passage of Helms's amendment to an NEA funding bill, and culminating momentarily in the acquittal, on charges of "pandering obscenity" and "the illegal use of a minor in nudity oriented materials," of the Cincinnati Contemporary Arts Center and its director for mounting the same exhibition.[5] What I failed to notice in 1982 was what Jesse Helms could not help but notice in 1989: that Mapplethorpe's work interrupts tradition in a way that Levine's does not. Whereas Weston's male nudes fit comfortably into a Western homosocial tradition, in which homoeroticism is incited only to be contained or disavowed, Mapplethorpe's pictures often depict eroticism as openly homosexual (a distinction that Helms's own amendment language paradoxically but strategically obscured).[6] Thus, whereas I saw Mapplethorpe's nudes only in the context of the other conventional genres of the artist's work—still lifes and portraits—Jesse Helms saw them in the context of the overtly homosexual images of Mapplethorpe's *X Portfolio.* The line that Mapplethorpe crossed, between the safely homosocial and the dangerously homosexual, was also a line between the aesthetics of traditional museum culture and the prerogatives of a self-defining gay subculture.

Although most of the "offending" pictures brought before the jury in Cincinnati were explicit S/M subjects from the *X Portfolio,* two were portraits of young children. One of these was a photograph of the naked young Jesse McBride, a picture whose innocence is obvious enough—and all the more so if we compare it to Weston's homoerotically charged pictures of Neil, taken when the boy was about the same age as Jesse McBride in Mapplethorpe's portrait. But this apparent innocence should alert us again to Helms's insistence on reading all of Mapplethorpe's pictures within the context of the artist's homosexuality. In the midst of the debates about legislative restrictions on the NEA, the *New York Times* quoted the senator as saying,

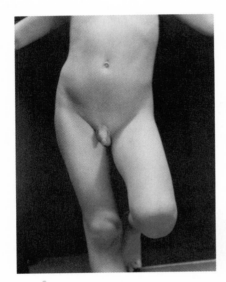

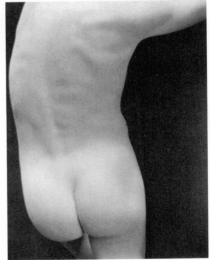

Sherrie Levine, *Untitled (After Edward Weston)*, 1981.

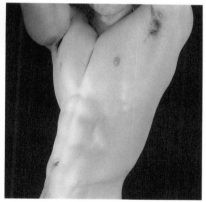

Robert Mapplethorpe, *Michael Reed*, 1987
(photo courtesy the Estate of Robert
Mapplethorpe).

Robert Mapplethorpe, *Charles*, 1985 (photo
courtesy the Estate of Robert
Mapplethorpe).

"Old Helms will win every time" on cutting Federal money for art projects with homosexual themes. "This Mapplethorpe fellow," said Mr. Helms, who pronounces the artist's name several ways, "was an acknowledged homosexual. He's dead now, but the homosexual theme goes throughout his work."[7]

The "scandal" of *Jesse McBride* is that it was taken by an openly gay man, a man who also took explicit pictures of "perverse" sex acts, a man who subsequently died of AIDS.

The Cincinnati prosecutors attempted to exploit Helms's contextualization by disallowing the contextualization I had urged in "Appropriating Appropriation": placing the offending photographs in relation to the exhibition as a whole, which would have allowed the jury to see classical nudes, still lifes, and a wide range of portraits.[8] Still, despite the prosecution's tactical success in isolating the photographs in question from Mapplethorpe's oeuvre, the defense won its case by reinscribing them within museum discourse. Expert witnesses for the defense—mostly museum officials—described Mapplethorpe's wider aesthetic preoccupations and detailed the photographs' "formal qualities," reducing them thereby to abstractions, lines and forms, light and shadow. Here is a description by Janet Kardon, *The Perfect Moment*'s curator, of Mapplethorpe's self-portrait in leather chaps and vest with a bull whip shoved up his rectum, which Kardon referred to as a "figure study":

The human figure is centered. The horizon line is two-thirds of the way up, almost the classical two-thirds to one-third proportions. The way the light is cast, so there's light all around the figure, it's very symmetrical, which is very characteristic of his flowers. . . . [9]

In a move that underscores the trial's many contradictions, the prosecution attempted to show that these very formal qualities could be deployed toward obscene ends. In Mapplethorpe's portrait of Jesse McBride, the child sits on the back of an overstuffed chair placed next to a refrigerator. Along the wall behind the chair, a molding intersects an electrical cord so as to form an arrow shape pointing, it could be said, in the direction of the boy's genitals. But when the prosecutor attempted to make this claim, the boy's mother simply remarked, "Refrigerators work by electricity."[10]

Evacuating meaning from Mapplethorpe's photographs was not, in any case, limited to confining them to the realm of pure formalism. Another kind of distortion was voiced at the Cincinnati trial by Robert Sobieszak, senior curator at the George Eastman House International Museum of Photography:

I would say they [the *X Portfolio* photographs] are works of art, knowing they are by Robert Mapplethorpe, knowing his intentions. They reveal in very strong, forceful ways a major concern of a creative artist . . . a troubled portion of his life that he was trying to come to grips with. It's that search for meaning, not unlike Van Gogh's.[11]

What is disclaimed here is Mapplethorpe's willing and active participation in a sexual subculture that we have no reason to believe he found "troubling" or was "trying to come to grips with."[12] Such a statement denies the subject's representation of his own sexual choices. By likening Mapplethorpe's work to that of Van Gogh—or, more accurately, to the Van Gogh of popular myth—Mapplethorpe's expression is rendered pathological; it thus achieves significance *because* of, rather than in spite of, its "troubling" subject matter.

So the line that Mapplethorpe's work crossed—between the aesthetics of museum culture and the prerogatives of a self-defining gay subculture—was redrawn to reinscribe the work safely within the museum. Although it was a successful tactical maneuver for the purposes of the obscenity trial, the aesthetic-merit defense made no case at all for the rights of sexual minorities to self-representation. At virtually no point in the widespread public debate about the censorship of artistic expression was anyone asked to speak on behalf of the subculture Mapplethorpe's work depicted and perhaps addressed.[13] And because Mapplethorpe had died of AIDS, he was unable to speak for himself.

∽

But what *is* that pun on "legs" in the Lawler photograph that hangs behind me? "Legs" is, of course, French for "bequest," and thus the label signals no more than what Lawler often captures in her "museum" photographs: those illusive indicators of an artwork's material history, something more than just what the artist portrayed, something less than a full account. But here, for the anglophone reader, Camando's legacy and the ballerina's legs linguistically combine in a sly hint about property and gender. To whom do these legs properly belong? Are they up for grabs? Lawler does not simply photograph the ballerina's legs, the legs Degas painted; she photographs the signs of a signifying system in which those legs are caught up.

And what of Jesse McBride's legs, or, more to the point, his little penis? Jesse Helms and the prosecutor in Cincinnati would have had us believe that the young boy's genitals are made the focus of all our attention. But the insinuation is dependent on something more than this particular photograph; it depends on placing the photograph in a broader representational matrix. In a piece for the Arts and Leisure section of the Sunday *New York Times,* Hilton Kramer wrote, "What one finds in many Mapplethorpe photographs is . . . so absolute and extreme a concentration on male sexual endowments that every other attribute of the human subject is reduced to insignificance. In these photographs, men are rendered as nothing but sexual—which is to say, homosexual—objects."[14] Without denying the homosexual specificity or even the "sexual objectification" of many of Mapplethorpe's photographs, I think we are nevertheless obliged to ask how it is that when a man is rendered as nothing but a sexual object, he thereby becomes a *homo*sexual object. Rendering the subject an object must be exclusively and unquestionably a male prerogative, for certainly when a woman is rendered nothing but a sexual object, we do not think of her, mutatis mutandis, as a lesbian object. Kramer assumes and underwrites a law of representation in which only a woman is properly a sexual object, the proper object of the male subject.[15]

How representation and subjectivity are explicitly and implicitly gendered has, of course, been the topic of feminist cultural work for nearly two decades; antihomophobic analysis has recently extended and complicated this feminist critique to include what is variously designated as sexuality (as distinct from gender), sexual orientation, or sexual object-choice.[16] The discussion of subjectivity in the essays that compose this book does not, however, comprehend these issues of sexual difference and sexuality; it is to that extent partial, in both senses of the word. When I wrote these essays, I understood the subject of representation in the traditional humanist sense as its *author,* standing in for universal *mankind,* and I wanted to displace that subject. I wanted to show that the creating subject was a fiction necessary to modern aesthetic understanding, and that what took its place in postmodern knowledge was the institution, if by institution we mean a discursive system. The museum is, in these essays, a figure for this system; at the same time it is shown to provide its cover: it installs the creating subject in its place.

᠊ᢙ᠊

My title essay outlines the book's project, a theory of postmodernism in the visual arts based on a Foucauldian archeology of the museum. It proposes that the modern epistemology of art is a function of art's seclusion in the museum, where art was made to appear autonomous, alienated, something apart, referring only to its own internal history and dynamics. As an instrument of art's reproduction, photography extended this idealism of art to a broader discursive dimension, an *imaginary* museum, a history of art. Photography itself, though, was excluded from the museum and art history because, virtually of necessity, it points to a world outside itself.

Thus, when photography is allowed entrance to the museum as an art among others, the museum's epistemological coherence collapses. The "world outside" is allowed in, and art's autonomy is revealed as a fiction, a construction of the museum. Although this discursive incoherence is what signals the advent of postmodernism, postmodernism is not only a matter of interpretive theory, it is also a matter of practice. What is at issue in "On the Museum's Ruins" is not merely the museum's long-postponed decision to admit the heterogeneity of photography but the fact that that heterogeneity is already *in* the museum, and represented as being there in Robert Rauschenberg's silkscreen works of the early 1960s. I designated those works postmodernist both because they expose that heterogeneity and because they do so by destroying the integrity of painting, hybridizing it, corrupting it with photographic images.

"On the Museum's Ruins" introduces a series of oppositions: postmodernism versus modernism, "archeology" versus art history, photography versus painting, hybridity versus integrity. In succeeding essays these oppositions are revised as, for example, a postmodernism of resistance versus a postmodernism of accommodation, materialist history versus historicism, practices versus works, contingency versus autonomy. Each essay performs a kind of balancing act, juxtaposing and interpreting—juxtaposing in order to interpret together—artworks, institutions, exhibitions, critical discourses, histories. The title essay's project is not so much realized as it is repeatedly reformulated. Throughout the decade during which these essays were written, cultural activity and the conditions of its production and reception changed rapidly, as did my own interests and positions. Although overlapping in their general concerns, the essays divide, more or less chronologically, according to three forms of critique, which correspond to the book's three sections: (1) the poststructuralist critique of authorship and authenticity, (2) the materialist critique of aesthetic idealism, and (3) the avant-garde critique of art's institutionalization.

Photography, a watershed—a watershed between modernism and postmodernism. Or so it seemed. The five essays composing the book's first section, "Photography in the Museum," were written between 1980 and 1982. Each seeks to bring into relation, with varying emphases, and with the purpose of theorizing a shift from modernism to postmodernism, the following phenomena: (1) the reclassification of photography as ipso facto an art form and its consequent "museumization," (2) the threat posed by photography's reclassification to the traditional modernist mediums and to the aesthetic theories that underwrite their primacy, and (3) the advent of new photographic practices that refuse the tenets of authorship and authenticity upon which photography is newly comprehended.

If modernist aesthetic theory and practice commence with the creation, during the early nineteenth century, of the museum as we know it, they also coincide with the invention of photography, whose mechanically determined images would haunt them. Painting, the principal museum art, developed throughout the modern period in antagonism to photography's descriptive powers, its wide dissemination, and its mass appeal. Isolated in the museum, painting increasingly shunned objective depiction, asserted its material uniqueness, became hermetic and difficult. It referred, according to formalist criticism, only to itself—"itself" indicating both its material essence and the self-enclosed history of the medium. But behind painting's self-referentiality, guaranteeing its particular meanings, stood the artist's subjectivity, for ultimately painting had to transcend its materiality and become human. The autonomy of art always defers, if only implicitly, to a prior autonomy, that of the sovereign human subject.

Photography could not so easily be granted such autonomy. More or less than an art form, banished from the museum except as an instrument, a tool, it pursued its course elsewhere, where its capacity for illustration and reproducibility could be usefully exploited—in journalism and advertising, in the physical sciences, in archeology and histories of art. Its meanings were secured not by a human subject but by the discursive structures in which it appeared. It referred not to itself or its own history but to a "world outside." But in spite of this, there were always photographers who lay claim to the artist's mantle. They imitated painting, manipulated prints, limited editions, foreswore utility, embraced artifice: in short, they invested their medium with the trappings of subjectivity, for which they were grudgingly granted a niche in the museum. As formalist theory took greater hold, however, it was not photography's imitation of painting that secured its place in the museum. Rather it was photography's fidelity to "itself." And thus, nearly 150 years after its invention in the 1830s, photography was *discovered,* discovered to have been art all the while. But what could this mean to the museum and to painting, which had hitherto resisted photography's allure?

This transition appeared to signal the reaffirmation, perhaps in bad faith, of the museum's founding premises and painting's self-confidence. The rhetoric of aesthetic autonomy and subjectivity was uneasily transferred to photography, while painting, in the guise of neoexpressionism, reclaimed its descriptive potential. Against this realignment, however, postmodern artists made other claims: that originality and authenticity are discursively produced by the museum; that subjective expression is an effect, not a source or guarantee, of aesthetic practices.

∽

If photography appeared to put the museum in crisis, it also appeared just in time to alleviate a crisis already felt. The economic recession of the mid-1970s shrank museums' operating and acquisition budgets, and photographs could be purchased, displayed, and loaned at far lower costs than could the museum's traditional objects. But the crisis was not merely economic; from the 1960s onward, contemporary art practices had strained the museum's resources not in monetary but in physical and ideological senses.

During the 1960s, minimal sculpture launched an attack on the prestige of both artist and artwork, granting that prestige instead to the situated spectator, whose self-conscious perception of the minimal object in relation to the site of its installation produced the work's meaning. The artist's own lowered prestige was exemplified by, but not limited to, the fact that minimal artworks were fabricated to specifications from readily available industrial materials. With the usual indicators of the artist's subjectivity in the craftsmanship of a work thus abandoned, the subjectivity experienced was the spectator's own. This condition of reception, in which meaning is made a function of the work's relationship to its site of exhibition, came to be known as site specificity, whose radicalism thus lay not only in the displacement of the artist-subject by the spectator-subject but in securing that displacement through the wedding of the artwork to a particular environment. The idealism of modernist art, in which the art object *in and of itself* was seen to have a fixed and transhistorical meaning, determined the object's placelessness, its belonging in no particular place, a no-place that was in reality the museum—the actual museum and the museum as a representation of the institutional system of circulation that also comprises the artist's studio, the commercial gallery, the collector's home, the sculpture garden, the public plaza, the corporate headquarters lobby, the bank vault. . . . Site specificity opposed that idealism—and unveiled the material system it obscured—by its refusal of circulatory mobility, its belongingness to a *specific* site.

But it is only the sense given to the word *specific* that would fully determine a break with modernism. For minimal sculptors, the interpolated context of the work of art generally resulted only in an extension of the aesthetic domain to the site itself. Even if the work could not be relocated from place to place, as is the case, for example, with earthworks, the materiality of the site was nevertheless taken to be generic—architecture, cityscape, landscape—and therefore neutral. It was only when artists recognized the site of art as *socially* specific that they began to oppose idealism with a materialism that was no longer phenomenologically—and thus still idealistically—grounded in matter or the body. This development, again intended as definitional for postmodernism, is taken up in my essay about Richard Serra's public sculpture, "Redefining Site Specificity." Of the essays here, it is the most explicitly Marxist in its interpretive framework.[17]

༤

Materialist history, especially as contemplated by Walter Benjamin, increasingly and perhaps paradoxically inflected the Foucauldian archeology of the museum that I initially proposed. The three essays in this book's final section employ these methods of historiography against the eclectic and revisionist historicism of an affirmative post-modernism. By the mid-1980s, postmodernism had come to be seen less as a critique of modernism than as a repudiation of modernism's own critical project, a perception that legitimized an "anything goes" pluralism. The term *postmodernism* described a situation in which both the present and the past could be stripped of any and all historical determinations and conflicts. Art institutions widely embraced this position, using it to reestablish art—even so-called postmodernist art—as autonomous, universal, timeless.

My response was to examine the institutions themselves, their representations of history and the ways their own history is repre-sented. Pursuing my earlier archeological project, I discovered that the museum's history was written much like art's, as a continuous evolution from ancient times. Locating the museum's origins in a universal impulse to collect and preserve mankind's aesthetic heri-tage, such history was unimpeded by knowledge that aesthetics is itself a modern invention and that collections differed vastly in their objects and classificatory systems at different historical junctures, up to and including the present. The three final essays take as their impetus, respectively, three "originary" institutions, the late Renais-sance *Wunderkammer,* the Fridericianum in Kassel, and Berlin's Altes Museum, not to uncover their true histories but to observe how they have been pressed into the service of contemporary museologi-cal historicism. What is at issue is the contemporary art of exhibi-tion: the construction of new museums and the expansion and

reorganization of existing ones to create a conflict-free representation of art history, and, concurrently, the effacement or co-optation
of current adversary art practices.

The question of adversary practices, the question of their relation to definitions and theories of postmodernism, is central to this
book. The "end" of the avant-garde, whether lamented by the Left
or gloated over by the Right, was generally seen as the condition of
postmodernism's possibility. I was skeptical. The practices I claimed
as postmodernist seemed to me to continue the unfinished avant-
garde project. Indeed, the prewar avant-garde appeared, through the
lens of a postmodernism critical of modernism, virtually as postmodernism *avant-la-lettre*. In this I both agreed with and differed
from Peter Bürger's *Theory of the Avant-Garde,* which makes a crucial distinction between modernist art—the autonomous art previously described—and the interventions of the avant-garde.
According to Bürger, with the advent of a fully modernist art for
art's sake, art's autonomy became institutionalized, whereupon the
avant-garde sought both to contest art-as-institution and to grant art
a social purpose:

The concept 'art as an institution'. . . refers to the productive and distribu-
tive apparatus and also to ideas about art that prevail at a given time and
that determine the reception of works. The avant-garde turns against
both—the distribution apparatus on which the work of art depends, and the
status of art in bourgeois society as defined by the concept of autonomy.
Only after art, in nineteenth-century Aestheticism, has altogether detached
itself from the praxis of life can the aesthetic develop "purely." But the
other side of autonomy, art's lack of social impact, also becomes recognizable. The avant-gardist protest, whose aim it is to reintegrate art into the
praxis of life, reveals the nexus between autonomy and the absence of any
consequences.

When the avant-gardistes demand that art become practical once again,
they do not mean that the contents of works of art should be socially signif-

icant. The demand is not raised at the level of the contents of individual works. Rather, it directs itself to the way art functions in society, a process that does as much to determine the effect that works have as does the particular content. . . . The avant-gardistes proposed the sublation of art—sublation in the Hegelian sense of the term: art was not to be simply destroyed, but transferred to the praxis of life where it would be preserved, albeit in a changed form.[18]

For Bürger, though, this is a *historical* project that failed: art's sublation into the praxis of life did not occur "and presumably cannot occur in bourgeois society unless it be as a false sublation of autonomous art."[19] The avant-garde's failure is recognizable in the recuperation of its interventions as autonomous works of art. This is the function of what Bürger calls the neo-avant-garde, which, in adopting avant-garde techniques in the aftermath of the original project's demise, "institutionalizes the *avant-garde as art* and thus negates genuinely avant-gardiste intentions."[20]

Bürger's view of the postwar avant-garde (his neo-avant-garde) differs significantly from mine.[21] As I see it, contemporary artists began, at about the same time Bürger published his book in Germany (the early 1970s), to learn and apply the very lessons of the historical avant-garde that Bürger theorizes. The challenge to art-as-institution is, if anything, more explicit in the work of, say, Marcel Broodthaers, Hans Haacke, or Louise Lawler than it is in the practices of dada and surrealism that Bürger cites. At the same time, the ability of the institution to co-opt and neutralize such challenges is also recognized, in both art and criticism. A number of my essays seek to reveal the falsifications necessary to forge an institutional history of modernism free of the conflicts posed by avant-garde art, whether historical or contemporary.

But there are problems that my own essays share with Bürger's position. Bürger locates the failure of the avant-garde in its inability to return art to social purpose and furthermore sees this failure as determined by the continuation of bourgeois hegemony.[22]

Similarly, my own essays limit the efficacy of postmodernist practice to a critique of art-as-institution, only intimating the apparently still-foreclosed possibility of art's integration into social practice. This would suggest—falsely I think—that revealing the institutionalization of art is not already a social practice with real consequences. More seriously, it suggests that art can only play a useful role in society once society itself has been thoroughly transformed, which assumes that art is merely reflective, not productive of social relations. Bürger's and my positions are both constrained by a vangardism central to modernism's own radical claims. In this sense, my theory of postmodernism is internally contradictory, positing both a rupture with modernism and a continuity of one of modernism's most salient features.

Bürger's commitment to vangardism is not limited to deferring the realization of art's practical potential to a revolutionary social order. It can be discerned, as well, in his unquestioning repetition of the Frankfurt School condemnation of popular culture. For Bürger, what he still calls the culture industry is the very antithesis of the avant-garde because it brings about "the false elimination of the distance between art and life."[23] Relying on the work of Walter Benjamin, my position is less rigid on this count, but my essays stop short of a necessary analysis of the postmodernist challenge to the uncompromising dist̲ ̲ ̲ ̲tion between "high" and "low" culture
̲ ̲ ̲ ̲ ̲ ̲ ntinuing to shore up that distinction.[24]

ᔕ

finally revealed to me the limits of
sm. By the time I completed the
ion ("This Is Not a Museum of Art,"
ctively involved in the grassroots
s. My engagement in direct-action
nt a break with the positions
rew out of an attempt to adapt
thetic responses to AIDS, which

New Museum,

in my view are divided between two distinct trends: what Bürger referred to as changes at the level of the contents of individual works and changes in the way art functions in society. The former trend includes traditional artworks that take AIDS as subject matter— paintings, plays, novels, poems "about" AIDS; the latter consists of cultural participation in activist politics, most often using agitprop graphics and documentary video.[25] Such work eludes the museum, not because it is never shown there but because it is made outside the institution's compass. Arising out of a collective movement, AIDS activist art practices articulate, actually *produce*, the politics of that movement. Often anonymously and collectively made; appropriating techniques of "high art," popular culture, and mass advertising; aimed at and constitutive of specific constituencies; relevant only to local and transitory circumstances; useless for preservation and posterity—is this art not an example of the "sublation of art into the praxis of life"?

Or perhaps the question should be, Is this not postmodern art? From the vantage point of these practices, postmodernism looks rather different from its theorization in this book. Indeed, I now think it would be more accurate to say of the essays published here that they are about the end of modernism. Contemporary art's critique of the museum and the modern aesthetic it produces still "belongs" to the museum, even if reluctantly, just as my analysis of those practices still engages with the problems of modernism. In "Mapping the Postmodern," Andreas Huyssen makes a similar point about the relation of poststructuralist theory to postmodernism:

I think we must begin to entertain the notion that rather than offering a *theory of postmodernity* and developing an analysis of contemporary culture, French theory provides us primarily with an *archeology of modernity,* a theory of modernism at the stage of its exhaustion. It is as if the creative powers of modernism had migrated into theory and come to full self-consciousness in the poststructuralist text—the owl of Minerva spreading its wings at the fall of dusk. Poststructuralism offers a theory of modernism characterized by *Nachträglichkeit,* both in the psychoanalytic and the historical sense.[26]

This is certainly true of my essays, as they are initially inspired by Foucault's early work, whose stated objective is an archeology of modernism. What follows from this realization is a shift in both the objects and methods of inquiry. Confronting aesthetic responses to AIDS, it is impossible to stay within the museum, and not only because the most forceful responses rarely appear there. AIDS activist art does not seek primarily to interrupt our notion of art itself but instead to intervene in a wider arena of representation: the mass media, medical discourse, social policy, community organizing, sexual identity. . . . Thus any attempt to assess and theorize this work will have to place it in relation not merely to aesthetics but to the full range of discourses it engages. Only a hybrid approach such as that of cultural studies—which proceeds locally, but against the grain of disciplinary knowledges; theoretically, but through a tension among competing theories—would seem suited to such a task.

The narrowness of focus in my essays on the practices and institutions of contemporary art entails a skepticism about totalizing postmodern theory, whereby every cultural act becomes some sort of symptom of a larger condition—fragmentation, schizophrenia, nostalgia, amnesia. What worried me most about such formulations was their suppression of difference and conflict, their inability to distinguish the critique from what is criticized. But my narrowness of focus also resulted in the parochialism, partiality, and vangardism I've already mentioned. Remaining within the world of high art, neglecting all forms of difference but those of aesthetic function, I was unable to comprehend the genuine significance of postmodernism as, precisely, the eruption of difference itself within the domains of knowledge. This is not the same thing as the collapse of coherence through heterogeneity and the incursions of the "world outside," but neither is it a surface condition or a cultural logic built upon an economic foundation.[27]

∽

In the fall of 1988, the Museum of Modern Art staged a major exhibition of Nicholas Nixon's photographs, including a new series of
portraits of people with AIDS (PWAs). Each portrait comprised a
chronological sequence of pictures taken at intervals of a few weeks
and was considered complete only when its subject had died. The
photographs enraged me. Everything I had objected to about photography in the museum was contained in these pictures and the
critical commentary that accompanied them: the fetishization of
technique (Nixon's "achievement" was said to lie in his use of an
old-fashioned view camera to rework the snapshot aesthetic); the
insistence on the artist's subjectivity at the expense of that of his
subjects (Nixon's theme was a grand and universal one, the myster-
ies of life and death);[28] and the obliteration of every type of social
relation that produced the images, from the interaction of photographer and subject to the failure of government to respond to an epidemic that disproportionately affected "marginal" populations.
What forced me to consider writing about these photographs,
though, was not that they posed anew the problem of photography
in the museum but that they so faithfully reproduced mass media
stereotypes about what are so callously called "AIDS victims": their
otherness, their isolation, their desperation, their inevitable decline
and death. Seeing what I saw, AIDS activists protested Nixon's
show and demanded different pictures: "PWAs who are vibrant,
angry, loving, sexy, beautiful, acting up and fighting back."[29]

But I had seen yet a different picture, Stashu Kybartas's video-
tape *Danny,* a loving portrait of a young gay man with AIDS, his
skin covered with Kaposi's sarcoma lesions, his face bloated from
chemotherapy, already dead when the tape was completed. In the
video's apostrophizing voice-over, Kybartas, who pictures himself,
too, mourns a man he clearly found sexually appealing. Seeing
Danny made obvious to me, by utter contrast, what Nixon's ugly
photographs had so perfectly—and so unconsciously—condensed

from media stereotypes: "These are not images that are intended to overcome our fear of disease and death, as is sometimes claimed. Nor are they meant only to reinforce the status of the PWA as victim or pariah, as we often charge. Rather, they are, precisely, *phobic* images, images of the terror at imagining the person with AIDS as still sexual."[30] I came to understand much more about Nixon's photographs than their possession by the museum, which transmutes documentary specificity into aesthetic generality. What I came to understand was that this transmutation constitutes a very particular and very significant social effect, that of inciting sexual fear and loathing while pretending to appeal to a common humanity.

The target of my critique of the museum is the formalism that it appeared inevitably to impose on art by removing it from any social context. But the critique itself is not entirely free of formalism, a formalism that substitutes the institution for the work of art, a vangardist formalism that cannot discern how changes "at the level of the contents of individual works" might in some cases lead to changes "in the way art functions in society," even when that art appears in a museum. A significant lesson of the controversy over Robert Mapplethorpe's photographs is that their social effects far exceeded their formal congruence with "art photography" and its insistence on the creative subject. What is occluded by the institution's emphasis on the subject *behind* representation is more than the historical, institutional structures that fabricate the creating subject; what is also, crucially, occluded is the gendered, sexually oriented, and otherwise designated subject effected by, constituted in representation through, those structures. If Hilton Kramer decried Mapplethorpe's "reduction" of the human subject to a sexual object, it was not, as he might think or might wish us to think, because the photographs thereby dehumanize their sitters; it was because Kramer, solicited as viewing subject of the photographs, found himself in the position of a man gazing at another man's genitals. And if Robert Sobieszak felt called upon to defend the *X Portfolio* pictures' search for meaning, it is not because Mapplethorpe was trying to come to

Robert Mapplethorpe, *Untitled*, 1981 (photo
courtesy the Estate of Robert
Mapplethorpe.

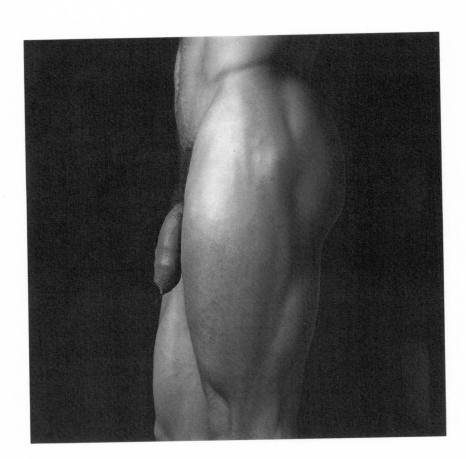

grips with a troubled portion of *his* life, but because Sobieszak, as viewer, found *himself* troubled. And finally, in a very different register indeed, if Kobena Mercer criticized Mapplethorpe's sexual objectification of *black* men—in Mercer's case, a critique grounded in, rather than disavowing, feminist theory—his complex revision of his initial criticism was impelled by the recognition of himself not only as the stereotyped object but also as the desiring subject of the representation.[31]

A genuinely postmodern critique of modernist formalism does not merely "move beyond discrete works of art to encompass their institutional framing conditions," as I imagined Louise Lawler's photograph illustrated of my own project. The institution does not exert its power only negatively—to remove the work of art from the praxis of life—but positively—to produce a specific social *relation* between artwork and spectator. Mapplethorpe's photographs do not abrogate that institutionally determined relation—which is why I compared them unfavorably with Sherrie Levine's postmodern appropriations. But they do take advantage of it, with the result not of rendering the depicted sitter a homosexual object but of momentarily rendering the male spectator a homosexual subject. And positions are occupied in the ensuing controversy as a function of our comfort in occupying this one.

∽

It is my hope that this book's critique of the museum provides a useful analysis of what might be called a discourse on the objects of knowledge. But there is another step that it does not take: an analysis of a discourse on the *subjects* of knowledge. This step is taken by Michel Foucault's work as it progresses from *The Order of Things* to *The History of Sexuality,* a trajectory that can also be characterized as progressing from an archeology of modernism toward a theory of postmodernism. The essays here are engaged with the former; my present concerns are with the latter. The dividing line is an epidemic that has claimed, among so many others, the life of Michel Foucault.

Notes

1. Douglas Crimp, "Positive/Negative: A Note on Degas's Photographs," *October,* no. 5 (Summer 1978), p. 100.

2. See "The Art of Exhibition," this volume.

3. Craig Owens, "The Discourse of Others: Feminists and Postmodernism," in *The Anti-Aesthetic: Essays on Postmodern Culture,* ed. Hal Foster (Port Townsend, Wash.: Bay Press, 1983), p. 73.

4. The compromise language of the notorious Helms amendment to the NEA/NEH appropriation bill stated, "None of the funds authorized to be appropriated for the National Endowment for the Arts or the National Endowment for the Humanities may be used to promote, disseminate, or produce materials which in the judgment of the National Endowment for the Arts or the National Endowment for the Humanities may be considered obscene, including but not limited to, depictions of sadomasochism, homo-eroticism, the sexual exploitation of children, or individuals engaged in sex acts and which, when taken as a whole, do not have serious literary, artistic, political or scientific value" (*Congressional Record—House,* 101st Congress, public law 101–121, October 23, 1989, p. H6407).

5. Among the best analyses of the issues at stake in these events are Carol Vance, "The War on Culture," *Art in America* 77, no. 9 (September 1989), pp. 39–43; and "Misunderstanding Obscenity," *Art in America* 78, no. 5 (May 1990), pp. 49–55.

6. I have written briefly of my failure of observation before, in "The Boys in My Bedroom," *Art in America* 78, no. 2 (February 1990), pp. 47–49. For an important account of the necessary distinction between homoeroticism and overt homosexuality in Western tradition and in contemporary debates about the canon, see Eve Kasofsky Sedgwick, *Epistemology of the Closet* (Berkeley and Los Angeles: University of California Press, 1990), esp. pp. 48–59.

7. Maureen Dowd, "Jesse Helms Takes No-Lose Position on Art," *New York Times,* July 28, 1989, p. B6.

8. In one of many biased rulings, Judge David J. Albanese refused the defense's motion to have the photographs at issue seen in relation to the whole exhibition. This was particularly damaging, since one can only prove obscenity, according to the Supreme Court's 1973 *Miller v. California* decision, if the work, *taken as a whole,* appeals to prurient interest. See Vance, "Misunderstanding Obscenity."

9. Quoted in Jayne Merkel, "Art on Trial," *Art in America* 78, no. 12 (December 1990), p. 47.

10. Quoted in ibid., p. 49.

11. Quoted in ibid., p. 47.

12. Compare the criticism of Mapplethorpe, made much earlier, by photography critic Ben Lifson: "I don't care who Mapplethorpe photographs. Every photographer has to depict or describe the milieu which fascinates him most. You've got to go where your passion lies, where your feelings are most in conflict. But Mapplethorpe's feelings are glossed over. There is no feeling in that work. Common sense tells us that those situations are charged with conflict" (Ben Lifson and Abigail Solomon-Godeau, "Photophilia," *October,* no. 16 [Spring 1981], p. 111).

13. The single exception that I know of, outside the gay press, of course, was the invitation—following my suggestion—of Gayle Rubin to speak at a symposium on Mapplethorpe organized by the Institute of Contemporary Art in Boston in the fall of 1990. Rubin is an active participant in the gay and lesbian S/M subculture in San Francisco, has published on the subject, and has long been at work on a doctoral dissertation on gay male S/M practices.

14. Hilton Kramer, "Is Art above the Laws of Decency?" *New York Times,* July 2, 1989, section 2, p. 7.

15. Allan Sekula makes this point by contrasting Kramer's attack on Mapplethorpe with his approval of a work by Gaston Lachaise: "We can find a similar reduction of the female subject to breasts and vagina in the work of Lachaise (*Breasts with Female Organ Between,* 1930–1932). Kramer argued, however, that 'even at his most extreme moments of expressiveness in dealing with the female figure, Lachaise conveys a sense of complete and unstrained mastery in realizing his sensations.' Kramer's notions of subjectivity seem to be quite gender-specific. Lachaise, of course can be claimed for a 'vitalist ideal' while Mapplethorpe stands condemned for 'social pathology'" (Allan Sekula, "Some American Notes," *Art in America* 78, no. 2 (February 1990), p. 43.

16. Of course, feminism is concerned with sexuality, and antihomophobic analysis must take account of questions of gender; nevertheless, it has been persuasively argued that the two forms of inquiry need to be conceptualized separately. See Gayle Rubin, "Thinking Sex: Notes for a Radical Theory of the Politics of Sexuality," in *Pleasure and Danger: Exploring Female Sexuality,* ed. Carole S. Vance (Boston: Routledge & Kegan Paul, 1984), pp. 287–319; and Sedgwick, *Epistemology,* esp. pp. 27–35.

17. The Museum of Modern Art, which had commissioned my essay for the catalogue of its Serra exhibition, reacted very strongly against the Marxist interpretation. Knowing that Serra supported the essay, however, and wanting to avoid controversy after the recent debacle over the decision by federal authorities to destroy Serra's *Tilted Arc,* the museum was in no position to refuse the text. In his catalogue preface, William Rubin, then Director of the Museum's Department of Painting and Sculpture, wrote, "Given the extraordinary circumstances of last spring's hearing on the fate of *Tilted Arc* and the outpouring of comment it occasioned, we felt it appropriate that the artist's position on these matters should be represented in the catalog in the way he personally deemed most effective. The Museum of Modern Art disagrees with the rhetorical tone and historical polemic of much that has been written about *Tilted Arc,* here as elsewhere. Yet, however differently our curators would argue for Serra's position, we have chosen, at an exceptionally embattled moment in the artist's career, to air this debate in the fashion he and his guest curator requested—thereby fulfilling one of the Museum's roles, as a forum for the widely differing ideas and opinions that give dynamism to public dialogue on the art of our time" ("Preface," *Richard Serra/Sculpture,* [New York: Museum of Modern Art, 1986], pp. 9–10). Needless to say, the position argued in my essay is my own, not Serra's or guest curator Rosalind Krauss's; nor was the particular argument requested as such by them. And since the museum's initial impulse was to refuse my text altogether or to force me to change it beyond recognition, it is the height of hypocrisy for Rubin to assert the museum's liberal role in providing a forum for differing ideas and opinions.

18. Peter Bürger, *Theory of the Avant-Garde,* trans. Michael Shaw (Minneapolis: University of Minnesota, 1984), pp. 22 and 49.

19. Ibid., p. 54.

20. Ibid., p. 58; see also footnote 4, p. 109.

21. Bürger, a literary critic, published *Theory of the Avant-Garde* in Germany in 1974, before much of the art discussed in my essays was well known or even produced.

22. Bürger nods to the greater potential of the Soviet avant-garde in the building of a socialist society; see Bürger, *Theory of the Avant-Garde*, footnote 21, p. 114.

23. Ibid., p. 50.

24. The most telling example of the museum's failure to reexamine its assumptions regarding the high art/popular culture divide was *High and Low: Modern Art and Popular Culture,* organized for the Museum of Modern Art in the fall of 1990 by Kirk Varnedoe and Adam Gopnik. The premise of the exhibition was simple: artists sometimes transform aspects of popular and mass culture into high art, just as they transform "primitive" art into high Western expression. *High and Low* was quite uniformly condemned in the press for its simple-minded thesis and for its wholesale exclusion of contemporary practices that break down the distinctions the museum so unthinkingly reiterated. Introducing a series of art historical essays on the subject of high and low in a companion volume to the exhibition catalogue, Varnedoe and Gopnik summarily dismiss the entire range of serious thinking about their subject, from Frankfurt School mass culture and aesthetic theory and

the cultural studies initiated during the 1960s at Birmingham to disparate contemporary feminist and postmodernist analyses: "Although an enormous body of writing about 'mass culture' and the avant-garde already existed, this corpus seemed disproportionately weighted by the work of commissars and scholiasts. The pronouncements of the theorists appeared all too frequently to be engaged, at best, in the skillful juggling of abstract concepts; and seemed, at worst, to insist on imposing dogmatic, narrow, and historically untenable (not to say untestable) categories on the complex realities of modern history" ("Introduction," in Kirk Varnedoe and Adam Gopnik, *Modern Art and Popular Culture: Readings in High & Low* [New York, Museum of Modern Art and Harry N. Abrams, 1990], p. 11. Scanning the book's index turns up not a single name in a list of writers one might expect to find: Theodor Adorno, Max Horkheimer, Walter Benjamin, Raymond Williams, Stuart Hall, Dick Hebdige, Laura Mulvey, Griselda Pollock, Meagan Morris, etc.

25. See Douglas Crimp, ed., *AIDS: Cultural Analysis/Cultural Activism* (Cambridge, Mass.: The MIT Press, 1988); and Douglas Crimp, with Adam Rolston, *AIDS Demo Graphics* (Seattle, Bay Press, 1990).

26. Andreas Huyssen, "Mapping the Postmodern," in *After the Great Divide: Modernism, Mass Culture, Postmodernism* (Bloomington and Indianapolis: Indiana University Press, 1986), p. 209.

27. I am referring to the foundationalist totalizing theory of postmodernism propounded most influentially by Fredric Jameson (*Postmodernism or The Cultural Logic of Late Capitalism* [Durham, N.C.: Duke University Press, 1991]) and to a book heavily indebted to Jameson's work: David Harvey, *The Condition of Postmodernity: An Enquiry into the Origins of Cultural Change* (Oxford: Basil Blackwell, 1989). For feminist critiques of these works, see Rosalyn Deutsche, "Men in Space," *Artforum* 28, no. 6 (February 1990), pp. 21–23; Rosalyn Deutsche, "Boys Town," *Environment and Planning D: Society and Space* 9, no. 1 (March 1991), pp. 5–30; Doreen Massey, "Flexible Sexism," *Environment and Planning D: Society and Space* 9, no. 1 (March 1991), pp. 31–57; Meaghan Morris, "The Man in the Mirror: David Harvey's 'Condition' of Postmodernity," *Theory, Culture & Society* 9 (1992), pp 253–279; Gillian Rose, review of Edward Soja's *Postmodern Geographies* and David Harvey's *The Condition of Postmodernity*, *Journal of Historical Geography* 17 (1991), pp. 118–121.

28. See Peter Galassi, *Nicholas Nixon: Pictures of People* (New York: Museum of Modern Art, 1988).

29. Quoted from the flier handed out at ACT UP's demonstration at the Museum of Modern Art, October 1988.

30. Douglas Crimp, "Portraits of People with AIDS," in *Cultural Studies*, ed. Lawrence Grossberg, Cary Nelson, and Paula Treichler (New York: Routledge, 1991), p. 130.

31. Kobena Mercer, "Skin Head Sex Thing," in *How Do I Look? Queer Film and Video*, ed. Bad Object Choices (Seattle: Bay Press, 1991), pp. 169–210.

PARIS NEW YORK ROME TOKYO

Once There Was a Little Boy and
Everything Turned Out Alright,
THE END

Salon Hodler, 1992

Edward Ruscha
Dreams #1, 1987
Acrylic on paper, 17 × 46"

To 420 from artist 3/14/89
To Thaddeus Ropac, Salzburg "Freud"
5/2/89
To Castelli Gallery, 578 Broadway, for
group drawing exhibit 9/26/89
Purchased by Leo Castelli 9/28/89
To LC apt 1/22/90

Roy Lichtenstein
Ball of Twine, 1963
Pencil and tusche on paper, 15 × 12½"

Gift to Leo Castelli from the artist 6/64
To LC apartment 6/24/64
To Philadelphia Museum for exhibit
(6/63–9/65)
To LC apartment 10/5/65
To Pasadena Museum (first museum retro-
spective 4/18–5/28/67), travels
To Walker Art Center (6/23–7/30/67)
To Stedelijk Museum, Amsterdam (10/5/67)
To LC apt 6/26/68
To Guggenheim Museum (first museum
retrospective in New York), travels
To Nelson Gallery of Art, Kansas City;
Seattle Art Museum; Columbus Gallery of
Fine Arts; and Museum of Contemporary
Art, Chicago
To LC apt 12/9/70
To Centre National d'Art Contemporaine,

Paris, retrospective drawing exhibition,
"Dessins sans bande," travels to National-
galerie, Staatliche Museen Preussischer
Kulturbesitz, Berlin
To Ohio State University 10/21/75
To Metropolitan Museum & Arts Center,
Miami 2/17/76
To LC apt 5/8/79
To MOMA "In Honor of Toiny Castelli:
Drawings from the Toiny, Leo and
Jean-Cristophe Castelli Collection"
(4/6–7/17/88)
To LC apt 1/24/89
To Guild Hall, East Hampton, "A View from
the Sixties: Selections from the Leo Castelli
Collection and the Michael and Ileana
Sonnabend Collection" (8/10–9/22/91)
To LC apt 10/29/91

Reception Area

Photography in the Museum

On the Museum's Ruins

> The German word *museal* [museumlike] has unpleasant overtones. It describes objects to which the observer no longer has a vital relationship and which are in the process of dying. They owe their preservation more to historical respect than to the needs of the present. Museum and mausoleum are connected by more than phonetic association. Museums are the family sepulchers of works of art.
>
> Theodor W. Adorno, "Valéry Proust Museum"

Reviewing the installation of nineteenth-century art in the Metropolitan Museum's new André Meyer Galleries, Hilton Kramer derided the inclusion of salon painting. Characterizing that painting as silly, sentimental, and impotent, Kramer went on to assert that, had the reinstallation been done a generation earlier, such pictures would have remained in the museum's storerooms, to which they had once so justly been consigned:

It is the destiny of corpses, after all, to remain buried, and salon painting was found to be very dead indeed.

But nowadays there is no art so dead that an art historian cannot be found to detect some simulacrum of life in its moldering remains. In the last decade, there has, in fact, arisen in the scholarly world a powerful subprofession that specializes in these lugubrious disinterments.[1]

Kramer's metaphors of death and decay in the museum recall Adorno's essay, in which the opposite but complementary experiences of Valéry and Proust at the Louvre are analyzed, except that Adorno insists upon this *museal* mortality as a necessary effect of an institution caught in the contradictions of its culture and therefore extending to every object contained there.[2] In contrast, Kramer, retaining his faith in the eternal life of masterpieces, ascribes the conditions of life and death not to the museum or the particular history of which it is an instrument but to the artworks themselves, their autonomous quality threatened only by the distortions that a particular misguided installation might impose. He therefore wishes to explain "this curious turnabout that places a meretricious little picture like Gérôme's *Pygmalion and Galatea* under the same roof with masterpieces on the order of Goya's *Pepito* and Manet's *Woman with a Parrot.* What kind of taste is it—or what standard of values—that can so easily accommodate such glaring opposites?"

The answer is to be found in that much-discussed phenomenon—the death of modernism. So long as the modernist movement was understood to be thriving, there could be no question about the revival of painters like Gérôme or Bouguereau. Modernism exerted a moral as well as an aesthetic authority that precluded such a development. But the demise of modernism has left us with few, if any, defenses against the incursions of debased taste. Under the new post-modernist dispensation, anything goes. . . .

It is as an expression of this post-modernist ethos . . . that the new installation of 19th-century art at the Met needs . . . to be understood. What we are given in the beautiful André Meyer Galleries is the first comprehensive account of the 19th century from a post-modernist point of view in one of our major museums.[3]

We have here an example of Kramer's moralizing cultural conservatism disguised as progressive modernism. But we also have an interesting estimation of the museum's discursive practice during the

Installation of paintings by Eduoard Manet
in the André Meyer Galleries, Metropolitan
Museum of Art, 1982 (photo Louise
Lawler).

period of modernism and its present transformation. Kramer's analysis fails, however, to take into account the extent to which the museum's claims to represent art coherently have already been opened to question by the practices of contemporary—postmodernist—art.

One of the first applications of the term *postmodernism* to the visual arts occurs in Leo Steinberg's "Other Criteria" in the course of a discussion of Robert Rauschenberg's transformation of the picture surface into what Steinberg calls a "flatbed," referring, significantly, to a printing press.[4] This flatbed picture plane is an altogether new kind of picture surface, one that effects, according to Steinberg, "the most radical shift in the subject matter of art, the shift from nature to culture."[5] That is to say, the flatbed is a surface that can receive a vast and heterogeneous array of cultural images and artifacts that had not been compatible with the pictorial field of either premodernist or modernist painting. (A modernist painting, in Steinberg's view, retains a "natural" orientation to the spectator's vision, which the postmodernist picture abandons.) Although Steinberg, writing in 1968, did not have a precise notion of the far-reaching implications of the term *postmodernism,* his reading of the revolution implicit in Rauschenberg's art can be both focused and extended by taking his designation seriously.

Steinberg's essay suggests important parallels with the "archeological" enterprise of Michel Foucault. Not only does the term *postmodernism* imply the foreclosure of what Foucault would call the episteme, or archive, of modernism, but even more specifically, by insisting on the radically different kinds of picture surfaces upon which different kinds of data can be accumulated and organized, Steinberg selects the very figure that Foucault employed to represent the incompatibility of historical periods: the tables on which their knowledge is formulated. Foucault's archeology involved the replacement of such unities of historicist thought as tradition, influence, development, evolution, source, and origin with concepts such as discontinuity, rupture, threshold, limit, and transformation.

Thus, in Foucauldian terms, if the surface of a Rauschenberg painting truly involves the kind of transformation Steinberg claims it does, then it cannot be said to evolve from or in any way be continuous with a modernist painting surface.[6] And if Rauschenberg's flatbed pictures are experienced as producing such a rupture or discontinuity with the modernist past, as I believe they do and as I think do the works of many other artists of the present, then perhaps we are indeed experiencing one of those transformations in the epistemological field that Foucault describes. But it is not, of course, only the organization of knowledge that is unrecognizably transformed at certain moments in history. New institutions of power as well as new discourses arise; indeed, the two are interdependent. Foucault analyzed modern institutions of confinement—the asylum, the clinic, and the prison—and their respective discursive formations—madness, illness, and criminality. There is another such institution of confinement awaiting archeological analysis—the museum —and another discipline—art history. They are the preconditions for the discourse that we know as modern art. And Foucault himself suggested the way to begin thinking about this analysis.

༄

The beginning of modernism is often located in Manet's work of the early 1860s, in which painting's relationship to its art-historical precedents was made shamelessly obvious. Titian's *Venus of Urbino* is meant to be as recognizable a vehicle for the picture of a modern courtesan in Manet's *Olympia* as is the unmodeled pink paint that composes her body. Just one hundred years after Manet thus rendered painting's relationship to its sources self-consciously problematic,[7] Rauschenberg made a series of pictures using images of Velázquez's *Rokeby Venus* and Rubens's *Venus at Her Toilet*. But Rauschenberg's references to old-master paintings are effected entirely differently from Manet's; whereas Manet duplicated the pose, composition, and certain details of the original in a painted transformation, Rauschenberg simply silkscreened photographic

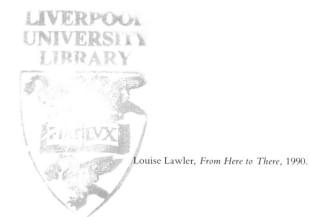

Louise Lawler, *From Here to There*, 1990.

reproductions of the originals onto surfaces that might also contain such images as trucks and helicopters. If trucks and helicopters did not find their way onto the surface of *Olympia,* it was obviously not only because such products of the modern age had not yet been invented; it was also because the structural coherence that made an image-bearing surface legible as a picture at the threshold of modernism differs radically from the pictorial logic that obtains at the beginning of postmodernism. Just what it is that constitutes the particular logic of a Manet painting is suggested by Foucault in an essay about Flaubert's *Temptation of St. Anthony:*

Déjeuner sur l'Herbe and *Olympia* were perhaps the first "museum" paintings, the first paintings in European art that were less a response to the achievement of Giorgione, Raphael and Velázquez than an acknowledgment (supported by this singular and obvious connection, using this legible reference to cloak its operation) of the new and substantial relationship of painting to itself, as a manifestation of the existence of museums and the particular reality and interdependence that paintings acquire in museums. In the same period, *The Temptation* was the first literary work to comprehend the greenish institutions where books are accumulated and where the slow and incontrovertible vegetation of learning quietly proliferates. Flaubert is to the library what Manet is to the museum. They both produced works in a self-conscious relationship to earlier paintings or texts—or rather to the aspect in painting or writing that remains indefinitely open. They erect their art within the archive. They were not meant to foster the lamentations—the lost youth, the absence of vigor, and the decline of inventiveness—through which we reproach our Alexandrian age, but to unearth an essential aspect of our culture: every painting now belongs within the massive surface of painting and all literary works are confined to the indefinite murmur of writing.[8]

At a later point in the essay, Foucault says that "*Saint Anthony* seems to summon *Bouvard and Pécuchet,* at least to the extent that the latter stands as its grotesque shadow." If *The Temptation* points to the library as the generator of modern literature, then *Bouvard and Pécuchet* fingers it as the dumping ground of an irredeemable classical culture. *Bouvard and Pécuchet* is a novel that systematically parodies the inconsistencies, the irrelevancies, the foolishness of received ideas in the mid-nineteenth century. Indeed, a "Dictionary of Received Ideas" was to make up part of a second volume of Flaubert's last, unfinished novel.

Bouvard and Pécuchet is the narrative of two loony Parisian bachelors who, at a chance meeting, discover between themselves a profound sympathy and also learn that they are both copy clerks. They share a distaste for city life and particularly for their fate of sitting behind desks all day. When Bouvard inherits a small fortune, the two buy a farm in Normandy to which they retire, expecting there to meet head-on the reality that was denied them in the half-life of their Parisian offices. They begin with the notion that they will farm their farm, at which they fail miserably. From agriculture they move to the more specialized field of arboriculture. Failing that, they decide on garden architecture. To prepare themselves for each new profession, they consult various manuals and treatises, in which they are perplexed to find contradictions and misinformation of all kinds. The advice they read is either confusing or utterly inapplicable; theory and practice never coincide. Undaunted by their successive failures, however, they move on inexorably to the next activity, only to find that it too is incommensurate with the texts that purport to represent it. They try chemistry, physiology, anatomy, geology, archeology—the list goes on. When they finally succumb to the fact that the knowledge they've relied on is a mass of haphazard contradictions quite disjunct from the reality they'd sought to confront, they revert to their initial task of copying. Here is one of Flaubert's scenarios for the end of the novel:

They copy papers haphazardly, everything they find, tobacco pouches, newspapers, posters, torn books, etc. (real items and their imitations. Typical of each category).

Then, they feel the need for a taxonomy, they make tables, antithetical oppositions such as "crimes of the kings and crimes of the people."—blessings of religion, crimes of religion. Beauties of history, etc.; sometimes, however, they have real problems putting each thing in its proper place and suffer great anxieties about it.

—Onward! Enough speculation! Keep on copying! The page must be filled. Everything is equal, the good and the evil. The farcical and the sublime—the beautiful and the ugly—the insignificant and the typical, they all become an exaltation of the statistical. There are nothing but facts—and phenomena.

Final bliss.[9]

In an essay about *Bouvard and Pécuchet,* Eugenio Donato argues persuasively that the emblem for the series of heterogeneous activities of the two bachelors is not, as Foucault and others have claimed, the library-encyclopedia, but rather the museum. This is not only because the museum is a privileged term in the novel itself but also because of the absolute heterogeneity the museum gathers together. It contains everything the library contains, and it contains the library as well:

If Bouvard and Pécuchet never assemble what can amount to a library, they nevertheless manage to constitute for themselves a private museum. The museum, in fact, occupies a central position in the novel; it is connected to the characters' interest in archeology, geology, and history and it is thus through the *Museum* that questions of origin, causality, representation, and symbolization are most clearly stated. The *Museum,* as well as the questions it tries to answer, depends upon an archeological epistemology. Its representational and historical pretensions are based upon a number of metaphysical assumptions about origins—archeology intends, after all, to be a science of the *archēs*. Archeological origins are important in two ways: each archeological artifact has to be an original artifact, and these original artifacts must in turn explain the "meaning" of a subsequent larger history. Thus, in Flaubert's caricatural example, the baptismal font that Bouvard and Pécuchet discover has to be a Celtic sacrificial stone, and Celtic culture has in turn to act as an original master pattern for cultural history.[10]

Bouvard and Pécuchet derive from the few stones that remain from the Celtic past not only all of Western culture but the "meaning" of that culture as well. Those menhirs lead them to construct the phallic wing of their museum:

In former times, towers, pyramids, candles, milestones and even trees had a phallic significance, and for Bouvard and Pécuchet everything became phallic. They collected swing-poles of carriages, chair-legs, cellar bolts, pharmacists' pestles. When people came to see them they would ask: "What do you think that looks like?" then confide the mystery, and if there were objections, they shrugged their shoulders pityingly.[11]

Even in this subcategory of phallic objects, Flaubert maintains the heterogeneity of the museum's artifacts, a heterogeneity that defies the systematization and homogenization that knowledge demanded.

The set of objects the *Museum* displays is sustained only by the fiction that they somehow constitute a coherent representational universe. The fiction is that a repeated metonymic displacement of fragment for totality, object to label, series of objects to series of labels, can still produce a representation which is somehow adequate to a nonlinguistic universe. Such a fiction is a result of an uncritical belief in the notion that ordering and classifying, that is to say, the spatial juxtaposition of fragments, can produce a representational understanding of the world. Should the fiction disappear, there is nothing left of the *Museum* but "bric-a-brac," a heap of meaningless and valueless fragments of objects which are incapable of substituting themselves either metonymically for the original objects or metaphorically for their representations.[12]

This view of the museum is what Flaubert figures through the comedy of *Bouvard and Pécuchet*. Founded on the disciplines of archeology and natural history, both inherited from the classical age, the museum was a discredited institution from its very inception. And the history of museology is a history of the various attempts to deny the heterogeneity of the museum, to reduce it to a homogeneous system or series. The faith in the possibility of ordering the museum's "bric-a-brac," echoing that of Bouvard and Pécuchet, persists until today. Reinstallations such as that of the Metropolitan's nineteenth-century collection in the André Meyer Galleries, particularly numerous throughout the 1970s and the 1980s, are testimonies to that faith. What so alarmed Hilton Kramer is that the criterion for determining the order of aesthetic objects in the museum throughout the era of modernism—the "self-evident" quality of masterpieces—has been abandoned, and as a result "anything goes." Nothing could testify more eloquently to the fragility of the museum's claims to represent anything coherent at all.

∽

In the period following World War II, the greatest monument to the museum's mission is André Malraux's *Museum without Walls*. If *Bouvard and Pécuchet* is a parody of received ideas in the mid-nineteenth century, the *Museum without Walls* is the hyperbolic expression of such ideas in the mid-twentieth. The claims that Malraux exaggerates are those of "art history as a humanistic discipline."[13] For Malraux finds in the notion of style the ultimate homogenizing principle, indeed the essence of art, hypostatized, interestingly enough, through the medium of photography. Any work of art that can be photographed can take its place in Malraux's supermuseum. But photography not only secures the admittance of various objects, fragments of objects, details of objects to the museum, it is also the organizing device: it reduces the now even vaster heterogeneity to a single perfect similitude. Through photographic reproduction a cameo takes up residence on the page next to a painted tondo or a sculpted relief; a detail of a Rubens in Antwerp is compared to that of a Michelangelo in Rome. The art historian's slide lecture and the art history student's slide comparison exam inhabit the museum without walls. In a recent example provided by one of our eminent art historians, the oil sketch for a small detail of a cobblestone street in *Paris—A Rainy Day,* painted in the 1870s by Gustave Caillebotte, occupies the left-hand screen while a painting by Robert Ryman from the *Winsor* series of 1966 occupies the right, and presto! they are revealed to be one and the same.[14] But precisely what kind of knowledge is it that this artistic essence, style, can provide? Here is Malraux:

In our Museum Without Walls, picture, fresco, miniature, and stained-glass window seem of one and the same family. For all alike—miniatures, frescoes, stained glass, tapestries, Scynthian plaques, pictures, Greek vase paintings, "details" and even statuary—have become "color-plates." In the process they have lost their properties as *objects;* but, by the same token, they have gained something: the utmost significance as to *style* that they can possibly acquire. It is hard for us clearly to realize the gulf between the performance of an Aeschylean tragedy, with the instant Persian threat and Salamis looming across the Bay, and the effect we get from reading it; yet, dimly albeit, we feel the difference. All that remains of Aeschylus is his genius. It is the same with figures that in reproduction lose both their original significance as objects and their function (religious or other); we see them only as works of art and they bring home to us only their makers' talent. We might almost call them not "works" but "moments" of art. Yet diverse as they are, all these objects . . . speak for the same endeavor; it is as though an unseen presence, the spirit of art, were urging all on the same quest. . . . Thus it is that, thanks to the rather specious unity imposed by photographic reproduction on a multiplicity of objects, ranging from the statue to the bas-relief, from bas-reliefs to seal-impressions, and from these to the plaques of the nomads, a "Babylonian style" seems to emerge as a real entity, not a mere classification—as something resembling, rather, the life-story of a great creator. Nothing conveys more vividly and compellingly the notion of a destiny shaping human ends than do the great styles, whose evolutions and transformations seem like long scars that Fate has left, in passing, on the face of the earth.[15]

All of the works that we call art, or at least all of them that can be submitted to the process of photographic reproduction, can take their place in the great superoeuvre, art as ontology, created not by men and women in their historical contingencies but by Man in his very being. This is the comforting "knowledge" to which the *Museum without Walls* gives testimony. And concomitantly, it is the deception to which art history is most deeply, if often unconsciously, committed.

But Malraux makes a fatal error near the end of his *Museum:* he admits within its pages the very thing that had constituted its homogeneity; that thing is, of course, photography. So long as photography was merely a *vehicle* by which art objects entered the imaginary museum, a certain coherence obtained. But once photography itself enters, an object among others, heterogeneity is reestablished at the heart of the museum; its pretensions to knowledge are doomed. For even photography cannot hypostatize style from a photograph.

∽

In Flaubert's "Dictionary of Received Ideas" the entry under "Photography" reads, "Will make painting obsolete. (See Daguerreotype.)" And the entry for "Daguerreotype" reads, in turn, "Will take the place of painting. (See Photography.)"[16] No one took seriously the possibility that photography might usurp painting. Less than half a century after photography's invention such a notion was one of those received ideas to be parodied. In our century, until recently, only Walter Benjamin gave credence to the notion, claiming that inevitably photography would have a truly profound effect on art, even to the extent that the art of painting might disappear, having lost its all-important aura through mechanical reproduction.[17] A denial of this power of photography to transform art continued to energize modernist painting through the immediate postwar period in America. But then in the work of Rauschenberg photography began to conspire with painting in its own destruction.

Installation of *Robert Rauschenberg: The Silk-screen Paintings 1962–64*, Whitney Museum of American Art, December 7, 1990–March 17, 1991 (photos Louise Lawler).

Although it is only with slight discomfort that Rauschenberg
was called a painter throughout the first decade of his career, when
he systematically embraced photographic images in the early 1960s
it became less and less possible to think of his work as painting. It
was instead a hybrid form of *printing*. Rauschenberg had moved
definitively from techniques of *production* (combines, assemblages) to
techniques of *reproduction* (silk screens, transfer drawings). And this
move requires us to think of Rauschenberg's art as postmodernist.
Through reproductive technology, postmodernist art dispenses with
the aura. The fiction of the creating subject gives way to a frank
confiscation, quotation, excerptation, accumulation, and repetition
of already existing images.[18] Notions of originality, authenticity, and
presence, essential to the ordered discourse of the museum, are
undermined. Rauschenberg steals the *Rokeby Venus* and screens her
onto the surface of *Crocus,* which also contains pictures of mosqui-
toes and a truck, as well as a reduplicated Cupid with a mirror. She
appears again, twice, in *Transom,* now in the company of a helicopter and repeated images of water towers on Manhattan rooftops. In
Bicycle she appears with the truck of *Crocus* and the helicopter of
Transom, but now also with a sailboat, a cloud, and an eagle. She
reclines just above three Merce Cunningham dancers in *Overcast III*
and atop a statue of George Washington and a car key in *Breakthrough.* The absolute heterogeneity that is the purview of photography, and through photography, the museum, is spread across the
surface of Rauschenberg's work. Moreover, it spreads from work to
work.

Malraux was enraptured by the endless possibilities of his
Museum, by the proliferation of discourses it could set in motion,
establishing ever new stylistic series simply by reshuffling the photographs. That proliferation is enacted by Rauschenberg: Malraux's
dream has become Rauschenberg's joke. But, of course, not everyone gets the joke, least of all Rauschenberg himself, judging from
the proclamation he composed for the Metropolitan Museum's
Centennial Certificate in 1970:

André Malraux with the photographic
plates for *The Museum without Walls* (photo
Paris Match/Jarnoux).

Treasury of the conscience of man.
Masterworks collected, protected and
celebrated commonly. Timeless in
concept the museum amasses to
concertise a moment of pride
serving to defend the dreams
and ideals apolitically of mankind
aware and responsive to the
changes, needs and complexities
of current life while keeping
history and love alive.

This certificate, containing photographic reproductions of masterpieces of art—without the intrusion of anything else—was signed by
the Metropolitan Museum officials.

Robert Rauschenberg, *Centennial Certificate,*
Metropolitan Museum of Art, 1969 (The Met-
ropolitan Museum of Art, Florence and
Joseph Singer Collection, 1969).

Notes

1.   Hilton Kramer, "Does Gérôme Belong with Goya and Monet?" *New York Times,* April 13, 1980, section 2, p. 35.

2.   Theodor W. Adorno, "Valéry Proust Museum," in *Prisms,* trans. Samuel and Shiery Weber (London: Neville Spearman, 1967), pp. 173–186.

3.   Kramer, "Does Gérôme Belong," p. 35.

4.   Leo Steinberg, "Other Criteria," in *Other Criteria* (New York: Oxford University Press, 1972), pp. 55–91. This essay is based on a lecture presented at the Museum of Modern Art, New York, in March 1968.

5.   Ibid., p. 84.

6.   See Rosalind Krauss's discussion of the radical difference between the cubist collage and Rauschenberg's "reinvented" collage in "Rauschenberg and the Materialized Image," *Artforum* 13, no. 4 (December 1974), pp. 36–43.

7.   Not all art historians would agree that Manet made the relationship of painting to its sources problematic. That is, however, the initial assumption of Michael Fried's "Manet's Sources: Aspects of his Art, 1859–1865" (*Artforum* 7, no. 7 [March 1969], pp. 28–82), whose opening sentences read, "If a single question is guiding for our understanding of Manet's art during the first half of the 1860s, it is this: What are we to make of the numerous references in his paintings of those years to the work of the great painters of the past?" (p. 28). In part, Fried's presupposition that Manet's references to earlier art were *different,* in their "literalness and obviousness," from the ways in which Western painting had previously used sources led Theodore Reff to attack Fried's essay, saying, for example, "When Reynolds portrays his sitters in attitudes borrowed from famous pictures by Holbein, Michelangelo and Annibale Carracci, wittily playing on their relevance to his own subject; when Ingres deliberately refers in his religious compositions to those of Raphael, and in his portraits to familiar examples of Greek sculpture or Roman painting, do they not reveal the same historical consciousness that informs Manet's early work?" (Theodore Reff, "'Manet's Sources': A Critical Evaluation," *Artforum* 8, no. 1 [September 1969], p. 40). As a result of this denial of difference, Reff is able to continue applying to modernism art-historical methodologies devised to explain past art, for example that which explains the very particular relationship of Italian Renaissance art to the art of classical antiquity.

It was a parodic example of such blind application of art-historical methodology to the art of Rauschenberg that occasioned this essay: in a lecture by the critic Robert Pincus-Witten, the source of Rauschenberg's *Monogram* (an assemblage that employs a stuffed angora goat) was said to be William Holman Hunt's *Scapegoat!*

8. Michel Foucault, "Fantasia of the Library," in *Language, Counter-Memory, Practice,* trans. Donald F. Bouchard and Sherry Simon (Ithaca: Cornell University Press, 1977), pp. 92–93.

9. Quoted in Eugenio Donato, "The Museum's Furnace: Notes Toward a Contextual Reading of *Bouvard and Pécuchet,*" in *Textual Strategies: Perspectives in Post-Structuralist Criticism,* ed. Josué V. Hararu (Ithaca: Cornell University Press, 1979), p. 214.

10. Ibid., p. 220. The apparent continuity between Foucault's and Donato's essays here is misleading, inasmuch as Donato is explicitly engaged in a critique of Foucault's archeological methodology, claiming that it implicates Foucault in a return to a metaphysics of origins. Foucault himself moved beyond his "archeology" as soon as he had codified it in *The Archeology of Knowledge* (New York: Pantheon Books, 1969).

11. Gustave Flaubert, *Bouvard and Pécuchet,* trans. A. J. Krailsheimer (New York: Penguin Books, 1976), pp. 114–115.

12. Donato, "The Museum's Furnace," p. 223.

13. The phrase is Erwin Panofsky's; see his article "The History of Art as a Humanistic Discipline," in *Meaning in the Visual Arts: Papers in and on Art History* (Garden City, N.Y.: Doubleday Anchor Books, 1955), pp. 1–25.

14. This comparison was first presented by Robert Rosenblum in a symposium entitled "Modern Art and the Modern City: From Caillebotte and the Impressionists to the Present Day," held in conjunction with the Gustave Caillebotte exhibition at the Brooklyn Museum in March 1977. Rosenblum published a version of his lecture, although only works by Caillebotte were illustrated. The following excerpt will suffice to give an impression of the comparisons Rosenblum drew: "Caillebotte's art seems equally in tune with some of the structural innovations of recent nonfigurative painting and sculpture. His embracing, in the 1870s, of the new experience of modern Paris . . . involves fresh ways of seeing that are surprisingly close to our own decade. For one, he seems to have polarized more than any of his Impressionist contemporaries the extremities of the random and the ordered, usually juxtaposing these contrary modes in the same work. Parisians in city and country come and go in open spaces, but within their leisurely movements are grids of arithmetic, technological regularity. Crisscrossing or parallel patterns of steel girders move with an A-A-A-A beat along the railing of a bridge. Checkerboards of square pavement stones map out the repetitive grid systems we see in

Warhol or early Stella, Ryman or Andre. Clean stripes, as in Daniel Buren, suddenly impose a cheerful, primary aesthetic order upon urban flux and scatter" (Robert Rosenblum, "Gustave Caillebotte: The 1970s and the 1870s," *Artforum* 15, no. 7 [March 1977], p. 52). When Rosenblum again presented the Ryman-Caillebotte slide comparison in a symposium on modernism at Hunter College in March 1980, he admitted that it was perhaps what Panofsky would have called a pseudomorphism.

15. André Malraux, *The Voices of Silence,* trans. Stuart Gilbert, Bollingen Series, no. 24 (Princeton: Princeton University Press, 1978), pp. 44, 46.

16. Flaubert, *Bouvard and Pécuchet,* pp. 321, 300.

17. See Walter Benjamin, "The Work of Art in the Age of Mechanical Reproduction," in *Illuminations,* trans. Harry Zohn (New York: Schocken Books, 1969), pp. 217–251.

18. For an earlier discussion of these postmodernist techniques pervasive in recent art, see Douglas Crimp, "Pictures," *October,* no. 8 (Spring 1979), pp. 75–88.

The Museum's Old, the Library's
New Subject

> All the arts are based on the presence of man, only photography
> derives an advantage from his absence.
>
> André Bazin, "The Ontology of the Photographic Image"

For the fiftieth anniversary of the Museum of Modern Art, William S. Lieberman, sole survivor of the museum's founding regime associated with the directorship of Alfred Barr, mounted the exhibition *Art of the Twenties*. The exhibition's focus was presumably chosen not only to celebrate the decade in which MOMA was born but also because it would necessarily draw on every department of the museum: Film, Photography, Architecture and Design, Drawings, Prints and Illustrated Books, as well as Painting and Sculpture. Indeed, a major impression left by the show was that aesthetic activity in the 1920s was wholly dispersed across the various mediums, that painting and sculpture exercised no hegemony at all. The arts clearly on the ascendant, not only in Paris but more tellingly in Berlin and Moscow, were photography and film, agitprop posters, and other functionally designed objects. With only a few exceptions— Miró, Mondrian, Brancusi—painting and sculpture appear to have been very nearly usurped. Duchamp's *Large Glass*—not, of course, included in the exhibition—may well be the decade's most significant work, and one is hard pressed to define its medium in relation to traditional categories.

Art of the Twenties was all the more interesting and appropriate for the museum's anniversary year, coming as it did at the end of another decade in which painting and sculpture had been displaced by other aesthetic options. And yet, if it is possible to assess the 1970s as a time of traditional painting and sculpture's demise, it is

Installation views of *Art of the Twenties*,
Museum of Modern Art, November 14,
1979–January 22, 1980 (photos courtesy
The Museum of Modern Art, New York).

equally possible to see it as the decade of an extraordinary resurgence of those modes, just as the 1920s can alternately be understood as a time of extreme conservative backlash in the arts—when, for example, after the radical achievement of analytic cubism, Picasso returned to traditional representation in his so-called neoclassical period.[1] That radical moves should be accompanied by or cause reaction is not surprising, but the degree to which such reaction is currently embraced, even to the extent of obscuring radical departures, is alarming.

In MOMA's annual report for its jubilee year, the museum's president and director gave less attention to *Art of the Twenties* than to two of the year's other major events, both of which helped create the first substantial operating surplus in the museum's history. These were the sale, after many legal and public-relations difficulties, of the museum's "air rights" to a real estate developer for $17,000,000 as the most crucial aspect of the museum's expansion program; and the biggest blockbuster the museum had ever staged, *Pablo Picasso: A Retrospective,* which boasted nearly a thousand artworks and over a million visitors. One other celebratory event was singled out by the museum's top officials as being of particular importance: the exhibition of photographs by Ansel Adams, one of the founding fathers of MOMA's Department of Photography—the first such department in any art museum, as they proudly point out.[2]

The big real estate deal, the blockbuster retrospective of the twentieth century's leading candidate for the title "artistic genius," the fêting of the best-selling living photographer (a print of Adams's *Moonrise, Hernandez, New Mexico* recently sold for $22,000)[3]—the significance of the conjunction of these events can hardly be lost on anyone forced to cope with the social realities of the current New York art world.[4] In comparison, the importance of *Art of the Twenties* begins to pale; perhaps the exhibition must after all be seen merely as the swan song of the museum's first era and its curator, who subsequently moved to the Metropolitan Museum.

The notion of art as bound by and deeply engaged in its particular historical moment, as radically departing from the age-old conventions of painting and sculpture, as embracing new technologies for its production—all of this could apparently be swept aside by a notion of art as bound only by the limitations of individual human creativity. Modern art could now be understood as art had seemingly always been understood, as embodied in the masterpieces invented by the master artist: *Picasso*—the man's signature adorned the T-shirts of thousands on the streets of New York that summer, evidence, one supposes, that they had attended the spectacle and were proud to have thus paid homage to a man of genius. But these T-shirt-clad museum goers were themselves part of another spectacle, the spectacle of response. The myths, the clichés, the platitudes, the *idées reçues* about artistic genius—appropriately signified by this *signature*—were never so resoundingly reaffirmed, not only by the mass media, from whom it was to have been expected, but by the museum itself, by curators, dealers, critics, and by artists. The very suggestion that there might be something suspicious, perhaps regressive, about this response was dismissed as misanthropic naysaying.

A short five years earlier, in a text on contemporary art intended for art-school audiences, I had written that Duchamp had replaced Picasso as the early-twentieth-century artist most relevant to contemporary practice.[5] Now, it seems, I'd have to eat those words. In a special "Picasso Symposium" devoted to responses to the MOMA retrospective, *Art in America* asked various art-world personalities to give their views. Here is that of the recently successful painter Elizabeth Murray: "Picasso is the avant-garde artist of our time. . . . He truly says you can do anything."[6] Her fellow painter, the former critic Bruce Boice, elaborates on the same point:

Picasso seems to have had no fear. He just did whatever he wanted to do, and obviously there was a lot he wanted to do. . . . For me to speak about what I find so astounding about Picasso is to speak of what is most fundamental to being a painter. Being a painter should be the easiest thing in the world because there are and can be no rules. All you have to do is do whatever you want to do. You can just, and you must, make everything up.[7]

This, then, is the lesson of Picasso. There are no constraints, whether these are construed as conventions, languages, discourses, ideologies, institutions, histories. There is only freedom, the freedom to invent at will, to do whatever you want. Picasso is the avant-garde artist of *our* time because, after so much tedious discussion about history and ideology, about the death of the author, he provides the exhilarating revelation that we are free after all.

This creative freedom fantasized by contemporary artists and confirmed for them by the spectacle of a thousand Picasso inventions is seconded by art historians. A typical response is that of John Richardson, writing in the favored organ of the U.S. literary establishment, the *New York Review of Books*.[8] Calling Picasso "the most prodigious and versatile artist of all time," Richardson rehearses the biography of artistic genius from its beginnings in the transcendence of the mere child prodigy by "an energy and a sensibility that are astonishingly mature" through the "stylistic changes that revolutionized the course of twentieth century art" to the "poignant" late works, with their "mixture of self-mockery and megalomania." Richardson's assessment is perhaps uncharacteristic in only one respect. He claims that "up to the day of Picasso's death in 1973 the power was never switched off."

Absolutely characteristic, though, is Richardson's view that Picasso's is a subjective art, that "the facts of his life have more bearing on Picasso's art than is the case with any other great artist, except perhaps van Gogh." And so that we don't miss the meaning of any of these great works, Richardson insists that "every crumb of information should be gathered while there is time. In no other great life are the minutiae of gossip so potentially significant."[9]

It is, then, as if Duchamp's readymades had never been conceived, as if modernism's most radical developments, including

Picasso's own cubist collage, had never taken place, or at least as if their implications could be overlooked and the old myths of art fully revivified. The dead author has been reborn; *he* has returned with his full subjective power restored—as the contemporary artist puts it—to make it all up, to do whatever he wants. Duchamp's readymades had, of course, embodied the proposition that the artist invents nothing, that he or she only uses, manipulates, displaces, reformulates, repositions what history has provided. This is not to divest the artist of the power to intervene in, to alter or expand, discourse, only to dispense with the fiction that that power arises from an autonomous self existing outside history and ideology. The readymades propose that the artist cannot *make,* but can only *take* what is already there.

∽

It is precisely on this distinction—the distinction between making and taking—that the ontological difference between painting and photography is said to rest. The director of MOMA's department of photography, John Szarkowski, states it simply enough:

The invention of photography provided a radically new picture-making process—a process based not on synthesis but on selection. The difference was a basic one. Paintings were *made* . . . but photographs, as the man on the street puts it, were *taken*.[10]

But MOMA's jubilee photographer, Ansel Adams, is uncomfortable with this predatory view of photography. How could the artist Adams wants to call a "photopoet" be a common thief?

The common term "*taking* a picture" is more than just an idiom; it is a symbol of exploitation. "*Making* a picture" implies a creative resonance which is essential to profound expression.

My approach to photography is based on my belief in the vigor and values of the world of nature—in the aspects of grandeur and of the minutiae all about us. I believe in growing things, and in the things which have grown and died magnificently. I believe in people and in the simple aspects of human life, and in the relation of man to nature. I believe man must be free, both in spirit and in society, that he must build strength into himself, affirming the "enormous beauty of the world" and acquiring the confidence to see and to express his vision. And I believe in photography as one means of expressing this affirmation, and of achieving an ultimate happiness and faith.[11]

There is really less contradiction of Szarkowski's position in Adams's Sierra Club humanism, however, than there appears to be. For in both cases there is ultimately a matter of faith in the medium to act as just that, a *medium* of the artist's subjectivity. So, for example, Adams writes,

A great photograph is a full expression of what one feels about what is being photographed in the deepest sense, and is, thereby, a true expression of what one feels about life in its entirety. And the expression of what one feels should be set forth in terms of simple devotion to the medium—a statement of utmost clarity and perfection possible under the conditions of creation and production.[12]

Compare Szarkowski:

An artist is a man who seeks new structures in which to order and simplify his sense of the reality of life. For the artist photographer, much of his sense of reality (where the picture starts) and much of his sense of craft or structure (where the picture is completed) are anonymous and untraceable gifts from photography itself.[13]

By construing photography ontologically, as a medium of subjectivity, Adams and Szarkowski contrive a fundamentally modernist position for it, duplicating in nearly every respect theories of modernist autonomy articulated earlier in this century for painting. In so doing, they ignore the plurality of discourses in which photography has participated. Everything that has determined its multiple practice is set aside in favor of *photography itself*. Thus reorganized, photography is readied to be funneled through a new market, ultimately to be housed in the museum.

ဢ

Several years ago, Julia van Haaften, a librarian in the Art and Architecture Division of the New York Public Library, became interested in photography. As she studied what was then known about this vast subject, she discovered that the library itself owned many books containing vintage photographic prints, especially from the nineteenth century, and she hit on the idea of organizing an exhibition of this material culled from the library's collections. She gathered books illustrated with photographs from throughout the library's many different divisions, books about archeology in the Holy Lands and Central America, about ruined castles in England and Islamic ornament in Spain; illustrated newspapers of Paris and London; books of ethnography and geology; technical and medical manuals.[14] In preparing this exhibition the library realized for the first time that it owned an extraordinarily large and valuable collection of photographs—for the first time, because no one had previously inventoried these materials under the single category of photography. Until then, the photographs had been so thoroughly dispersed throughout the library's extensive resources that it was only through patient research that van Haaften was able to track them down. And furthermore, it was only at the time she installed her exhibition that photography's prices were beginning to skyrocket. So although books with original plates by Maxime Du Camp or Francis Frith might now be worth a small fortune, ten or fifteen years ago they weren't even worth enough to merit placing them in the library's Rare Books Division.

Julia van Haaften now has a new job. She is director of the New York Public Library's Photographic Collections Documentation Project, an interim step on the way to the creation of a new division to be called Art, Prints, and Photographs, which will consolidate the old Art and Architecture Division with the Prints Division, adding to them photographic materials culled from all other library departments.[15] These materials are thus to be reclassified according to their newly acquired value, the value that is now attached to the "artists" who made the photographs. Thus, what was once housed in the Jewish Division under the classification "Jerusalem" will eventually be found in Art, Prints, and Photographs under the classification "Auguste Salzmann." What was Egypt will become Beato, or Du Camp, or Frith; Pre-Columbian Middle America will be Désiré Charnay; the American Civil War, Alexander Gardner and Timothy O'Sullivan; the cathedrals of France will be Henri LeSecq; the Swiss Alps, the Bisson Frères; the horse in motion is now Muybridge; the flight of birds, Marey; and the expression of emotions forgets Darwin to become Guillaume Duchenne de Boulogne.

What Julia van Haaften is doing at the New York Public Library is just one example of what is occurring throughout our culture on a massive scale. And thus the list goes on, as urban poverty becomes Jacob Riis and Lewis Hine, portraits *of* Delacroix and Manet become portraits *by* Nadar and Carjat, Dior's New Look becomes Irving Penn, and World War II becomes Robert Capa. For if photography was invented in 1839, it was only *discovered* in the 1960s and 1970s—photography, that is, as an essence, photography *itself.* Szarkowski can again be counted on to put it simply:

The pictures reproduced in this book [*The Photographer's Eye*] were made over almost a century and a quarter. They were made for various reasons, by men of different concerns and varying talent. They have in fact little in common except their success, and a shared vocabulary: these pictures are unmistakably photographs. The vision they share belongs to no school or aesthetic theory, but to photography itself.[16]

It is in this text that Szarkowski attempts to specify the particulars of "photographic vision," to define those things that are specific to photography and to no other medium. In other words, Szarkowski's ontology of photography makes photography a *modernist* medium in Clement Greenberg's sense of the term—an art form that can distinguish itself in its essential qualities from all other art forms. And it is according to this view that photography is now being redefined and redistributed. Photography will hereafter be found in departments of photography or divisions of art and photography. Thus ghettoized, it will no longer primarily be *useful* within other discursive practices; it will no longer serve the purposes of information, documentation, evidence, illustration, reportage. The formerly plural field of photography will henceforth be reduced to the single, all-encompassing *aesthetic.* Just as paintings and sculptures acquired a new-found autonomy, relieved of their earlier functions, when they were wrested from the churches and palaces of Europe and consigned to museums in the late eighteenth and early nineteenth centuries, so now photography acquires *its* autonomy as it too enters the museum. But we must recognize that in order for this new aesthetic understanding to occur, other ways of understanding photography must be dismantled and destroyed. Books about Egypt will literally be torn apart in order that photographs by Francis Frith may be framed and placed on the walls of museums. Once there, photographs will never look the same. Whereas we may formerly have looked at Cartier-Bresson's photographs for the information they conveyed about the revolution in China or the Civil War in Spain, we will now look at them for what they tell us about the artist's style of expression.

∽

This consolidation of photography's formerly multiple practices, this formation of a new epistemological construct in order that we may now *see* photography, is only part of a much more complex redistribution of knowledge taking place throughout our culture.

This redistribution is associated with the term *postmodernism,* although most people who employ the word have very little idea what, exactly, they're naming or why they even need a new descriptive category. In spite of the currency of its use, *postmodernism* has thus far acquired no agreed-upon meaning at all. For the most part, it is used in only a negative sense, to say that modernism is over. And where it is used in a positive sense, it is used as a catch-all, to characterize anything and everything that is happening in the present. So, for example, Douglas Davis, who uses the term very loosely, and relentlessly, says of it,

"Post-modern" is a negative term, failing to name a "positive" replacement, but this permits pluralism to flourish (in a word, it permits *freedom,* even in the marketplace). . . . "Post-modern" has a reactionary taint—because "Modern" has come to be acquainted with "now"—but the "Tradition of the New" requires a strong counter-revolution, not one more forward move.[17]

Indeed, counterrevolution, pluralism, the fantasy of artistic freedom—all of these are, for many, synonymous with postmodernism. And they are right to the extent that in conjunction with the end of modernism all kinds of regressive symptoms are appearing. But rather than characterizing these symptoms as postmodernist, I think we should see them as the forms of a retrenched, a petrified, reductive modernism. They are, I think, the morbid symptoms of modernism's demise.

Photography's entrance into the museum on a vast scale, its reevaluation according to the epistemology of modernism, its new status as an autonomous art—this is what I mean by the symptoms of modernism's demise. For photography is not autonomous, and it is not, in the modernist sense, an art. When modernism was a fully operative paradigm of artistic practice, photography was necessarily seen as too contingent—too constrained by the world that was photographed, too dependent upon the discursive structures in which it

was embedded—to achieve the self-reflexive, entirely conventional-
ized form of modernist art. This is not to say that no photograph
could ever be a modernist artwork; the photographs in MOMA's
Art of the Twenties show were ample proof that certain photographs
could be as self-consciously about photographic language as any
modernist painting was about painting's particular conventions.
That is why MOMA's photography department was established in
the first place. Szarkowski is the inheritor of a department that
reflected the modernist aesthetic of Alfred Stieglitz and his followers. But it has taken Szarkowski and *his* followers to bestow retro-
spectively upon *photography itself* what Stieglitz had thought was
achieved by only a very few photographs.[18] For photography to be
understood and reorganized in such a way entails a drastic revision
of the paradigm of modernism, and it can happen only because that
paradigm has indeed become dysfunctional. Postmodernism may be
said to be founded in part on this paradox: it is photography's reevaluation as a modernist medium that signals the end of modernism.
Postmodernism begins when photography comes to pervert modernism.

꼬

If this entry of photography into the museum and the library's art
division is one means of photography's perversion of modernism—
the negative one—then there is another form of that perversion that
may be seen as positive, in that it establishes a wholly new and
radicalized artistic practice that truly deserves to be called postmodernist. For at a certain moment photography enters the practice of
art in such a way that it contaminates the purity of modernism's
separate categories, the categories of painting and sculpture. These
categories are subsequently divested of their fictive autonomy, their
idealism, and thus their power. The first positive instances of this
contamination occurred in the early 1960s, when Robert Rauschenberg and Andy Warhol began to silkscreen photographic images
onto their canvases. From that moment forward, the guarded autonomy of modernist art was under constant threat from the incursions

of the real world that photography readmitted to the purview of art. After over a century of art's imprisonment in the discourse of modernism and the institution of the museum, hermetically sealed off from the rest of culture and society, the art of postmodernism begins to make inroads back into the world. It is photography, in part, that makes this possible, while still guaranteeing against the compromising atavism of traditional realism.

Another story about the library will perhaps illustrate my point: I was once hired to do picture research for an industrial film about the history of transportation, a film that was to be made largely by shooting footage of still photographs; it was my job to find appropriate photographs. Browsing through the stacks of the New York Public Library where books on the general subject of transportation were shelved, I came across the book by Ed Ruscha entitled *Twentysix Gasoline Stations,* first published in 1963 and consisting of photographs of just that: twenty-six gasoline stations. I remember thinking how funny it was that the book had been miscatalogued and placed alongside books about automobiles, highways, and so forth. I knew, as the librarians evidently did not, that Ruscha's book was a work of art and therefore belonged in the art division. But now, because of the reconfigurations brought about by postmodernism, I've changed my mind; I now know that Ed Ruscha's books make no sense in relation to the categories of art according to which art books are catalogued in the library, and that that is part of their achievement. The fact that there is nowhere for *Twentysix Gasoline Stations* within the present system of classification is an index of the book's radicalism with respect to established modes of thought.

The problem with the view of postmodernism that refuses to theorize it and thereby confuses it with pluralism is that this view lumps together under the same rubric the symptoms of modernism's demise with what has positively replaced modernism. Such a view has it that the paintings of Elizabeth Murray and Bruce Boice —clearly academic extensions of a petrified modernism—are as

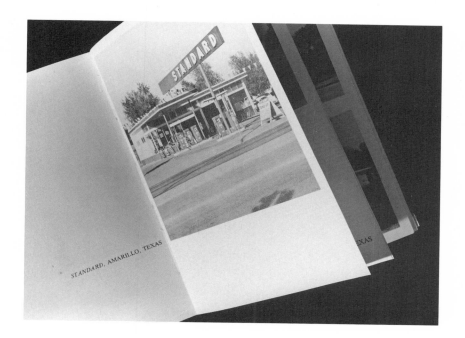

Ed Ruscha, *Twentysix Gasoline Stations*,
1962 (photos Louise Lawler).

MOBIL, WILLIAMS,

much manifestations of postmodernism as Ed Ruscha's books, which are just as clearly replacements of that modernism. For Ruscha's photographic books have escaped the categories through which modernism is understood just as they have escaped the art museum, which arose simultaneously with modernism and came to be its inevitable resting place. Such a pluralist view of postmodernism would be like saying of modernism at its founding moment that it was signaled by both Manet *and* Gérôme (and it is surely another symptom of modernism's demise that revisionist art historians are saying just that), or, better yet, that modernism is both Manet and Disdéri, that hack entrepreneur who made a fortune peddling photographic visiting cards, who is credited with the first extensive commercialization of photography, and whose utterly uninteresting photographs hang, as I write this essay, in the Metropolitan Museum of Art in an exhibition whose title is *After Daguerre: Masterworks from the Bibliothèque Nationale.*

Notes

1. For a detailed discussion of this between-the-wars reaction in relation to the recent return to representational painting, see Benjamin H. D. Buchloh, "Figures of Authority, Ciphers of Regression," *October,* no. 16 (Spring 1981), pp. 39–68.

2. "Museum of Modern Art Annual Report 1979–80," Museum of Modern Art, New York, 1980.

3. As this essay originally went to press in the spring of 1981, a mural-size print of *Moonrise* was sold for over $70,000. Ansel Adams died in 1984.

4. For an important discussion of the relations between real estate development and the art world, see Rosalyn Deutsche and Cara Gendel Ryan, "The Fine Art of Gentrification," *October,* no. 31 (Winter 1984), pp. 91–111.

5. Douglas Crimp, *Introduction to 1970s Art* (New York: Art Information Distribution, 1975).

6. Lawrence Alloway et al., "Picasso: A Symposium," *Art in America* 68, no. 10 (December 1980), p. 19.

7. Ibid., p. 17.

8. John Richardson, "Your Show of Shows," *New York Review of Books* 27, no. 12 (July 17, 1980), pp. 16–24.

9. For a critique of the prevailing view of Picasso's art as autobiography, see Rosalind Krauss, "In the Name of Picasso," *October,* no. 16 (Spring 1981), pp. 5–22.

10. John Szarkowski, "Introduction to *The Photographer's Eye*" (1966), in *The Camera Viewed: Writings on Twentieth-Century Photography,* vol. 2, ed. Peninah R. Petruck (New York: E. P. Dutton, 1979), p. 203.

11. Ansel Adams, "A Personal Credo," *American Annual of Photography,* vol. 58 (1948), p. 16.

12. Ibid., p. 13.

13. Szarkowski, "Introduction," pp. 211–212.

14. See Julia van Haaften, "'Original Sun Pictures': A Check List of the New York Public Library's Holdings of Early Works Illustrated with Photographs, 1844–1900," *Bulletin of the New York Public Library* 80, no. 3 (Spring 1977), pp. 355–415.

15. See Anne M. McGrath, "Photographic Treasures at the N.Y.P.L.," *AB Bookmans Weekly,* January 25, 1982, pp. 550–560. As of 1982, the photography collection, of which Julia van Haaften is the *curator,* was integrated into what is now called the Miriam and Ira D. Wallach Division of Art, Prints, and Photographs.

16. Szarkowski, "Introduction," p. 206.

17. Douglas Davis, "Post-Everything," *Art in America* 68, no. 2 (February 1980), p. 14. Davis's notion of freedom, like that of Picasso's fans, is the thoroughly

mythological one that recognizes no social differences determined by class, ethnicity, race, gender, or sexuality. It is therefore highly telling that when Davis thinks of freedom, the first thing that springs to his mind is "the marketplace." Indeed, his notion of freedom appears to be the Reagan-era version of it—as in "free" enterprise.

18.   For a history of MOMA's Department of Photography, see Christopher Phillips, "The Judgment Seat of Photography, *October,* no. 22 (Fall 1982), pp. 27–63.

The End of Painting

Painting has not always existed; we can determine when it began. And if its development and its moments of greatness can be drummed into our heads, can we not then also imagine its periods of decline and even its end, like any other idea?

Louis Aragon, "La peinture au defi"

The work of art is so frightened of the world at large, it so needs isolation in order to exist, that any conceivable means of protection will suffice. It frames itself, withdraws under glass, barricades itself behind a bullet-proof surface, surrounds itself with a protective cordon, with instruments showing the room humidity, for even the slightest cold would be fatal. Ideally the work of art finds itself not just screened from the world, but shut up in a vault, permanently and totally sheltered from the eye. And yet aren't such extreme measures, bordering on the absurd, already with us, everyday, everywhere, when the artwork is exhibited in those vaults called galleries, museums? Isn't it the very point of departure, the end, and the essential function of the work of art that it should be so exhibited?

Daniel Buren, *Reboundings*

On one of those rare occasions during the 1970s when Barbara Rose abandoned the pages of *Vogue* magazine in order to say something really serious about the art of our time, she did so to vent her anger at an exhibition called *Eight Contemporary Artists,* held at the Museum of Modern Art in the fall of 1974.[1] Although she found the work in the show "bland and tepid" and therefore something "normally one would overlook," she felt compelled to speak out because this show was organized by our most prestigious institution of modern art, and, for that reason alone, it became significant. But the work was bland and tepid to Rose only from an aesthetic standpoint; it was more potent as politics:

For some time I have felt that the radicalism of Minimal and Conceptual art is fundamentally political, that its implicit aim is to discredit thoroughly the forms and institutions of dominant bourgeois culture. . . . Whatever the outcome of such a strategy, one thing is certain: when an institution as prestigious as the Museum of Modern Art invites sabotage, it becomes party, not to the promulgation of experimental art, but to the passive acceptance of disenchanted, demoralized artists' aggression against art greater than their own.[2]

The particular saboteur who seems most to have captured Rose's attention in this case is Daniel Buren, whose work for MOMA consisted of his familiar striped panels, cut to conform to the windows facing the garden, and affixed to the corridor wall facing those windows, and again to the garden wall, with leftover fragments displaced to a billboard and a gallery entrance in SoHo. Impressed though she is by the cogency of Buren's arguments about the ideology imposed by the museum, Rose is nevertheless perplexed that Buren would want his work to appear in one, which seems to her like having his cake and eating it too. For illumination on this question, she turns to an interview with William Rubin, director of MOMA's Department of Painting and Sculpture. In the interview, published in a 1974 issue of *Artforum,* Rubin explains that museums are essentially compromise institutions invented by bourgeois democracies to reconcile the larger public with art conceived within

Installation of work by Daniel Buren for
Eight Contemporary Artists, Museum of
Modern Art, October 7, 1974–January 5,
1975 (photos courtesy The Museum of
Modern Art, New York).

the compass of elite private patronage. This situation, Rubin suggests, might be coming to an end, making the museum irrelevant to the practices of contemporary art.

Perhaps, looking back 10, 15, 30 years from now, it will appear that the modernist tradition really did come to an end within the last few years, as some critics suggest. If so, historians a century from now—whatever name they will give to the period we now call modernism—will see it beginning shortly after the middle of the 19th century and ending in the 1960s. I'm not ruling this out; it may be the case, but I don't think so. Perhaps the dividing line will be seen as between those works which essentially continue an easel painting concept and that grew up associated with bourgeois democratic life and was involved with the development of private collections as well as the museum concept—between this and, let us say, Earthworks, Conceptual works and related endeavors, which want another environment (or should want it) and, perhaps, another public.[3]

Rose assumes that Buren is one of those artists whose work wants (or should want) another environment. After all, his text "Function of the Museum," which she quotes, is a polemic against the confinement of artworks in the museum.[4] But if Buren's work had not appeared in the museum, if it had not taken the museum as its point of departure and as its referent, the very issues Rose ponders in her essay would not have arisen. It is fundamental to Buren's work that it function in complicity with those very institutions it seeks to make visible as the necessary condition of the artwork's intelligibility. This is the reason that his work not only appears in museums and galleries but also poses as painting. It is only thereby possible for his work to ask, What makes it possible to see a painting? What makes it possible to see a painting *as a painting?* And, under such conditions of its presentation, to what end painting?

But Buren's work runs a great risk by posing as painting, the risk of invisibility. Since everything to which Buren's work points as being cultural, historical, is so easily taken to be natural, many people look at Buren's paintings the way they look at all paintings, vainly asking them to render up their meanings *about themselves*. And since they categorically refuse to do so, since they have, by design, no internal meaning, they simply disappear. Thus, Rose, for example, sees Buren's work at the Museum of Modern Art only as "vaguely resembling Stella's stripe paintings."[5] But if Rose is myopic on matters of painting, blind to those questions about painting that Buren's work poses, this is because she, like most people, still *believes* in painting.

☞

> One must really be engaged in order to be a painter. Once obsessed by it, one eventually gets to the point where one thinks that humanity could be changed by painting. But when that passion deserts you, there is nothing else left to do. Then it is better to stop altogether. Because basically painting is pure idiocy.
>
> Gerhard Richter, in conversation with Irmeline Lebeer

As testimony to her faith in painting, Rose organized her own exhibition of contemporary art five years after the MOMA show. *American Painting: The Eighties* (the title is oracular: her show was mounted in the fall of 1979) expressly intended to demonstrate that throughout that grim period of the 1960s and the 1970s, when art seemed to her so bent on self-destruction, intent as it was on those extra-art concerns gathered together under the rubric *politics*—that throughout that period there had been "a generation of holdouts" against "disintegrating morality, social demoralization, and lack of conviction in the authority of tradition."[6] These noble survivors, painters all, were "maintaining a conviction in quality and values, a belief in art as a mode of transcendence, a worldly incarnation of the ideal."

As it happens, Rose's evidence of this keeping of the faith was extremely unconvincing, and her exhibition became an easy target for hostile critics. Biased as her selection was toward hackneyed

Installation of *American Painting: The
Eighties*, Grey Art Gallery, New York, Sep-
tember 5–October 13, 1979 (photo courtesy
Grey Art Gallery).

recapitulations of late modernist abstraction, the show had the unmistakable look of Tenth Street art, twenty years later. Given the thousands of artists currently practicing the art of painting, Rose's selection was indeed parochial; certainly there is a lot of painting around that *looks* more original. Furthermore, favoring such a narrow range of painting at a time when pluralism was the critical byword, Rose virtually invited an unfavorable response. And so, as was to be expected, she was taken to task by various art journalists for whomever of their favorites she failed to include. Hilton Kramer's review asked, Where are the figurative painters? John Perreault's asked, Where are the pattern painters? And Roberta Smith's asked, Where is Jennifer Bartlett? But the crucial point is that no one asked, Why *painting?* To what end painting, now, at the threshold of the 1980s? And to that extent, Rose's show was a resounding success. It proved that faith in painting had indeed been fully restored. For, however much easel painting may have been in question in 1974 when Rubin was interviewed by *Artforum* and his museum exhibited *Eight Contemporary Artists,* by 1979 the question clearly had been withdrawn.

The rhetoric that accompanies this resurrection of painting is almost entirely reactionary: it reacts specifically against all those art practices of the 1960s and the 1970s that abandoned painting and worked to reveal the ideological supports of painting, as well as the ideology that painting, in turn, supports. And so, whereas almost no one agreed with the choices Rose made to demonstrate painting's renascence, almost everyone agreed with the substance, if not the details, of her rhetoric. Rose's catalogue text for *American Painting: The Eighties* is a dazzling collection of received ideas about the art of painting, and I want to suggest that painting knows only such ideas today. Here are a number of excerpts from Rose's essay, which I think we may take as provisional answers to the question, To what end painting in the 1980s?

Painting [is] a transcendental, high art, a major art, and an art of universal as opposed to topical significance. . . .

Only painting [is] genuinely liberal, in the sense of free. . . .

[Painting is] an expressive human activity . . . our only hope for preserving high art. . . .

[Painting] is the product exclusively of the individual imagination rather than a mirror of the ephemeral external world of objective reality. . . .

Illusion . . . is the essence of painting. . . .

Today, the essence of painting is being redefined not as a narrow, arid and reductive anti-illusionism, but as a rich, varied capacity to birth new images into an old world. . . .

[Painting's] capacity [is] to materialize an image . . . behind the proverbial looking-glass of consciousness, where the depth of the imagination knows no bounds. . . .

Not innovation, but originality, individuality and synthesis are the marks of quality in art today, as they always have been. . . .

Art is labor, physical human labor, the labor of birth, reflected in the many images that appear as in a process of emergence, as if taking form before us. . . .

The liberating potential of art is . . . a catharsis of the imagination. . . .

These paintings are clearly the works of rational adult humans, not a monkey, not a child, or a lunatic. . . .

[The tradition of painting is] an inner world of stored images ranging from Altamira to Pollock.

For Rose, then, painting is a high art, a universal art, a liberal art, an art through which we can achieve transcendence and catharsis. Painting has an essence, and that essence is illusionism, the capacity to render images conjured up by the boundless human imagination. Painting is a great unbroken tradition that encompasses the entire known history of man. Painting is, above all, human.

All of this stands in direct opposition to the art of the previous two decades, for which I am using Daniel Buren's work as the example, that sought to contest the myths of high art, to declare art, like all other forms of endeavor, to be contingent upon the material, historical world. Moreover, this art attempted to discredit the myth of man and the humanist conventions growing out of that myth. For, indeed, these *are* the supports of the dominant bourgeois culture. They are the very hallmarks of bourgeois ideology.

But if the art of the 1960s and the 1970s contested the myth of man with an open assault on the artist as unique creator, there was another phenomenon that had initiated that assault in the visual arts at the founding moment of modernism, a phenomenon from which painting has been in retreat since the mid-nineteenth century. That phenomenon is, of course, photography.

⌇

You know exactly what I think of photography. I would like to see it make people despise painting until something else will make photography unbearable.

Marcel Duchamp, in a letter to Alfred Stieglitz

"From today painting is dead": it is now nearly a century and a half since Paul Delaroche is said to have pronounced that sentence in the face of the overwhelming evidence of Daguerre's invention. But even though the death warrant has been periodically reissued throughout the era of modernism, no one seems to have been entirely willing to execute it; life on death row lingered to longevity. But during the 1960s, painting's terminal condition finally seemed impossible to ignore. The symptoms were everywhere: in the work of painters themselves, all of whom seemed to be reiterating Ad Reinhardt's claim that he was "just making the last paintings anyone could make" or allowing their paintings to be contaminated with such alien elements as photographic images; in minimal sculpture, which provided a definitive rupture with painting's unavoidable ties to a centuries-old idealism; in all those other mediums to which artists turned as, one after another, they abandoned painting. The dimension that had always resisted even painting's most dazzling feats of illusionism—time—now became the dimension in which artists staged their activities, as they embraced film, video, and performance. And, after waiting out the entire era of modernism, photography reappeared, finally to claim its inheritance. The appetite for photography in the past decade has been insatiable. Artists, critics, dealers, curators, and scholars have defected from their former pursuits in droves to take up this enemy of painting. Photography may have been *invented* in 1839, but it was only *discovered* in the 1970s.

But "What's All This about Photography?"[7] Now this question is asked again, and in the very terms employed by Lamartine, also nearly a century and a half ago: "But wherein does its human conception lie?"[8] Lamartine's argument is rehearsed this time by Richard Hennessy, one of Rose's American painters of the 1980s, and published in *Artforum,* the very journal that had so faithfully and lucidly chronicled those radical developments of the 1960s and the 1970s that had signaled painting's demise, but which more recently has given testimony that painting is born again. Hennessy against photography is characteristic of this new revivalist spirit:

The role of intention and its poetry of human freedom is infrequently discussed in relation to art, yet the more a given art is capable of making intention felt, the greater are its chances of being a fine, and not a minor or applied, art. Consider the paintbrush. How many bristles or hairs does it have? Sometimes 20 or less, sometimes 500, a thousand—more. When a brush loaded with pigment touches the surface, it can leave not just a single mark, but the marks of the bristles of which it is composed. The "Yes, I desire this" of the stroke is supported by the choir of bristles—"Yes, *we* desire this." The whole question of touch is rife with spiritual associations.[9]

Imagine the magnitude of that choir, bristling so with desire as to produce a deafening roar of hallelujahs, in the particular case of Robert Ryman's *Delta* series, paintings that employed

a very wide brush, 12 inches. I got it specially—I went to a brush manufacturer and they had this very big brush. I wanted to pull the paint across this quite large surface, 9 feet square, with this big brush. I had a few failures at the beginning. Finally, I got the consistency right and I knew what I was doing and how hard to push the brush and pull it and what was going to happen when I did. That's kind of the way to begin. I didn't have anything else in mind, except to make a painting.[10]

Juxtaposed against Hennessy's panegyric, Ryman's words sound prosaic indeed. There is in his language, as in his paintings, a strict adherence to the matter at hand. His conception of painting is reduced to the stark physical components of painting-as-object. The systematic, single-minded, persistent attempt to rid painting once and for all of its idealist trappings lends Ryman's work its special place during the 1960s as, again, "just the last paintings anyone can make." And this is, as well, their very condition of possibility. Ryman's paintings, like Buren's, make visible the most literal of painting's *material* conventions: its supporting surface, its stretcher, its frame, the wall on which it hangs. But, more significantly, his paintings, unlike Buren's, make visible the mechanical activity of applying the brush strokes, as they are manifestly lined up, one after the other, left to right, say, or top to bottom, until the surface is, simply, painted.

The revivalism of current painting, which Hennessy's text so perfectly articulates, depends, of course, on reinvesting those strokes with human presence, a metaphysics of the human touch. "Painting's quasi-miraculous mode of existence is produced . . . by its mode of facture. . . . *Through the hand:* this is the crucial point."[11] This faith in the healing powers of the hand, the facture that results from the laying on of hands, echoes throughout Rose's catalogue essay, which pays special homage to Hennessy's attack on photography. The unifying principle in the aesthetic of Rose's painters is that their work "defines itself in conscious opposition to photography and all forms of mechanical reproduction which seek to deprive the art work of its unique 'aura.'" For Rose, elimination of the human touch can only express "the self-hatred of artists. . . . Such a powerful wish to annihilate personal expression implies that the artist does not love his creation." What distinguishes painting from photography is this "visible record of the activity of the human hand, as it builds surfaces experienced as tactile."

To counter the euphoria over photography's reappearance, Hennessy finally directs our attention to Velázquez's *Las Meninas,* which he sees as a "description of the photographic process, in which we become the camera." We are to understand, although it is stated ever so subtly, that we pay homage to this particular painting for its celebrated facture. Hennessy tells us of Velázquez that "he looks at us, almost as if we might be his subjects" as "his hand, hovering between palette and canvas, holds"—what else?—"a brush." Hennessy describes this painting with the most dazzling of metaphors, tropes of which he and Rose are particularly fond, for they consider painting essentially a metaphorical medium. He says, for example, that it is "a gift we will never finish unwrapping," "a city without ramparts, a lover who needs no alibi," in which "the play of gazes, in front, behind, past and toward us, weaves a web about us, bathing us in murmuring consciousness. We are the guests of the mighty, the august, in rank and spirit. We stand at the center of their implied world, and are ourselves the center of attention. Velázquez has admitted us into his confidence."[12]

Stripped of its fatuous metaphors and its reverential tone, Hennessy's description of *Las Meninas* might suggest a rather more persuasive discussion of this painting, which composes the opening chapter of *The Order of Things.* As Michel Foucault describes it, this is indeed a painting in which the artist, on the one hand, and the spectator, on the other, have usurped the position of the subject, who is displaced to the vague reflection in the mirror on the rear wall of Velázquez's studio. For within the seventeenth century's theory of representation, these parallel usurpations and displacements were the very ground of representation's possibility.

It may be that, in this picture, as in all the representations of which it is, as it were, the manifest essence, the profound invisibility of what one sees is inseparable from the invisibility of the person seeing—despite all mirrors, reflections, imitations, and portraits. . . .

Perhaps there exists in this picture by Velázquez the representation, as it were, of Classical representation, and the definition of the space it opens up to us. And, indeed, representation undertakes to represent itself here in all its elements, with its images, the eyes to which it is offered, the faces it makes visible, the gestures that call it into being. But there, in the midst of this dispersion which it is simultaneously grouping together and spreading out before us, indicated compellingly from every side, is an essential void: the necessary disappearance of that which is its foundation—of the person it resembles and the person in whose eyes it is only a resemblance. This very subject—which is the same—has been elided. And representation, freed from the relation that was impeding it, can offer itself as representation in its pure form.[13]

What Foucault sees when he looks at this painting, then, is the way representation functioned in the classical period, a period that came to an end, in Foucault's archeological analysis of history, at the beginning of the nineteenth century, when our own age, the age of modernism, began. And, of course, if this era of history came to an end, so too did its means of understanding the world, of which *Las Meninas* is a particularly fine example.

For Hennessy, however, *Las Meninas* does not signal a *particular* historical period with its *particular* mode of knowledge. Instead, *Las Meninas* is, more than it is anything else, a great painting, governed not by history but by creative genius, which is ahistorical, eternal, like man himself. This position—that of an entrenched historicism—

is the very one that Foucault is determined to overturn. From such a position, painting is understood to have an eternal essence, of which *Las Meninas* is one instance, the marks on the walls of Altamira another, the poured skeins of Jackson Pollock another. "From Altamira to Pollock"—the phrase encapsulates the argument that people have always had the impulse to create paintings; how, then, can it even be suggested that they could stop in, say, 1965?

But what is it that makes it possible to look at the paleolithic markings on the walls of a cave, a seventeenth-century court portrait, and an abstract expressionist canvas and say that they are all *the same thing?* that they all belong to the same category of knowledge? How did this historicism of art get put into place?

ও

There was a time when, with few exceptions, works of art remained generally in the same location for which they were made. However, now a great change has occurred that, in general as well as specifically, will have important consequences for art. Perhaps there is more cause than ever before to realize that Italy as it existed until recently was a great art entity. Were it possible to give a general survey, it could then be demonstrated what the world has now lost when so many parts have been torn from this immense and ancient totality. What has been destroyed by the removal of these parts will remain forever a secret. Only after some years will it be possible to have a conception of that new art entity which is being formed in Paris.

Johann Wolfgang von Goethe, introduction to the *Propyläen*

The new art entity being formed in Paris (literally, of course, the Louvre), which Goethe foresaw as early as 1798, was the art entity we now call modernism, if by modernism we mean not merely a period style but an entire epistemology of art. Goethe foresaw that art would be seen in a way that was radically different from his own way of understanding it, which would in turn become, for us, a secret. The great art entity that was symbolized for Goethe by Italy, which we might call art in situ, or art before the invention of the art museum, simply no longer exists for us. And this is not only because art was stolen from the places for which it had been made and sequestered in art museums but also because for us the art entity is held in another kind of museum, the kind that André Malraux called *Imaginary*. That museum consists of all those works of art that can be submitted to mechanical reproduction and, thus, to the discursive practice that mechanical reproduction has made possible: art history. With art history, the art entity that Goethe called Italy is forever lost. That is to say—and this must be emphasized because from within an epistemological field, even as it begins to be eroded, it is always difficult to see its workings—that art as we think about it *only came into being* in the nineteenth century, with the birth of the museum and the discipline of art history, for these share the same time span as modernism (and, not insignificantly, photography). For us, then, art's natural end is in the museum, or, at the very least, in the imaginary museum, that idealist space that is art with a capital *A*. The idea of art as autonomous, as separate from everything else, as destined to take its place in *art* history, is a development of modernism. And it is an idea of art that contemporary painting upholds, destined as it, too, is to end up in the museum.

Within this conception of art, painting is understood ontologically: it has an origin and an essence. Its historical development can be plotted in one long, uninterrupted sweep from Altamira to Pollock and beyond, into the 1980s. Within this development, painting's essence does not change; only its outward manifestation—known to art historians as style—changes. Art history ultimately reduces painting to a succession of styles—personal styles, period styles, national styles. And, of course, these styles are unpredictable in their vicissitudes, governed as they are by the individual choices of painters expressing their "boundless imaginations."

A recent instance of such a stylistic shift, and its reception, exemplifies this art-historical view of painting and how it functions in support of the continued practice of painting. The shift occurs during the late 1970s in the work of Frank Stella. Although it could be said that this shift was presaged in every earlier stylistic change in Stella's work after the black paintings of 1959, Stella's move to the flamboyantly idiosyncratic constructed works of the past several years is by comparison a kind of quantum leap, and as such it has been taken as sanction for much of that recent painting that declares its individualism thorough the most ostentatious eccentricities of shape, color, material, and image. Indeed, at the Whitney Museum Biennial exhibition of 1979, one of Stella's new extravaganzas, which was set up as the spectator's first encounter as the elevator doors opened on the museum's fourth floor, became an emblem for everything else that was displayed on that floor—a collection of paintings that were surely intended to be read as deeply personal expressions, but which looked like so many lessons dutifully learned from the master.

But apart from Stella's imitators, how can the phenomenon of his recent work be accounted for? If we remember that it was Stella's earliest paintings that signaled to his colleagues that the end of painting had finally come (I am thinking of such deserters of the ranks of painters as Dan Flavin, Donald Judd, Sol LeWitt, and Robert Morris), it seems fairly clear that Stella's own career is a prolonged agony over the incontestable implications of those works, as he has retreated further and further from them, repudiating them more vociferously with each new series. The late 1970s paintings are truly hysterical in their defiance of the black paintings; each one looks like a tantrum, shrieking and sputtering that the end of painting *has not come*. Moreover, it is no longer even *as paintings* that Stella's new works argue so tenaciously for the continued life of the medium. The irony of Stella's recent enterprise is that he is able to point at painting only from the distance of a peculiar hybrid object, an object that may well *represent* a painting but can hardly legitimately *be* a painting. This is not a wholly uninteresting enterprise, this defiance of the end of painting, but surely its only interest is in such a reading, for conceived as renewal, Stella's recent works are, as Gerhard Richter said of painting, pure idiocy.

Installation of *Frank Stella: The Black Paintings,* Baltimore Museum of Art, November 23, 1976–January 23, 1977 (photo courtesy Baltimore Museum of Art).

Frank Stella, *Shards IV*, 1983, as seen from
outside the lobby of 375 Hudson Street,
New York (owner Tishman–Speyer, primary tenant Saatchi, Saatchi & Compton)
(photo Louise Lawler).

Nevertheless, it is as renewal that they are understood. Here, for example, is Stella's friend Philip Leider, expressing the art-world majority opinion:

In these most recent works, Stella, throwing open the doors to much that had hitherto seemed to him forbidden—figure-ground dichotomies, composition, gestural paint-handling, etc.—has achieved for abstraction a renewed animation, life, vitality, that has already about it something of the sheerly miraculous. One would have to be blind not to see it, catatonic not to feel it, perverse not to acknowledge it, spiritless not to admire it.[14]

Leider's insistence on our belief in miracles, echoing that of Hennessy and Rose, is perhaps symptomatic of the real contemporary condition of painting: only a miracle can prevent it from coming to an end. Stella's paintings are not miracles, but perhaps their sheer desperation is an expression of painting's need for a miracle to save it.

Leider anticipates my skepticism in his apology for Stella's recent work, assuming that, as usual, a major change of style will be met with resistance:

Every artist who hopes to attain a major change in style, within abstraction especially, must prepare himself for a period in which he will have to "compromise with his own achievements." During this period he can expect to lose friends and stop influencing youth. . . . It is a matter of having taken things as far as possible only to find oneself trapped in an outpost of art, with work threatening to come to a standstill, thin and uncreative. At such a point he must compromise with the logic of his own work in order to go on working at all—it is either that or remain prisoner of his own achievement forever, face those sterile repetitions that stare at us from the late works of Rothko, Still, Braque.[15]

Opinions about the late works of Rothko, Still, and Braque aside, sterile repetitions may, under the present circumstances of

art, have their own value. This is, of course, the premise of Daniel
Buren's work, which has never, since he began his activities in
1965, evidenced a single stylistic change.

☙

It is no longer a matter of criticizing works of art and their meaning,
aesthetic, philosophical, or otherwise. It is no longer a matter even of
knowing how to make a work of art, an object, a painting; how to
become inserted in the history of art, nor even of asking oneself the
question whether it is interesting or not, essential or ridiculous, to
create a work of art, how, if you are or desire to be an artist (or if you
challenge that word), to fit in with the game so as to play it with your
own tools, and to the best of your ability. It is no longer a matter
even of challenging the artistic system. Neither is it a matter of taking
delight in one's interminable analysis. The ambition of this work is
quite different. It aims at nothing less than abolishing the code that
has until now made art what it is, in its production and in its
institutions.

Daniel Buren, *Reboundings*

Buren's work has been exhibited more extensively than that of any
other painter in the past decade. And although it has been seen in
galleries and museums, as well as in the streets, all over the developed world, perhaps by more people than have seen the work of
any other contemporary artist, it has thus far remained invisible to
all but a few. This paradox is testimony to the success of Buren's
gambit, as well as to the seemingly unshakable faith in painting—
which is to say, the code. When Buren decided in 1965 to make only
works in situ, always using 8.7-centimeter-wide vertical stripes,
alternating colored with white or transparent, he obviously made a
canny choice. For, just as he predicted, this format has not been
assimilable to the codes of art, regardless of how elastic those codes
have been in the past fifteen years. As we have seen, even such
bizarre hybrids as Stella's recent constructions can easily be taken for

Daniel Buren, Rue Jacob, Paris, April 1968
(photo Daniel Buren).

paintings, though certainly they are not, and as such they can be understood to continue painting-as-usual.

In a climate in which Stella's hysterical constructions can so readily be seen as paintings, it is understandable that Buren's works cannot. It is therefore not surprising that Buren is widely regarded as a conceptual artist who is unconcerned with the visible (or what Marcel Duchamp called the retinal) aspects of painting. But Buren has always insisted specifically on the visibility of his work, the necessity for it to be *seen*. For he knows only too well that when his stripes are seen as painting, painting will be understood as the "pure idiocy" that it is. At the moment when Buren's work becomes visible, the code of painting will have been abolished and Buren's repetitions can stop: the end of painting will have been finally acknowledged.

Notes

1. *Eight Contemporary Artists,* an exhibition of the work of Vito Acconci, Alighiero Boetti, Daniel Buren, Hanne Darboven, Jan Dibbets, Robert Hunter, Brice Marden, and Dorothea Rockburne, organized by Jennifer Licht at the Museum of Modern Art, New York, October 9, 1974–January 5, 1975.

2. Barbara Rose, "Twilight of the Superstars," *Partisan Review* 41, no. 4 (Winter 1974), p. 572.

3. Lawrence Alloway and John Coplans, "Talking with William Rubin: 'The Museum Concept Is Not Infinitely Expandable,'" *Artforum* 13, no. 2 (October 1974), p. 52.

4. Daniel Buren, "Function of the Museum," *Artforum* 12, no. 1 (September 1973), p. 68.

5. Rose, "Twilight of the Superstars," p. 569.

6. Barbara Rose, *American Painting: The Eighties* (Buffalo: Thorney-Sidney Press, 1979), n.p. All following quotations from Barbara Rose are taken from her essay in this catalogue.

7. This question is the title of an essay by Richard Hennessy published in *Artforum* 17, no. 9 (May 1979), pp. 22–25.

8. Quoted in "Photography: A Special Issue" (editorial), *October,* no. 5 (Summer 1978), p. 3.

9. Hennessy, "What's All This," p. 22.

10. Robert Ryman, in Phyllis Tuchman, "An Interview with Robert Ryman," *Artforum* 9, no. 9 (May 1971), p. 49.

11. Hennessy, "What's All This," p. 23 (italics original).

12. Ibid., p. 25.

13. Michel Foucault, *The Order of Things* (New York: Pantheon, 1970), p. 16.

14. Philip Leider, *Stella since 1970* (Fort Worth: Fort Worth Art Museum, 1978), p. 98.

15. Ibid., pp. 96–97.

The Photographic Activity of Postmodernism

> It is a fetishistic, fundamentally anti-technical notion of art with
> which theorists of photography have tusseled for almost a century,
> without, of course, achieving the slightest result. For they sought
> nothing beyond acquiring credentials for the photographer from the
> judgment-seat which he had already overturned.
>
> Walter Benjamin, "A Short History of Photography"

That photography had overturned the judgment-seat of art is a fact
that modernism found it necessary to repress, and so it seems that
we may accurately say that postmodernism constitutes a return of
the repressed. Postmodernism represents a specific breach with
modernism, with those institutions that are the preconditions for
and shape the discourse of modernism. The institutions can be
named at the outset: first, the museum; then, art history; and,
finally, in a more complex sense, because modernism depends on
both its presence and its absence, photography. Postmodernism is
about art's dispersal, its plurality, by which I do not mean pluralism.
Pluralism entails the fantasy that art is free, free of other discursive
practices and institutions, free above all, of history. And this fantasy
of freedom can be maintained because every work of art is held to
be absolutely unique and original. Against this pluralism of originals, I want to speak of the plurality of copies.

In an essay of 1979 called "Pictures," in which I first found it
useful to employ the term *postmodernism,* I attempted to sketch a
background to the work of a group of younger artists who were just
beginning to exhibit in New York.[1] I traced the genesis of their
concerns to what had been pejoratively labeled the theatricality of
minimal sculpture and the extensions of that theatrical position into

the art of the 1970s.[2] I suggested that the aesthetic mode that was exemplary during the 1970s was performance art—all those works that were constituted in a specific situation and for a specific duration; works for which it could be said literally that you had to be there; works, that is, that assumed the presence of a spectator in front of the work as the work took place, thereby privileging the spectator instead of the artist.

In my attempt to continue the logic of the development I was outlining, I came eventually to a stumbling block. What I wanted to explain was how to get from this condition of presence—the *being there* necessitated by performance—to the kind of presence that is possible only through the absence that we know to be the condition of representation. For what I was writing about was work that had taken on, after half a century of its repression, the question of representation. I effected that transition with a kind of fudge, an epigraph quotation suspended between two sections of the text. The quotation, taken from one of the ghost tales of Henry James, was a false tautology, which played on the double, indeed antithetical, meaning of the word *presence:* "The presence before him was a presence."

What I just said was a fudge was perhaps not really that, but rather it was a hint of something crucial about the work I was describing, which I would like now to elaborate. In order to do so, I want to add a third definition to the word *presence.* To the notion of presence that is about *being there,* being in front of, and the notion of presence that Henry James uses in his ghost stories, the presence that is a ghost and therefore really an absence, the presence that is *not there,* I want to add the notion of presence as a kind of increment to being there, a ghostly aspect of presence that is its excess, its supple-

Jack Goldstein, *Two Fencers*, Salle Patino,
Geneva, 1977.

ment. This notion of presence is what we mean when we say, for example, that Laurie Anderson is a performer with presence. We mean by such a statement not simply that she is there, in front of us, but that she is more than there, that in addition to being there, she has presence. If we think of Laurie Anderson in this way, it might seem a bit odd, because Laurie Anderson's particular presence is effected through the use of reproductive technologies that really make her quite absent, or only there as the kind of presence that Henry James meant when he said, "The presence before him was a presence."

This is the kind of presence that I attributed to the performances of Jack Goldstein, such as *Two Fencers,* and to which I would add the performance by Robert Longo called *Surrender.* These performances were little else than presences, performed tableaux that were there in the spectator's space but that appeared ethereal, absent. They had the odd quality of holograms, very vivid and detailed and present and at the same time ghostly, absent. Goldstein and Longo are artists whose work, together with that of a great number of their contemporaries, approaches the question of representation through photographic modes, particularly all those aspects of photography that have to do with reproduction, with copies, and with copies of copies. The peculiar presence of this work is effected through absence, through its unbridgeable distance from the original, from even the possibility of an original. Such presence is what I attribute to the kind of photographic activity I call postmodernist.

This quality of presence would seem to be just the opposite of what Walter Benjamin had in mind when he introduced the notion of aura into the language of criticism. For the aura has to do with the presence of the original, with authenticity, with the unique existence of the work of art in the place in which it happens to be. It is that aspect of the work that can be put to the test of chemical analysis or connoisseurship, that aspect that the discipline of art history, at least in its guise as *Kunstwissenschaft,* is able to prove or disprove, and that aspect, therefore, that either admits the work of art into or banishes it from the museum. For the museum has no truck with fakes or copies or reproductions. The presence of the artist in the work must be detectable; that is how the museum knows it has something authentic.

But it is this very authenticity, Benjamin tells us, that is inevitably depreciated through mechanical reproduction, diminished through the proliferation of copies. "That which withers in the age of mechanical reproduction is the aura of the work of art," is the way Benjamin puts it.[3] But, of course, the aura is not an ontological category as employed by Benjamin but rather a historical one. It is not something a handmade work has that a mechanically made work does not have. In Benjamin's view, certain photographs have an aura, whereas even a painting by Rembrandt loses its aura in the age of mechanical reproduction. The withering away of the aura, the dissociation of the work from the fabric of tradition, is an *inevitable* outcome of mechanical reproduction. This is something we have all experienced. We know, for example, the impossibility of experiencing the aura of such a picture as the *Mona Lisa* as we stand before it at the Louvre. Its aura has been utterly depleted by the thousands of times we've seen its reproduction, and no degree of concentration will restore its uniqueness for us.

It would seem, though, that if the withering away of the aura is an inevitable fact of our time, then equally inevitable are all those projects to recuperate it, to pretend that the original and the unique are still possible and desirable. And this is nowhere more apparent than in the field of photography itself, the very culprit of mechanical reproduction.

Benjamin granted a presence or aura to only a very limited number of photographs. These were photographs of the so-called primitive phase, the period prior to photography's commercialization after the 1850s. He said, for example, that the people in these early photographs "had an aura about them, a medium which mingled with their manner of looking and gave them a plenitude and security."[4] This aura seemed to Benjamin to be a product of two things: the long exposure time during which the subjects grew, as it were, into the images and the unique, unmediated relationship between the photographer, who was "a technician of the latest school," and the sitter, who was "a member of a class on the ascendant, replete with an aura which penetrated to the very folds of his bourgeois overcoat or bow-tie."[5] The aura in these photographs, then, is not to be found in the presence of the photographer in the photograph in the way that the aura of a painting is determined by the presence of the painter's unmistakable hand in his or her picture. Rather, it is the presence of the subject, of what is photographed, "the tiny spark of chance, of the here and now, with which reality has, as it were, seared the character of the picture."[6] For Benjamin, then, the connoisseurship of photography is an activity diametrically opposed to the connoisseurship of painting; it means looking not for the hand of the artist but for the uncontrolled and uncontrollable intrusion of reality, the absolutely unique and even magical quality not of the artist but of his or her subject. And that is perhaps why it seemed to Benjamin so misguided that photographers began, after the commercialization of the medium, to simulate the lost aura through the application of techniques imitative of those of painting. His example was the gum bichromate process used in pictorial photography.

Although it may at first seem that Benjamin lamented the loss of the aura, the contrary is in fact true. Reproduction's "social significance, particularly in its most positive form, is inconceivable," he wrote, "without its destructive, cathartic aspect, its liquidation of the traditional value of the cultural heritage."[7] That was for him the greatness of Eugène Atget: "He initiated the liberation of the object from the aura, which is the most incontestable achievement of the recent school of photography."[8] "The remarkable thing about [Atget's] pictures . . . is their emptiness."[9]

This emptying operation, the depletion of the aura, the contestation of the uniqueness of the work of art, has been accelerated and intensified in the art of the past two decades. From the multiplication of silkscreened photographic images in the works of Rauschenberg and Warhol to the industrially manufactured, repetitively structured works of minimal sculptors, everything in radical artistic practice seemed to conspire in that liquidation of traditional cultural values that Benjamin spoke of. And because the museum is the institution that was founded on those values, whose job it is to sustain those values, it has faced a crisis of considerable proportions. One symptom of that crisis is the fact that our museums, around 1970, one after another abdicated responsibility toward contemporary artistic practice and turned with nostalgia to the art that had previously been relegated to their storerooms. Revisionist art history soon began to be vindicated by "revelations" of the achievements of academic artists and minor figures of all kinds.

By the mid–1970s another, more serious symptom of the museum's crisis appeared, the one I have already mentioned: the various attempts to recuperate the auratic. These attempts are manifest in two contradictory phenomena: the resurgence of expressionist painting and the triumph of photography-as-art. The museum has embraced both of these phenomena with equal enthusiasm.

Little, I think, needs to be said about the return to a painting of personal expression. We see it everywhere we turn. The marketplace is glutted with it. It comes in all guises—pattern painting, new-image painting, neoconstructivism, neoexpressionism; it is pluralist, to be sure. But within its individualism, this painting is utterly conformist on one point: its hatred of photography. In a manifesto-like text for the catalogue of her *American Painting: The Eighties,* Barbara Rose wrote,

The serious painters of the eighties are an extremely heterogeneous group— some abstract, some representational. But they are united on a sufficient number of critical issues that it is possible to isolate them as a group. They are, in the first place, dedicated to the preservation of painting as a transcendental high art, and an art of universal as opposed to local or topical significance. Their aesthetic, which synthesizes tactile with optical qualities, defines itself in conscious opposition to photography and all forms of mechanical reproduction which seek to deprive the art work of its unique "aura." It is, in fact, the enhancement of this aura, through a variety of means, that painting now self-consciously intends—either by emphasizing the artist's hand, or by creating highly individual visionary images that cannot be confused either with reality itself or with one another.[10]

That this kind of painting should so clearly see mechanical reproduction as the enemy is symptomatic of the threat to inherited ideas (the only ideas known to this painting) posed by the photographic activity of postmodernism. But in this case it is also symptomatic of a more limited and internecine threat: the one posed to painting when photography itself suddenly acquires an aura. Now it's not only a question of ideology; now it's real competition for the acquisition budget and wall space of the museum.

But how is it that photography has suddenly had conferred upon it an aura? How has the plenitude of copies been reduced to the scarcity of originals? And how do we know the authentic from its reproduction?

Enter the connoisseur. But not the connoisseur of photography, of whom the type is Walter Benjamin, or, closer to us, Roland Barthes. Neither Benjamin's "spark of chance" nor Barthes's "third meaning" would guarantee photography's place in the museum.[11] The connoisseur needed for this job is the old-fashioned art historian with his chemical analyses and, more important, his stylistic analyses. To authenticate photography requires all the machinery of art history and museology, with a few additions and more than a few sleights of hand. To begin, there is, of course, the incontestible rarity of age, the vintage print. Certain techniques, paper types, and chemicals have passed out of use, and thus the age of a print can easily be established. But this kind of certifiable rarity is not what interests me, nor is its parallel in contemporary photographic practice, the limited edition. What interests me is the subjectivization of

Louise Lawler, *Arranged by Barbara and
Eugene Schwartz; Desk Light by Ernesto
Gismondi*, 1982. Photographs by August
Sander, one by Ansel Adams, sculpture by
Robert Smithson.

photography, the ways in which the connoisseurship of the photograph's "spark of chance" is converted into a connoisseurship of the photograph's style. For now, it seems, we can detect the photographer's hand after all, except, of course, that it is the eye, his or her unique vision (although it can also be the hand; one need only listen to the partisans of photographic subjectivity describe the mystical ritual performed by the photographer in the darkroom).

I realize, of course, that in raising the question of subjectivity I am reviving the central debate in photography's aesthetic history—between the straight and the manipulated print, or the many variations on that theme. But I do so here in order to point out that the recuperation of the aura of photography would in fact subsume under the banner of subjectivity *all* of photography, the photography whose source is the human mind and the photography whose source is the world around us, the most thoroughly manipulated photographic fictions and the most faithful transcriptions of the real, the directorial and the documentary, the mirrors and the windows,[12] *Camera Work* in its infancy, *Life* in its heyday. But these are only the terms of style and mode of the agreed-on spectrum of photography-as-art. The restoration of the aura, the consequent collecting and exhibiting, does not stop there. It is extended to the carte-de-visite, the fashion plate, the advertising shot, the anonymous snap or polaroid. At the origin of each there is an Artist, and therefore each can find its place on the spectrum of subjectivity. For it has long been a commonplace of art history that realism and expressionism are only matters of degree, matters, that is, of style.

The photographic activity of postmodernism operates, as we might expect, in complicity with these modes of photography-as-art, but it does so only in order to subvert or exceed them. And it does so precisely in relation to the aura, not, however, to recuperate it, but to displace it, to show that it too is now only an aspect of the copy, not the original. A group of young artists working with photography have addressed photography's claims to originality, showing those claims for the fiction they are, showing photography to be

always a *representation*, always–already–seen. Their images are pur-
loined, confiscated, appropriated, *stolen*. In their work, the original
cannot be located, is always deferred; even the self that might have
generated an original is shown to be itself a copy.

In a characteristic gesture, Sherrie Levine begins a statement
about her work with an anecdote that is very familiar:

Since the door was only half closed, I got a jumbled view of my mother
and father on the bed, one on top of the other. Mortified, hurt, horror-
struck, I had the hateful sensation of having placed myself blindly and completely in unworthy hands. Instinctively and without effort, I divided
myself, so to speak, into two persons, of whom one, the real, the genuine
one, continued on her own account, while the other, a successful imitation
of the first, was delegated to have relations with the world. My first self
remains at a distance, impassive, ironical, and watching.[13]

Not only do we recognize this as a description of something
we already know—the primal scene—but our recognition might
extend even further to the Moravia novel from which it has been
lifted. For Levine's autobiographical statement is only a string of
quotations pilfered from others, and if we might think this a strange
way of writing about one's own working methods, then perhaps we
should turn to the work it describes.

At a recent exhibition, Levine showed six photographs of a
nude youth. They were simply rephotographed from the famous
series by Edward Weston of his young son Neil, available to Levine
as a poster published by the Witkin Gallery. According to copyright
law, the images belong to Weston—or now to the Weston estate. I
think, to be fair, however, we might just as well give them to
Praxiteles, for if it is the *image* that can be owned, then surely these
belong to classical sculpture, which would put them in the public
domain. Levine has said that when she showed her photographs to a
friend, he remarked that they only made him want to see the originals. "Of course," she replied, "and the originals make you want to

see that little boy, but when you see the boy, the art is gone." The desire that is initiated by that representation does not come to closure around that little boy, is not at all satisfied by him. The desire of representation exists only insofar as it can never be fulfilled, insofar as the original always is deferred. It is only in the absence of the original that representation can take place. And representation takes place because it is always already there in the world *as* representation. It was, of course, Weston who said that the photograph must be visualized in full before the exposure is made.[14] Levine has taken the master at his word and in so doing has shown him what he really meant. The a priori Weston had in mind was not really in his mind at all; it was in the world, and Weston only copied it.

This fact is perhaps even more crucial in those series by Levine where that a priori image is not so obviously confiscated from high culture—by which I intend both Weston and Praxiteles—but from the world itself, where nature poses as the antithesis of representation. The images that Levine confiscated from books of photographs by Andreas Feininger and Elliot Porter show scenes of nature that are utterly familiar. They suggest a new interpretation of Roland Barthes's description of the tense of photography as the "having been there."[15] The presence that such photographs have for us is the presence of déjà vu, nature as already having been seen, nature as representation.

If Levine's photographs occupy a place on that spectrum of photography-as-art, that place would be at the farthest reaches of straight photography, not only because the photographs she appropriates operate within that mode but also because she does not manipulate her photographs in any way; she merely, and literally, *takes* photographs. At the opposite end of that spectrum is the photography that is self-consciously composed, manipulated, fictionalized, the so-called directorial mode, in which we find such *auteurs* of photography as Duane Michaels and Les Krims. The strategy of this mode is to use the apparent veracity of photography against itself, creating one's fictions through the appearance of a seamless reality

Louise Lawler, *Arranged by Carl Lobell at Weil, Gotshal, and Manges*, 1982. Photographs by Cindy Sherman.

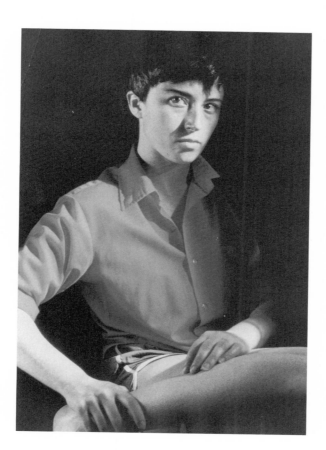

Cindy Sherman, *Untitled*, 1982 (photo courtesy Metro Pictures, New York).

into which has been woven a narrative dimension. Cindy Sherman's photographs function within this mode, but only in order to expose an unwanted aspect of that fiction, for the fiction Sherman discloses is the fiction of the self. Her photographs show that the supposed autonomous and unitary self out of which those other "directors" would create their fictions is itself nothing other than a discontinuous series of representations, copies, and fakes.

Sherman's photographs are all self-portraits in which she appears in disguise enacting a drama whose particulars are withheld. This ambiguity of narrative parallels the ambiguity of the self that is both actor in the narrative and creator of it. For though Sherman is literally self-created in these works, she is created in the image of already known feminine stereotypes; her self is therefore understood as contingent on the possibilities provided by the culture in which Sherman participates, not by some inner impulse. As such, her photographs reverse the terms of art and autobiography. They use art not to reveal the artist's true self but to show the self as an imaginary construct. There is no real Cindy Sherman in these photographs; there are only the guises she assumes. And she does not create these guises; she simply chooses them in the way that any of us do. The pose of authorship is dispensed with not only through the mechanical means of making the image but also through the effacement of any continuous, essential persona or even recognizable visage in the scenes.

The aspect of our culture that is most thoroughly manipulative of the roles we play is, of course, mass advertising, whose photographic strategy is to disguise the directorial mode as a form of documentary. Richard Prince steals the most frank and banal of these images, which register, in the context of photography-as-art, as a kind of shock. But ultimately their rather brutal familiarity gives way to strangeness, as an unintended and unwanted dimension of fiction reinvades them. By isolating, enlarging, and juxtaposing fragments of commercial images, Prince points to their invasion by these ghosts of fiction. Focusing directly on the commodity fetish,

Richard Prince, window installation,
Printed Matter, New York, 1980 (photo
courtesy Metro Pictures, New York).

using the master tool of commodity fetishism, Prince's rephotographed photographs take on a Hitchcockian dimension; the commodity becomes a clue. It has, we might say, acquired an aura, only
now it is a function not of presence but of absence, severed from an
origin, from an originator, from authenticity. In our time, the aura
has become only a presence, which is to say, a ghost.

Notes

1. Douglas Crimp, "Pictures," *October,* no. 8 (Spring 1979), pp. 75–88. This essay is a revised version of the catalogue for an exhibition of the same title that I organized for Artists Space, New York, in the fall of 1977.

2. The famous condemnation of minimal sculpture's theatricality is Michael Fried's "Art and Objecthood," *Artforum* 5, no. 10 (June 1967), pp. 12–23.

3. Walter Benjamin, "The Work of Art in the Age of Mechanical Reproduction," in *Illuminations,* trans. Harry Zohn (New York: Schocken Books, 1969), p. 221.

4. Walter Benjamin, "A Short History of Photography," trans. Stanley Mitchell, *Screen* 13, no. 1 (Spring 1972), p. 18.

5. Ibid., p. 19.

6. Ibid., p. 7.

7. Benjamin, "Work of Art," p. 221.

8. Benjamin, "Short History", p. 20.

9. Ibid., p. 21.

10. Barbara Rose, *American Painting: The Eighties* (Buffalo: Thoren-Sidney Press, 1979), n.p.

11. Photography's "third meaning" is theorized in Roland Barthes, "The Third Meaning: Research Notes on Some Eisenstein Stills," in *Image—Music—Text,* trans. Stephen Heath (New York: Hill and Wang, 1977), pp. 52–68.

12. I refer here to John Szarkowski, *Mirrors and Windows: American Photography since 1960* (New York: Museum of Modern Art, 1978).

13. Sherrie Levine, unpublished statement, 1980.

14. Weston's notion that the photograph must be *previsualized* is stated in many variations throughout his large body of writings. It first appears at least as early as his "Random Notes on Photography" of 1922. See Peter C. Bunnell, ed., *Edward Weston on Photography* (Salt Lake City: Peregrim Smith Books, 1983).

15. See Roland Barthes, "Rhetoric of the Image," in *Image—Music—Text,* pp. 32–51.

Appropriating Appropriation

The strategy of appropriation no longer attests to a particular stance toward the conditions of contemporary culture. To say this is both to suggest that appropriation *did* at first seem to entail a critical position and to admit that such a reading was altogether too simple. Appropriation, pastiche, quotation—these methods extend to virtually every aspect of our culture, from the most cynically calculated products of the fashion and entertainment industries to the most committed critical activities of artists, from the most clearly retrograde works (Michael Graves's buildings, Hans Jürgen Syberberg's films, Robert Mapplethorpe's photographs, David Salle's paintings) to the most seemingly progressive practices (Frank Gehry's architecture, Jean-Marie Straub and Danièle Huillet's cinema, Sherrie Levine's photography, Roland Barthes's texts). If all aspects of the culture use this new operation, then the operation itself cannot indicate a specific reflection upon the culture.

The very ubiquity of a new mode of cultural production does, however, underscore the fact that there has been an important cultural shift in recent years, a shift that I still want to designate as that between modernism and postmodernism, even if the latter term is utterly confusing in its current usages. *Postmodernism* will perhaps begin to acquire meaning beyond the simple naming of a *Zeitgeist* when we are able to employ it to make distinctions within all the various practices of appropriation. What I would like to do here, then, is to suggest some ways in which these distinctions might be approached.

To begin, I should perhaps look more closely at the assertions of the regressive/progressive character of the uses of appropriation by the artists previously named. How, for example, can we distinguish Graves's use of pastiche from that of Gehry? For the sake of convenience, let us take the most famous building by each architect—Graves's Portland Public Services Building and Gehry's own house in Santa Monica. The Portland building displays an eclectic mix of past architectural styles drawn generally from the orbit of classicism. But it is an already eclectic classicism to which Graves turns—the neoclassicism of Boullée and Ledoux, the pseudoclassicism of Art Deco public buildings, occasional flourishes of beaux-arts pomp. Gehry's house, in contrast, appropriates only a single element from the past. It is not, however, an element of style; it is an already existing 1920s clapboard house. This house is then collaged with (surrounded by, shot through with) mass-produced, from-the-catalogue materials of the construction industry—corrugated iron, chain-link fence, plywood, asphalt.

Differences between these two practices are immediately obvious: Graves appropriates from the architectural past; Gehry appropriates laterally, from the present. Graves appropriates style; Gehry, material. What different readings result from these two modes of appropriation? Graves's approach to architecture returns to a premodernist understanding of the art as a creative combination of elements derived from a historically given vocabulary (these elements are also said to derive from nature, but nature as understood in the nineteenth century). Graves's approach is thus like that of beaux-arts architects, against whom modernist architects would react. Although there can be no illusion that the elements of style are originated by the architect, there is a very strong illusion indeed of the wholeness of the end product and of the architect's creative contribution to the uninterrupted, ongoing tradition of architecture.

Graves's eclecticism thus maintains the integrity of a self-enclosed history of architectural style, a pseudohistory immune to problematic incursions from real historical developments (one of which would be modern architecture, if it is considered as more than merely another style).

Gehry's practice, however, retains the historical lessons of modernism even as it criticizes modernism's idealist dimension from a postmodernist perspective. Gehry takes from history an actual object (the existing house), not an abstracted style. His use of present-day products of the building trade reflects on the current material conditions of architecture. Unlike the sandstone or marble that Graves uses or imitates, Gehry's materials cannot pretend to a timeless universality. Moreover, the individual elements of Gehry's house resolutely maintain their identities. They do not combine into an illusion of a seamless whole. The house appears as a collage of fragments, declaring its contingency as would a movie set seen on a sound stage (a comparison this house directly solicits), and these fragments never add up to a style. Gehry's house is a response to a specific architectural program; it cannot be indiscriminately reapplied in another context. Graves's vocabulary, on the other hand, will seem to him as appropriate to a tea kettle or a line of fabrics as to a showroom or a skyscraper.

What, then, becomes of these differences when applied to photography? Can analogous distinctions be made between the photographic borrowings of Robert Mapplethorpe on the one hand and Sherrie Levine on the other? Mapplethorpe's photographs, whether portraits, nudes, or still lifes (and it is not coincidental that they fall so neatly into these traditional artistic genres), appropriate the stylistics of prewar studio photography. Their compositions, poses, lighting, and even their subjects (*mondain* personalities, glacial nudes, tulips) recall *Vanity Fair* and *Vogue* at that historical juncture when such artists as Edward Stiechen and Man Ray contributed to those publications an intimate knowledge of international art photography. Mapplethorpe's abstraction and fetishization of objects refer, through the mediation of the fashion industry, to Edward Weston, while his abstraction of the *subject* refers to the neoclassical pretenses of George Platt Lynes. Just as Graves finds his style in a few carefully selected moments of architectural history, so Mapplethorpe constructs from his historical sources a synthetic "personal" vision that is yet another creative link in photographic history's endless chain of possibilities.

When Levine wished to make reference to Edward Weston and to the photographic variant of the neoclassical nude, she did so by simply rephotographing Weston's pictures of his young son Neil— no combinations, no transformations, no additions, no synthesis. Like the 1920s house that forms the core of Gehry's design, Weston's nudes are appropriated whole. In such an undisguised theft of already existing images, Levine lays no claim to conventional notions of artistic creativity. She makes use of the images, but not to constitute a style of her own. Her appropriations have only functional value for the particular historical discourses into which they are inserted. In the case of the Weston nudes, that discourse is the very one in which Mapplethorpe's photographs naively participate. In this respect, Levine's appropriation reflects on the strategy of appropriation itself—the appropriation by Weston of classical sculptural style; the appropriation by Mapplethorpe of Weston's style; the appropriation by the institutions of high art of both Weston and Mapplethorpe, indeed of photography in general; and finally, photography as a tool of appropriation. Using photography instrumentally as Levine does, she is not confined to the specific medium of photography. She can also appropriate paintings (or reproductions of paintings). In contrast, the rejection of photography as a possible tool guarantees the atavism of the painters' recent pastiches, since they remain dependent on modes of imitation/transformation that are no different from those practiced by nineteenth-century academicians. Like Graves and Mapplethorpe, such painters appropriate style, not material, except when they use the traditional form of collage. Only Levine has been canny enough to appropriate painting

Frank Gehry, *Frank Gehry House*, Santa
Monica, California, 1978 (photos Tim
Street-Porter/Esto).

Michael Graves, *The Portland Building*, 1980
(photo Proto Acme).

Michael Graves, tea kettle designed for
Alessi, 1985 (photo William Taylor).

Robert Mapplethorpe, *Thomas and Amos,*
1987 (photo courtesy the Estate of Robert
Mapplethorpe).

Robert Mapplethorpe, *Bird of Paradise*, 1981
(photo courtesy the Estate of Robert
Mapplethorpe).

Sherrie Levine, *Untitled (After Alexander Rodchenko: 3)*, 1987 (photo Zindman/ Fremont, courtesy Mary Boone Gallery).

Sherrie Levine, *Untitled (After Ilya Chasnick)*, 1984 (photo Zindman/Fremont, courtesy Mary Boone Gallery).

whole, in its material form, by staging, in collaboration with Louise Lawler, an exhibition at/of the studio of the late painter Dimitri Merinoff.

The centrality of photography within the current range of practices makes it crucial to a theoretical distinction between modernism and postmodernism. Not only has photography so thoroughly saturated our visual environment as to make the invention of visual images seem archaic, but it is also clear that photography is too multiple, too useful to other discourses, ever to be wholly contained within traditional definitions of art. Photography will always exceed the institutions of art, will always participate in nonart practices, will always threaten the insularity of art's discourse. In this regard, I want to return to the context in which photography first suggested to me the moment of transition to postmodernism.

In my essay "On the Museum's Ruins," I suggested that Robert Rauschenberg's works of the early 1960s threatened the museum's order of discourse. The vast array of objects that the museum had always attempted to systematize now reinvaded the institution as pure heterogeneity. What struck me as crucial was these works' destruction of the guarded autonomy of modernist painting through the introduction of photography onto the surface of the canvas. This move was important not only because it spelled the extinction of the traditional production mode but also because it questioned all the claims to authenticity according to which the museum determined its body of objects and its field of knowledge.

When the determinants of a discursive field begin to break down, a whole range of new possibilities for knowledge opens up that could not have been foreseen from within the former field. And in the years following Rauschenberg's appropriation of photographic images—his very real disintegration of the boundaries between art and nonart—a whole new set of aesthetic activities *did* take place. These activities could not be contained within the space of the museum or accounted for by the museum's discursive system. The crisis thus precipitated was met, of course, by attempts to deny that any significant change had occurred and to recuperate traditional forms. A new set of appropriations aided this recuperation: revivals of long-outmoded techniques such as painting *al fresco* (albeit on portable panels to ensure salability) and casting sculpture in bronze, rehabilitations of *retardataire* artists such as nineteenth-century *pompiers* and between-the-wars realists, and reevaluations of hitherto secondary products such as architects' drawings and commercial photography.

It was in relation to this last response to the museum's crisis—the wholesale acceptance of photography as a museum art—that it seemed to me a number of recent photographic practices using the strategy of appropriation functioned. Thus, Richard Prince's appropriation of advertising images, his thrusting unaltered pictures into the context of the art gallery, exactly duplicated—but in an undisguised manner—the appropriation by art institutions of earlier commercial photography. In like fashion, it appeared that the so-called directorial mode of art photography (which I prefer to call *auteur* photography) was wryly mocked by Laurie Simmons's setup shots of doll houses and plastic cowboys or by Cindy Sherman's ersatz film stills, which implicitly attacked auteurism by equating the known artifice of the actress in front of the camera with the supposed authenticity of the director behind it.

Certainly I did not expect this work simply to function as a programmatic or instrumental critique of the institutional force of the museum. Like Rauschenberg's pictures, all works made within the compass of existing art institutions will inevitably find their discursive life and actual resting place within those institutions. But when these practices begin, even if very subtly, to accommodate themselves to the desires of the institutional discourse—as in the case of Prince's extreme mediation of the advertising image or Sherman's abandonment of the movie still's *mise-en-scène* in favor of close-ups of the "star"—they allow themselves simply to enter that discourse (rather than to intervene within it) on a par with the very objects they had once appeared ready to displace. And in this way the strategy of appropriation becomes just another academic category—a thematic—through which the museum organizes its objects.[1]

A particularly illuminating example of the current conditions of art is provided again by the work of Rauschenberg. In his recent work he has returned to one of his early interests—photography. But now he uses photography not as a reproductive technology through which images can be transferred from one place in the culture to another—from, say, the daily newspaper to the surface of painting—but rather as an art medium traditionally conceived. Rauschenberg has become, in short, a photographer. And what does he find with his camera, what does he see through his lens, but all those objects in the world that look like passages from his own art. Rauschenberg thus appropriates his own work, converts it from material to style, and delivers it up in this new form to satisfy the museum's desire for appropriated photographic images.

Notes

1. The reference here was pointed: this essay was written for the catalogue of *Image Scavengers: Photography,* part of a double exhibition also including *Image Scavengers: Painting,* presented at the Institute of Contemporary Art, University of Pennsylvania, December 8, 1982–January 30, 1983, using "appropriation" as an organizing theme.

A Drinking Glass

Midnight Pasadena

Roche, Dinkeloo, & Assoc., Metropolitan Museum of Art, André Meyer
Gallery

The following year her glass "cage"
remained empty for the first two
weeks of the exhibition. When finally
exposed she was likened by one critic
to an "expelled foetus" which if
smaller " . . . one would be tempted
to pickle in a jar of alcohol."

Calder, Franzen, Oldenburg, The
Whitney, Philip Morris

The End of Sculpture

Redefining Site Specificity

I know that there is no audience for sculpture, as is the case with poetry and experimental film. There is, however, a big audience for products which give people what they want and supposedly need, and which do not attempt to give them more than they can understand.

Richard Serra, "Extended Notes from Sight Point Road"

It is better to be an enemy of the people than an enemy of reality.

Pier Paolo Pasolini, "Unhappy Youths"

The site was an old warehouse on the Upper West Side in Manhattan used by the Leo Castelli Gallery for storage; the occasion, an exhibition organized by minimal sculptor Robert Morris; the moment, December 1968. There, strewn upon the cement floor, affixed to or leaning against the brick walls, were objects that defied our every expectation regarding the form of the work of art and the manner of its exhibition. It is difficult to convey the shock registered then, for it has since been absorbed, brought within the purview of normalized aesthetics, and, finally, consigned to a history of an avant-garde now understood to be finished. But, for many of us who began to think seriously about art precisely because of such assaults on our expectations, the return to convention in the art of the 1980s can only seem false, a betrayal of the processes of thought that our confrontations with art had set in motion. And so we try again and again to recover that experience and to make it available to those who now complacently spend their Saturday afternoons in SoHo galleries viewing paintings that smell of fresh linseed oil and sculptures that are once again cast in bronze.

Of the things in that warehouse, certainly none was more defiant of our sense of the aesthetic object than Richard Serra's *Splashing*. Along the juncture where wall met floor, Serra had tossed molten lead and allowed it to harden in place. The result was not really an object at all; it had no definable shape or mass; it created no legible image. We could, of course, say that it achieved the negation of categories that Donald Judd had, some years earlier, ascribed to "the best new work": "neither painting nor sculpture."[1] And we could see that by effacing the line where the wall rose up perpendicular to the floor, Serra was obscuring a marker for our orientation in interior space, claiming that space as the ground of a different kind of perceptual experience. Our difficulty with *Splashing* was in trying to imagine its very possibility of continued existence in the world of art objects. There it was, attached to the structure of that old warehouse on the Upper West Side, condemned to be abandoned there forever or scraped off and destroyed. For to remove the work meant certainly to destroy it.

"To remove the work is to destroy the work." It is with this assertion that Serra sought to shift the terms of debate in a public hearing convened to determine the fate of *Tilted Arc*.[2] Serra's sculpture had been commissioned by the General Services Administration (GSA) Art-in-Architecture Program and permanently installed in the plaza of Jacob K. Javits Federal Building in Lower Manhattan during the summer of 1981. In 1985, a newly appointed GSA regional administrator presumed to reconsider its presence there, to ask whether it might be "relocated" elsewhere. In testimony after testimony at that hearing, artists, museum officials, and others pleaded the case for site specificity that Serra's assertion implied.

Richard Serra, *Splashing* and *Prop*, both
1968, installation Castelli Warehouse, New
York (photo Peter Moore).

The work was conceived for the site, built on the site, had become an integral part of the site, altered the very nature of the site. Remove it, and the work would simply cease to exist. But, for all its passion and eloquence, the testimony failed to convince the adversaries of *Tilted Arc*. To them the work was in conflict with its site, disrupted the normal views and social functions of the plaza, and, indeed, would be far more pleasant to contemplate in a landscape setting. There, presumably, its size would be less overwhelming to its surroundings, its rust-colored steel surface more harmonious with the colors of nature.

The larger public's incomprehension in the face of Serra's assertion of site specificity is the incomprehension of the radical prerogatives of a historic moment in art practice. "To remove the work is to destroy the work" was made self-evident to anyone who had seen *Splashing*'s literalization of the assertion, and it is that which provided the background of *Tilted Arc* for its defenders. But they could not be expected to explain, within the short time of their testimonies, a complex history that had been deliberately suppressed. The public's ignorance is, of course, an enforced ignorance, for not only is cultural production maintained as the privilege of a small minority, but it is not in the interests of the institutions of art and the forces they serve to produce knowledge of radical practices even for their specialized audience. And this is particularly the case for those practices whose goal is a materialist critique of the presuppositions of those very institutions. Such practices attempt to reveal the material conditions of the work of art, its mode of production and reception, the institutional supports of its circulation, the power relations represented by these institutions—in short, everything that is disguised by traditional aesthetic discourse. Nevertheless, these practices have subsequently been recuperated by that very discourse as reflecting just one more episode in a continuous development of modern art. Many of *Tilted Arc's* defenders, some representing official art policies, argued for a notion of site specificity that reduced it to a purely aesthetic category. As such, it was no longer germane to the presence of the sculpture on Federal Plaza. The specificity of *Tilted Arc*'s site is that of a particular public place. The work's material, scale, and form intersect not only with the formal characteristics of its environment but also with the desires and assumptions of a very different public from the one conditioned to the shocks of the art of the late 1960s. Serra's transfer of the radical implications of *Splashing* into the public realm, deliberately embracing the contradictions this transfer implies, is the real specificity of *Tilted Arc*.

When site specificity was introduced into contemporary art by minimal artists in the mid-1960s, what was at issue was the idealism of modern sculpture, its engagement of the spectator's consciousness with sculpture's own internal set of relationships. Minimal objects redirected consciousness back on itself and the real-world conditions that ground consciousness. The coordinates of perception were established as existing not only between the spectator and the work but among spectator, artwork, and the place inhabited by both. This was accomplished either by eliminating the object's internal relationships altogether or by making those relationships a function of simple structural repetition, of "one thing after another."[3] Whatever relationship was now to be perceived was contingent on the viewer's temporal movement in the space shared with the object. Thus the work belonged to its site; if its site were to change, so would the interrelationship of object, context, and viewer. Such a reorientation of the perceptual experience of art made the viewer, in effect, the subject of the work, whereas under the reign of modernist idealism this privileged position devolved ultimately on the artist, the sole generator of the artwork's formal relationships. The critique of idealism directed against modern sculpture and its illusory sitelessness was, however, left incomplete. The incorporation of place within the domain of the work's perception succeeded only in extending art's idealism to its surrounding site. Site was understood as specific only in a formal sense; it was thus abstracted, aestheticized. Carl Andre, who made the claim that sculpture, formerly equated with form and structure, was now to be equated with place, was asked about the implications of moving his works from one place to another. His reply: "I don't feel myself obsessed with the singularity of places. I don't think spaces are that singular. I think there are generic classes of spaces which you work for and toward. So it's not really a problem where a work is going to be in particular."[4] And Andre enumerated these spaces: "Inside gallery spaces, inside private dwelling spaces, inside museum spaces, inside large public spaces, and outside spaces of various kinds too."[5]

Andre's failure to see the singularity of the "generic classes of spaces" he "worked for and toward" was the failure of minimal art to produce a fully materialistic critique of modernist idealism. That critique, initiated in the art production of the following years, would entail an analysis of, and resistance to, art's institutionalization within the system of commerce represented by those spaces listed by Andre. If modern artworks existed in relation to no specific site and were therefore said to be autonomous, homeless, that was also the precondition of their circulation; from the studio to the commercial gallery, from there to the collector's private dwelling, thence to the museum or lobby of a corporate headquarters. The real material condition of modern art, masked by its pretense to universality, is that of the specialized luxury commodity. Engendered under capitalism, modern art became subject to the commodification from which nothing fully escapes. And in accepting the "spaces" of art's institutionalized commodity circulation as given, minimal art could neither expose nor resist the hidden material conditions of modern art.

That task was taken up in the work of artists who radicalized site specificity, artists as various as Daniel Buren and Hans Haacke, Michael Asher and Lawrence Weiner, Robert Smithson and Richard Serra. Their contributions to a materialist critique of art, their resistance to the "disintegration of culture into commodities,"[6] were fragmentary and provisional, the consequences limited, systematically opposed or mystified, ultimately overturned. What remains of this critique today are a history to be recovered and fitful, marginalized practices that struggle to exist at all in an art world more dedicated than ever before to commodity value.

That history cannot be recovered here; it can only be claimed as necessary for any genuine understanding of Richard Serra's *Splashing* and what he was to make afterward. We need hardly be reminded of the dangers inherent in divorcing art practices from the social and political climates in which they took place; in this case, the very mention of the year 1968 as the date of *Splashing* should serve sufficient notice. The following paragraphs, written in France by Daniel Buren just one month after the events of May 1968 and published the following September, may provide a reminder of the political consciousness of artists of the period.

We can find challenges to tradition back in the 19th century—indeed (considerably) earlier. And yet since then countless traditions, academicisms, countless new taboos and new schools have been created and overthrown!

Why? Because those phenomena against which the artist struggles are only epiphenomena or, more precisely, they are only the superstructures built on the base that conditions art and is art. And art has changed its traditions, it academicisms, its taboos, its schools, etc., at least a hundred times, because it is the vocation of what is on the surface to be changed, endlessly, and so long as we don't touch the base, nothing, obviously, is fundamentally, *basically,* changed.

And that is how art evolves, and that is how there can be art history. The artist challenges the easel when he paints a surface too large to be supported by the easel, and then he challenges the easel and the overlarge surface by turning out a canvas that's also an object, and then just an object; and then there is the object to be made in place of the object made, and then a mobile object or an untransportable object, etc. This is said merely by way of example, but intended to demonstrate that if there is a possible challenge it cannot be a formal one, it can only be basic, on the level of art and not on the level of the forms given to art.[7]

The Marxist terminology of Buren's text locates him in a political tradition very different from that of his American colleagues. Moreover, among the artists of his generation Buren has been the most systematic in his analysis of art in relation to its economic and ideological bases, and thus he has reached a far more radical conclusion: that the changes wrought on art within practice must be "basic," not "formal." In spite of Richard Serra's continued work with the "forms given to art," however, he has incorporated important components of a materialist critique. These include his attention to the processes and divisions of labor, to art's tendency toward the conditions of consumption, and the false separation of private and public spheres in art's production and reception. Although Serra's work is not systematic or consistent in this regard, even the contradictory manner in which he has taken a critical position has produced reactions that are often perplexed, outraged, sometimes violent. Determined to build his work outside the confines of art institutions, Serra has frequently met with the opposition of public officials and their surrogates, who have been quick to manipulate public incomprehension for their censorial purposes.[8]

The extraordinary status that has accrued to the work of art during the modern period is, in part, a consequence of the romantic myth of the artist as the most highly specialized, indeed unique, producer. That this myth obscures the social division of labor was recognized by minimal artists. Traditional sculpture's specialized craft and highly fetishized materials were opposed by minimalism with the introduction of objects industrially fabricated of ordinary materials. Dan Flavin's fluorescent lights, Donald Judd's aluminum boxes, and Carl Andre's metal plates were in no way products of the artist's hand. Serra, too, turned to industrial materials for his early sculpture, but at first he worked those materials himself or with the help of friends. Using lead and working at a scale proportionate to hand manipulation, he produced torn, cast, and propped pieces that were still evidence of the artist's activity, however much the processes Serra employed differed from the conventional crafts of carv-

Richard Serra, *Strike: To Roberta and Rudy*,
1969–1971, installation Lo Giudice Gallery,
New York (photo Peter Moore).

ing, modeling, and welding. But when Serra installed *Strike* in the Lo Giudice Gallery, New York, in 1971, his working procedure was transformed. *Strike* was only a single plate of hot-rolled steel, one inch thick, eight feet high, twenty-four feet long, and weighing nearly three tons. That steel plate was not, however, the work. To become the sculpture *Strike,* the steel plate had to occupy a site, to assume its position wedged into the corner of the gallery room, bisecting the right angle where wall met wall. But there is no operation of the artist's craft that would accomplish this simple fact. The steel's tonnage required an industrial process other than the one that produced the plate. That process, known as rigging, involves the application of the laws of mechanics, usually with the aid of machinery, "to put [material] in condition or position for use."[9] Beginning with *Strike,* Serra's work would require the professional labor of others, not only for the manufacture of the sculpture's material elements but also to "make" the sculpture, that is, to put it in its condition or position for use, to constitute the material *as* sculpture. This exclusive reliance on the industrial labor force (a force signaled with a very particular resonance in the sculpture's name) distinguishes Serra's production after the early 1970s as public in scope, not only because the scale of the work dramatically increased but because the private domain of the artist's studio could no longer be the site of production. The place where the sculpture would stand would be the place where it was made, and its making would be the work of others.

Characterizations of Serra's work as macho, overbearing, aggressive, oppressive, seek to return the artist to the studio, to reconstitute him as the work's sole creator, and thereby to deny the role of industrial processes in his sculpture. Whereas any large-scale sculpture requires such processes, whereas even the manufacture of paint and canvas require them, the labor that has been expended in them is nowhere to be discerned in the finished product. That labor has been mystified by the artist's own "artistic" labor, transformed by the artist's magic into a luxury commodity. Serra not only refuses to perform the mystical operations of art but also insists on confronting the art audience with materials that otherwise never appear in their raw state. Serra's materials, unlike those of the minimal sculptors, are materials used only for the means of production. They normally appear to us transformed into finished products or, more rarely, into the luxury goods that are works of art.[10]

This conflict between the product of heavy industry, which is unavailable for luxury consumption, and the sites of its exhibition, the commercial gallery and museum, intensified as Serra developed the implications of *Strike* toward the total negation of the normal functions of gallery spaces. Rather than subserviently taking their cues from the formal conditions of room spaces, as site-specific works tied to purely aesthetic ideas began to do, Serra's sculptures worked not "for and toward" but against those spaces. The enormous steel-plate walls of *Strike, Circuit* (1972), and *Twins* (1972) took on new dimensions with *Slice* (1980), *Waxing Arcs* (1980), *Marilyn Monroe—Greta Garbo* (1981), and *Wall to Wall* (1983). These dimensions were also assumed in the horizontal steel-plate works *Delineator* (1974) and *Elevator* (1980) and the forged-steel block pieces *Span* (1977) and *Step* (1982). Testing and straining against the outer limits of structural, spatial, visual, and circulatory capacity, these works pointed to another sort of specificity of the site of art, its specific historical origins in the bourgeois interior. For if the historical form of the modern artwork was conceived for its function in adorning that private interior space, if the museum goer could always imagine the painting by Picasso or the sculpture by Giacometti transposed back inside the private dwelling, it was hardly so comfortable a thought to imagine a steel wall slicing through one's living room. "Inside private dwelling spaces" would no longer be congenial sites for Serra's sculpture, and thus another of art's private domains was defeated by Serra's use of heavy industrial materials and their mode of deployment. At the same time, art's institutional exhibition spaces, surrogates of the private domicile, were revealed as determining, constraining, and drastically limiting art's possibilities.

Rigging Richard Serra's *Circuit* for *Documenta 5*, Kassel, 1972.

Rigging Richard Serra's *Elevator*, The Hudson River Museum, Yonkers, 1980 (photo Jon Abbott).

By the time Serra installed these later works in commercial galleries and museums, he had already transferred much of his activity out-of-doors into the landscape and cityscape. The sheer implausibility of the indoor works, shoehorned into clean white rooms, imposes the terms of a truly public sculptural experience within the confines of the usually private site. In effect, Serra reversed the direction generally taken by sculpture as it ventures into public space, the direction concisely spelled out in one critic's statement of resignation: "All we can ever do is put private art in public places."[11] Unwilling, as we shall see, to accept this calcified idea of private versus public, Serra insists rather on bringing the lessons learned on the street, as it were, back into the gallery. In the process, the gallery goer (*Marilyn Monroe—Greta Garbo* is subtitled "A Sculpture for Gallery Goers") is made excruciatingly aware of the gallery's limitations, of the stranglehold it exerts on the experience of art. By turning the tables on the gallery, holding the gallery hostage to sculpture, Serra defies the gallery's authority, declares it a site of struggle. That the terms of this struggle hinge in part on questions of the private versus the public site of art is demonstrated by *Slice,* installed in the Leo Castelli Gallery on Greene Street, New York, in 1980. A continuous curve of steel plates, 10 feet high and over 124 feet long, the sculpture sliced through the gallery's deep space and lodged itself into the two corners of one of the long walls. The room was thereby divided into two noncommunicating areas, an area on the convex side of the curve, which we may designate as public, and a concave interior "private" area. Entering the gallery from the street, the gallery goer followed the curve from an expansive open space through the compression where the curve closed in closer to the long wall and then opened out again into the gallery's back wall. The sensation was that of being on the outside, cut off from the real function of the gallery, unable to see its operations, its office, its personnel. Leaving the gallery and reentering through the door off the lobby, the gallery goer was now "inside," confined in the concavity of the curve, privy to the gallery's commercial deal-

Richard Serra, *Slice*, 1980, installation Leo
Castelli Gallery, New York (photos Bevan
Davies).

ings. In thus experiencing the two sides of *Slice* as extraordinary different spatial sensations, neither imaginable from the other, one also experienced the always present and visible but never truly apparent relations between the gallery as a space of viewing and as a space of commerce. In installing a work that could not partake of the commercial possibilities of commodity circulation, Serra was nevertheless able to make that condition of the gallery a part of the work's experience, if only in abstract, sensory terms.

But possibilities of disrupting the power of galleries to determine the experience of art are exceedingly limited, dependent as they are on the willingness of the contested institution. This is also true, of course, for museums, even though the latter might claim greater neutrality with respect to all art practices, even those that question the privatization of culture as a form of property. The museum, however, in the benevolence of this neutrality, simply substitutes an ideologically constituted concept of private expression for the gallery's commercial concept of private commodities. For the museum as an institution is constituted to produce and maintain a reified history of art based on a chain of masters, each offering his private vision of the world. Although his work does not participate in this myth, Serra is aware that within the museum it will be seen that way in any case:

In all my work the construction process is revealed. Material, formal, contextual decisions are self-evident. The fact that the technological process is revealed depersonalizes and demythologizes the idealization of the sculptor's craft. The work does not enter into the fictitious realm of the "master." . . . My works do not signify any esoteric self-referentiality. Their construction leads you into their structure and does not refer to the artist's persona. However, as soon as you put a work into a museum, its label points first to the author. The visitor is asked to recognize "the hand." Whose work is it? The institution of the museum invariably creates self-referentiality, even where it's not implied. The question, how the work functions, is not asked. Any kind of disjunction the work might intend is eclipsed. The problem of self-referentiality does not exist once the work enters the public domain. How the work alters a given site is the issue, not the persona of the author. Once the works are erected in a public space, they become other people's concerns.[12]

When Serra first moved out of the institutions of art, he moved very far indeed. It was 1970. Robert Smithson had built the *Spiral Jetty* in the Great Salt Lake in Utah; Michael Heizer had carved *Double Negative* into the Virginia River Mesa of Nevada; Serra himself was planning *Shift,* the large outdoor work in King County, Canada. For all the excitement generated by the development of earthworks, however, Serra found such isolated sites unsatisfactory. An urban artist working with industrial materials, he discovered that the vast and inevitably mythologized American landscape was not his concern, nor were the pathos and mock heroism of working in isolation from an audience. "No," he said, "I would rather be more vulnerable and deal with the reality of my living situation."[13] Serra negotiated with New York City officials for a site in the city, and eventually they granted him a permit to construct a work in an abandoned dead-end street in the Bronx. There, in 1970, Serra built *To Encircle Base Plate Hexagram, Right Angles Inverted,* a circle of steel angle, twenty-six feet in diameter, embedded in the surface of the street. Half the circle's circumference was a thin line, one inch wide; the other half, the angle's flange, eight inches wide. From a distance, at street level, the work was invisible; only when the viewer came directly upon it did the work materialize. Standing within its circumference, the viewer could reconstruct its sculptural bulk, half buried under grade. There was, however, a second approach, also from a distance, from which the work was visible in a different way. The dead-end street gave onto stairways leading up to an adjoining street at a higher level; from there the street below appeared as a "canvas" upon which the steel circle was "drawn." This reading of figure against ground, rather than reconstructing material bulk *in* the ground, worried Serra, seeming to him once again to evoke the

Rigging *To Encircle Base Plate Hexagram,*
Right Angles Inverted, The Bronx, New
York, 1970 (photo Gianfranco Gorgoni).

pictorialism into which sculpture always tended to lapse, a pictorialism he wished to defeat with the sheer materiality and duration of experience of his work. Moreover, this deceptive pictorialism coincided with another way of reading the sculpture that Serra did not foresee and that came to represent for him a fundamental deception against which he would position his work. That deception was the *image* of the work as against the actual experience of it.

To Encircle's site was, as Serra described it, "sinister, used by the local criminals to torch cars they'd stolen."[14] Clearly those "local criminals" were not interested in looking at sculpture—pictorial or not—and it was Serra's misconception that anyone from the art world was interested enough in sculpture to venture into that "sinister" outpost in the Bronx. The work existed, then, in precisely the form in which earthworks exist for most people—as documents, photographs. They are transferred back into the institutional discourses of art through reproduction, one of the most powerful means through which art has been abstracted from its contexts throughout the modern era. For Serra, the whole point of sculpture is to defeat this surrogate consumption of art, indeed to defeat consumption altogether and to replace it with the experience of art in its material reality:

If you reduce sculpture to the flat plane of the photograph, you're passing on only a residue of your concerns. You're denying the temporal experience of the work. You're not only reducing the sculpture to a different scale for the purposes of consumption, but you're denying the real content of the work. At least with most sculpture, the experience of the work is inseparable from the place in which the work resides. Apart from that condition, any experience of the work is a deception.

But it could be that people want to consume sculpture the way they consume paintings—through photographs. Most photographs take their cues from advertising, where the priority is high image content for an easy Gestalt reading. I'm interested in the experience of sculpture in the place where it resides.[15]

Serra's attempts to enforce the difference between an art for consumption and a sculpture to be experienced in the place where it resides would, however, embroil him in constant controversy. The first work Serra proposed for a truly public location was never allowed to occupy the site for which it was intended. After winning a competition in 1971 for a sculpture for the Wesleyan University campus in Middletown, Connecticut, Serra's *Sight Point* was ultimately rejected by the university's architect as "too large and too close to the campus's historical building."[16] It was, of course, just this size and proximity that Serra wanted. *Sight Point* is one of a number of large-scale works that employ the principles developed in the early prop pieces, principles of construction that rely on the force of gravity. But at their greatly increased scale and in their particular public settings, these works no longer use those principles merely to oppose the formal relationships obtaining in modernist sculpture; now they come into conflict with another form of construction, that of the architecture of their surroundings. Rather than playing the subsidiary role of adornment, focus, or enhancement of their nearby buildings, they attempt to engage the passerby in a new and critical reading of the sculptures' environment. By revealing the processes of their construction only in the active experience of sequential viewing, Serra's sculptures implicitly condemn architecture's tendency to reduce to an easily legible image, collapsed into, precisely, a facade. It is that reduction to facade, the pictorial product of the architects' drawing board, site of the architect's expressive mastery, that, presumably, the Wesleyan University architect wanted to protect for the campus's "historical building."[17]

When asked what *Sight Point* (1971–1975) lost by being built in the back court of the Stedelijk Museum in Amsterdam instead of its intended location, Serra replied simply: "What happened with *Sight Point* was that it lost all relationship to a pattern of circulation, which was a major determinate for its original location at Wesleyan."[18] Serra recognized that even public art was generally granted only the function of aesthetic enhancement in the seclusion of museumlike sites, removed from normal circulation patterns and placed, as it were, on ideological pedestals:

Usually you're offered places which have specific ideological connotations, from parks to corporate and public buildings and their extensions such as lawns and plazas. It's difficult to subvert those contexts. That's why you have so many corporate baubles on Sixth Avenue [New York], so much bad plaza art that smacks of IBM, signifying its cultural awareness. . . . But there is no neutral site. Every context has its frame and its ideological overtones. It's a matter of degree. There is one condition that I want, which is a density of traffic flow.[19]

It was just such a density of traffic flow that Serra found for *Terminal* (1977), erected in the very center of the German city of Bochum in the central hub of commuter traffic. "The streetcars miss it by a foot and a half."[20]

Terminal is a prop construction of four identical trapezoidal plates of Cor-Ten steel, forty-one feet high. The plates were manufactured at the Thyssen steelworks in the nearby town of Hattingen, in the Ruhr industrial district of which Bochum is one of the major cities. Although *Terminal* was initially built in Kassel for *Documenta 6*, Serra meant the work for its present site, in part because he wanted it located in the center of the steel-producing district where its plates were manufactured.[21] This social specificity of its site, however, would cause a furor over *Terminal*.

At first the work aroused a response not unusual for Serra's public sculpture: graffiti identifying it as a toilet or warning of rats, letters to the editors of local newspapers deploring the huge expenditure of city funds and declaring the work ugly and inappropriate. As the controversy grew and city council elections neared, the Christian Democratic party (CDU) seized upon the issue as a focus for its political campaign against the firmly entrenched Social Democrats, who had voted to purchase the work for the city. Vying for the votes of steelworkers, who constitute a large bloc of the region's

Richard Serra, *Terminal*, 1977, Bochum
(photos Alexander von Berswordt-
Wallrabe).

Christian Democratic Party campaign
poster, Bochum, 1979.

electorate, the CDU printed campaign posters showing a photograph of *Terminal* montaged against one of a steel mill. The slogan
announced, "It cannot *always* be like this—CDU for Bochum." The
Christian Democrats' objections to *Terminal* are extremely revealing
of the issues raised in Serra's public sculptures, especially insofar as
his abstract vocabulary intersects with explicit social and material
conditions. It is therefore worth quoting at length from the press
release issued by the CDU stating its position on *Terminal*:

The supporters of the sculpture refer to its great symbolic value for the
Ruhr district generally and for Bochum in particular as the home of coal
and steel. We believe the sculpture lacks important qualities that would
enable it to function as a symbol. Steel is a special material whose production demands great craftsmanship, professional and technical know-how.
The material has virtually unlimited possibilities for the differentiated, even
subtle treatment of both the smallest and the largest objects, both the sim-
plest and the most artistically expressive forms.

We do not believe this sculpture expresses any of these things since it
looks like a clumsy, undifferentiated, half-finished "ingot." No steelworker
can point to it positively, with pride.

Steel signifies boldness and elegance in the most varied constructions;
it does not signify monstrous monumentality. This sculpture is frightening
because of its awkward massiveness, untempered by any other attributes.
Steel is also a material that, to a great degree, suggests resilience, durability,
and resistance to rust. This is especially true of the high-quality steel produced in Bochum. This sculpture, made only of simple steel, is already
rusting and disgusting in appearance. Steel is a high-quality material developed from iron and so is not a true raw material. Yet this sculpture gives
the impression of raw material . . . extracted from the earth and given no
special treatment.

If, as its supporters claim, the sculpture is to symbolize coal and steel,
it must provide the possibility of positive identification for those concerned, that is, for the citizens of this area, especially the steelworkers. We
believe that all of the characteristics mentioned provide no positive chal-

lenge and identification. We fear the opposite will occur, that rejection and scorn will not only result initially but will intensify over time. That would be a burden not only for this sculpture but for all self-contained modern artworks. Such cannot be the goal of a responsible cultural policy.[22]

The hypocrisy of the Christian Democrats' claim to represent the steelworkers' interests hardly needs to be pointed out at a time when the German working class suffers from the increasingly brutal policies of that party, and the steelworkers were undeceived in this regard: the Social Democrats retained power in the region.[23] What is most important here, however, is the nature of the demand made on public art to provide the workers with symbols to which they can point with pride, with which they can positively identify. Hidden in this demand is the requirement that the artist symbolically reconcile the steelworkers to the brutal working conditions to which they are subjected. Steel, the material that the citizens of Ruhr district work with daily, is to be used by the artist only to symbolize boldness and elegance, resilience and durability, the unlimited possibilities for subtle treatment and expressive form. It is, in other words, to be disguised, made unrecognizable to those who have produced it. Serra's work flatly refuses this implicitly authoritarian symbolism, which would convert steel from raw material—although processed, steel is a raw material in the capitalist economic structure[24]—to a signifier of invincibility. Instead Serra presents the steelworkers with the very product of their alienated labor, untransformed into any symbol at all. If the workers are then repelled and heap scorn on *Terminal,* it is because they are already alienated from the material; for although they produced those steel plates or materials like them, they never owned them; the steelworkers have no reason whatsoever to take pride in or identify with any steel product. In asking the artist to give the workers a positive symbol, the CDU is really asking the artist to provide a symbolic form of consumption; for the CDU does not, in any case, wish to think of the worker as a worker, but rather as a consumer.[25]

The Bochum CDU's goal of a "responsible cultural policy" that would not be a burden for "self-contained modern artworks" parallels official public art policies in the United States that have emerged and expanded over the past twenty years. Taking for granted that art is private self-expression, these policies are concerned with the various possibilities of transferring such an art into the public realm without offending public expectations. In an essay tellingly entitled "Personal Sensibilities in Public Places," John Beardsley, who worked for the Art in Public Places Program of the National Endowment for the Arts and was commissioned to write a book about it, explains how the artists' private concerns can be made palatable for the public:

An artwork can become significant to its public through the incorporation of content relevant to the local audience, or by the assumption of an identifiable function. Assimilation can also be encouraged through a work's role in a larger civic improvement program. In the first case, recognizable content or function provides a means by which the public can become engaged with the work, though its style or form might be unfamiliar to them. In the latter, the work's identity as art is subsumed by a more general public purpose, helping to assure its validity. In both cases, the personal sensibilities of the artist are presented in ways that encourage widespread public empathy.[26]

One of Beardsley's prime examples of the empathy solicited through recognizable content involves a public much like that for *Terminal:*

[George] Segal was awarded his commission by the Youngstown Area Arts Council. He visited the city and toured its steel mills, finding the open hearth furnaces "staggeringly impressive." He decided to make steelworkers at an open hearth the subject of his sculpture, and used as models Wayman Paramore and Peter Kolby, two men selected by the steelworkers union from its membership. His commission coincided with a severe economic crisis in Youngstown during which a series of mill shutdowns eventually idled some 10,000 workers. Yet completion of the sculpture became a matter of civic pride. Numerous local businesses and foundations gave money; one of the steel companies donated an unused furnace. Labor unions assisted in fabricating and installing the work. One cannot escape the conclusion that the subject matter was largely responsible for this outpouring of public support. The people of Youngstown sought a monument to their principal industry, even as it collapsed around them. Segal's *Steelmakers* is a tribute to their tenacity.[27]

It is a cynical arts policy indeed that would condone, much less laud, a monument mythologizing work in steel mills when the real historical condition of the steelworkers is that of being forced into the industrial reserve army. Just whose tenacity does this work really pay tribute to? To the steelworkers hopelessly trying to maintain their dignity in the face of joblessness? Or to the society—including the business community, steel companies, and labor unions whose largess contributed to the work—that will go to any length to ensure that those steelworkers will never recognize the nature of the economic forces arrayed against them? Perhaps the CDU in Bochum would find Segal's *Steelmakers* insufficient as a symbol of the boldness and elegance of steel—the work is, after all, cast bronze—but it can certainly be said to fulfill their essential demand: that the sculpture reconcile the workers with their brutal conditions by giving them something with which they can positively identify. The fact that their identification is manipulated, that the workers' pride is only intended to make their slavery more tolerable, is precisely what such a cultural policy is concerted toward.[28] Needless to say, such a cultural policy, whether that of the Right in Germany or of the liberal arts establishment in the United States, finds the public sculpture of Richard Serra considerably more problematic. Conservatives in this country, who argue against all federal funding for culture, oppose Serra's work categorically, confident that when all public commissions are once again exclusively paid for by the private sector there will be no more room for such "malignant objects" (Serra's *Tilted Arc* is illustrated in an article of that title).[29] The cultural bureaucrats want, however, to appear more tolerant, hoping that "Serra's sculpture may eventually win a greater measure of acceptance within its community."[30]

That a difficult work of art requires time to ingratiate itself with its public was a standard line of defense of Serra's *Tilted Arc* during the public hearing of March 1985. Historical precedents of public outrage meeting now-canonical works of modern art became something of a leitmotif. But this deferral to the judgment of history was in fact a repudiation of history, a denial of the actual historical moment in which *Tilted Arc* confronted its public in all its specificity as well as a denial of Serra's intransigent rejection of the universal nature of the work of art. For to say that *Tilted Arc* would withstand the test of time is to reclaim for it an idealist position. The genuine importance of *Tilted Arc* can best be understood through an analysis of the crisis that it precipitated within established cultural policy.

Tilted Arc was built on a site that is public in a very particular sense. It inhabited a plaza flanked by a government office building housing federal bureaucracies and by the United States Court of International Trade. The plaza adjoins Foley Square, the location of New York City's federal and state courthouses. *Tilted Arc* was thus situated in the very center of the mechanisms of state power. The Jacob K. Javits Federal Building and its plaza are nightmares of urban development, official, anonymous, overscaled, inhuman. The plaza is a bleak, empty area, whose sole function is to shuttle human traffic in and out of the buildings. Located at one corner of the plaza is a fountain that cannot be used, since the wind-tunnel effect of the huge office tower would drench the entire plaza with water. Serra's *Tilted Arc,* a 12-foot-high steel-plate wall, 120 feet long and tilted slightly toward the office building and the trade courthouses, swept across the center of the plaza, dividing it into two distinct areas. Employing material and form that contrasted radically with both the

Richard Serra, *Tilted Arc*, Federal Plaza,
New York (photos David Aschkenas,
Glenn Speigelman).

Demonstration at Federal Plaza, New York,
June 6, 1984, against U.S. Immigration and
Naturalization Service policies regarding
Central American refugees (video Dee Dee
Halleck).

Destruction of *Tilted Arc* by the General
Services Administration, New York, March
15, 1989 (photo Jennifer Kotter).

vulgarized International Style architecture of the federal structures and the beaux-arts design of the old Foley Square courthouses, the sculpture imposed a construction of absolute difference within the conglomerate of civic architecture. It engaged the passerby in an entirely new kind of spatial experience that was counterposed against the bland efficiency established by the plaza's architects. Although *Tilted Arc* did not disrupt normal traffic patterns—the shortest routes to the streets from the buildings were left clear—it did implant itself within the public's field of vision. Soliciting, even commanding attention, the sculpture asked the office workers and other pedestrians to leave their usual hurried course and follow a different route, gauging the curving planes, volumes, and sight lines that marked this place as the place of sculpture.

In reorienting the use of Federal Plaza from a place of traffic control to one of sculptural place, Serra once again used sculpture to hold its site hostage, to insist on the necessity for art to fulfill its own functions rather than those relegated to it by its governing institutions and discourses. For this reason, *Tilted Arc* was considered an aggressive and egotistical work, with which Serra placed his own aesthetic assumptions above the needs and desires of the people who had to live with his work. But insofar as our society is fundamentally constructed on the principle of egotism, the needs of each individual coming into conflict with those of all other individuals, Serra's work did nothing other than present us with the truth of our social condition. The politics of consensus that ensures the smooth functioning of our society is dependent on the shared belief that all individuals are unique but can exist in harmony with one another by assenting to the benign regulation of the state. The real function of the state, however, is not the defense of the citizen in his or her true individuality but the defense of private property—the defense, that is, precisely of the conflict between individuals.[31] Within this politics of consensus, the artist is expected to play a leading role, offering a unique "private sensibility" in a manner properly universalized so as to ensure feelings of harmony. The reason Serra is accused of egotism, when other artists who put their "private sensibilities in public places" are not, is that his work cannot be seen to reflect his private sensibility in the first place. And once again, when the work of art refuses to play the prescribed role of falsely reconciling contradictions, it becomes the object of scorn. A public that has been socialized to accept the atomization of individuals and the false dichotomy of private and public spheres of existence cannot bear to be confronted with the reality of its situation. And when the work of public art rejects the terms of consensus politics within the very purview of the state apparatus, the reaction is bound to be censorial. Not surprisingly, the coercive power of the state, disguised as democratic procedure, was soon brought to bear on *Tilted Arc*. At the show trial staged to justify the work's removal, the most vociferous opposition to the work came not from the public at large but from representatives of the state, from judges of the courts and heads of federal bureaucracies whose offices are in the Federal Building.[32]

From the moment *Tilted Arc* was installed on Federal Plaza in 1981, Chief Judge Edward D. Re of the U.S. Court of International Trade began the campaign to have it removed.[33] Preying on the people's impotence in controlling their degraded social environment in a city where that control is granted only to property owners, Judge Re held out the deceptive promise of pleasant social activities, which he claimed could not take place on the plaza unless the steel wall was removed. With accusations that an elitist art world had foisted its experiments upon them, many office workers signed petitions for *Tilted Arc*'s removal. But the judge and his fellow civil servants really had a very different view of the public from the beneficent one that saw people gathering to listen to music on their lunch breaks. One the one hand, the public consisted for them of competitive individuals who could be manipulated to fight it out among themselves over the crumbs of social activity dishonestly offered to them. On the other hand, they were the frightening individuals lurking on the other side of the wall, lying in wait for the judge as he left the protection of his chambers and ventured out into the public realm. In one of the many letters written to the GSA complaining of the sculpture, Judge Re made his fears explicit: "By no means of minor importance is the loss of efficient security surveillance. The placement of this wall across the plaza obscures the view of security personnel, who have no way of knowing what is taking place on the other side of the wall."[34]

Judge Re's attitude toward the people was further elaborated during the GSA hearing by one of those security personnel. Her testimony is worth excerpting at some length, since it gives a clear and chilling sense of the state's current regard for its citizens:

My main purpose here is to present you the aspects, from the security angle, which affect us in the execution of our duties here. The *Arc* is what I consider to be a security hazard or a disadvantage. My main contention is that it presents a blast wall effect. . . . It's 120 feet long, 12 feet high, and it's angled in a direction towards both federal buildings, 1 Federal Plaza and 26 Federal Plaza. The front curvature of the design is comparable to devices which are used by bomb experts to vent explosive forces. . . . The purpose of these . . . bomb devices is to vent explosions upward. This one could vent an explosion both upward and in an angle toward both buildings. . . .

Most of the time the wall was closer to the building. It would, of course, take a larger bomb than [those] which have been previously used to destroy enough for their purposes; but it is possible, and lately we are expecting the worst in the federal sector. . . . Most people express their opinions against us in either violent ways or with graffiti and those types of ways. . . . The wall—pardon, the *Tilted Arc*—is used more for graffiti purposes than any of the other walls. . . . Most of the graffiti is done on the other side where we cannot view it.

Loitering for illegal purposes is another problem we experience, and we do have the problem with drug dealings which we cannot see from our side of the building. We, by the way, only concern ourselves with the federal side of the building.[35]

If a public sculpture can have projected on it such an explicit statement of the contempt in which the public is held by the state, it has
served a historical function of great consequence. We now have
written into the public record, for anyone who wishes to read it, the
fact that the "federal sector" expects only the worst from us, that we
are all considered potential loiterers, graffiti scribblers, drug dealers,
terrorists. When *Tilted Arc* is converted, in the paranoid vision of a
state security guard, into a "blast wall," when the radical aesthetics
of site-specific sculpture are reinterpreted as the site of political
action, public sculpture can be credited with a new level of achievement. That achievement is the redefinition of the site of the work of
art as the site of political struggle. Determined to "be vulnerable and
deal with the reality of his living situation," Richard Serra has found
himself again and again confronted with the contradictions of that
reality. Unwilling to cover up those contradictions, Serra runs the
risk of uncovering the true specificity of the site, which is always a
political specificity.

Notes

1. Donald Judd, "Specific Objects," *Arts Yearbook,* no. 8 (1965), p. 74.

2. Serra's actual assertion on this occasion was, "To remove *Tilted Arc,* therefore, is to destroy it"; see Clara Weyergraf-Serra and Martha Buskirk, eds., *The Destruction of* Tilted Arc: *Documents* (Cambridge, Mass., The MIT Press, 1991), p. 67. Held March 6–8, 1985, at the Ceremonial Courtroom, International Court of Trade, One Federal Plaza, New York, the hearing on the removal of *Tilted Arc* took place before a panel consisting of William J. Diamond, Regional Administrator, General Services Administration; Gerald Turetsky, Acting Deputy Regional Administrator, GSA; Paul Chistolini, Public Building Services, GSA; and two outside panelists, Thomas Lewin of the law firm Simpson, Thacher and Bartlett, and Michael Findlay of the auction house of Christie, Manson and Woods. On April 10, 1985, the panel in a four-to-one vote recommended relocation of *Tilted Arc.* This recommendation was adopted by Dwight A. Ink, Acting Director of the United States General Services Administration, Washington, D.C., and on May 31, 1985, he announced his decision to relocate the sculpture.

3. Judd, "Specific Objects," p. 82.

4. Quoted in Phyllis Tuchman, "An Interview with Carl Andre," *Artforum* 7, no. 10 (June 1970), p. 55.

5. Ibid.

6. Walter Benjamin, "Eduard Fuchs, Collector and Historian," trans. Kingsley Shorter, in *One-Way Street* (London: New Left Books, 1979), p. 360.

7. Daniel Buren, "Peut-il Enseigner l'Art?" *Galerie des Arts* (September 1968). Translated from the French by Richard Miller.

8. There have been several attempts to remove Serra's work from public sites. Soon after the decision to remove *Tilted Arc* was announced, St. Louis City Alderman Timothy Dee introduced a bill to the Board of Aldermen that would, if passed, allow city voters to decide whether *Twain* (1974–1982), a work in downtown St. Louis, should be removed. According to *The Riverfront Times* (St. Louis), September 6–10, 1985, p. 6A, Dee said, "The problem is the real gap between *regular people*—my constituents and the overwhelming majority—and the *elitist art community,* who decide to do something because they've all invested in certain artists" (italics added). The most thoroughly documented case is that of the Christian Democratic party of Bochum, West Germany, against *Terminal* (1977). For this case, see *Terminal von Richard Serra: Eine Dokumentation in 7 Kapiteln* (Bochum: Museum Bochum, 1980), and my discussion in this chapter. In addition, a number of major commissions awarded to Serra have never been built, owing to opposi-

tion to the work from architects and city officials. These include works for the Pennsylvania Avenue Development Corporation in Washington, D.C., the Centre Georges Pompidou in Paris, and works for outdoor sites in Madrid; Marl, West Germany; and Peoria, Illinois. *Sight Point* (1971–75), commissioned for Wesleyan University campus, was not built there. For a discussion of the difficulties Serra has faced in building his work in public, see Douglas Crimp, "Richard Serra's Urban Sculpture: An Interview," in *Richard Serra: Interviews, Etc. 1970–1980* (Yonkers, N.Y.: The Hudson River Museum, 1980), pp. 163–187.

9. *Webster's Eighth New Collegiate Dictionary* (Springfield, Mass., 1979), p. 989.

10. In volume 2 of *Capital,* Karl Marx divides the total mass of commodities into a two-department system for the purposes of explaining reproduction. Department 1 consists of the means of production: raw materials, machinery, building, etc.; Department 2 consists of consumer goods. Later Marxists have added to this scheme Department 3 to designate those goods that do not play a role in the reproduction of the working class since they are intended for consumption only by the capitalist classes. Department 3 includes luxury goods, art, and weapons. For a discussion of this relation between art and arms, see Ernest Mandel, *Late Capitalism,* trans. Joris de Bres (London: Verso, 1978), especially chapter 9, "The Permanent Arms Economy and Late Capitalism."

11. Amy Goldin, "The Esthetic Ghetto: Some Thoughts about Public Art," *Art in America* 62, no. 3 (May–June 1974), p. 32.

12. Richard Serra, "Extended Notes from Sight Point Road," in *Richard Serra: Recent Sculpture in Europe 1977–1985* (Bochum: Galerie m, 1985), p. 12.

13. Quoted in Crimp, "Richard Serra's Urban Sculpture," p. 170.

14. Ibid., p. 168.

15. Ibid., p. 170.

16. Ibid., p. 175.

17. On this subject, see Yve-Alain Bois, "A Picturesque Stroll around Clara-Clara," *October,* no. 29 (Summer 1984), pp. 32–62; see also Richard Serra and Peter Eisenman, "Interview," *Skyline* (April 1983), pp. 14–17.

18. Quoted in Crimp, "Richard Serra's Urban Sculpture," p. 175.

19. Ibid., pp. 166, 168.

20. Richard Serra, in Annette Michelson, Richard Serra and Clara Weyergraf, "The Films of Richard Serra: An Interview," *October,* no. 10 (Fall 1979), p. 91.

21. Ibid.; In this interview, in the context of a discussion of the film *Steelmill/Stahlwerk* (1970) by Serra and Weyergraf, Serra discusses at length his experience working in steel mills. *Steelmill/Stahlwerk* was shot in the mill where the plates of *Terminal* were fabricated, although the shooting took place during the forging of *Berlin Block for Charlie Chaplin* (1977).

22. Press release, CDU representatives to the Bochum City Council, reproduced in *Terminal von Richard Serra,* pp. 35–38.

23. Since 1982, when the CDU came to power in West Germany, the unemployment rate has risen to a postwar record: as of 1985, there were 2.2 million registered

unemployed and an estimated 1.3 million unregistered job seekers. Hardest hit have been the areas such as the Ruhr district, where heavy industries are located. In October 1985, the Federation of German Labor Unions staged a week-long protest against the CDU's economic policies to coincide with the heated debates on the issue in the Bundestag. In these debates, the full range of the opposition attacked the CDU for contributing to the disintegration of social conditions in Germany.

24. In claiming that steel is not a raw material because it is produced from iron, the CDU attempts to mystify, through an appeal to a natural versus man-made distinction, the place of steel within capitalist production. Steel is, of course, a product of Department 1, used for producing the means of production; see note 10.

25. "To each capitalist, the total mass of all workers, with the exception of his own workers, appear not as workers but as consumers, possessors of exchange values (wages), money, which they exchange for his commodity." Karl Marx, *Gundrisse: Foundations of the Critique of Political Economy,* Marx Library ed., trans. Martin Nicolaus (New York: Vintage Books, 1973), p. 419. In the postwar period in Germany, attempts to reconcile the working class to its social conditions has operated precisely on the symbolic level, including language itself. Thus the words *Arbeiter* (worker) and *Arbeitklasse* (working class) are no longer used in official discussion, as Germany is now said to be a classless society. In this society, there are only *Arbeitnehmer* (one who *takes* work, employee) and *Arbeitgeber* (one who gives work, employer). The irony of this linguistic reversal is not lost on the workers, who, for their part, know perfectly well that it is the worker who is the giver of work (Arbeitgeber) and the employer who is the taker of work (Arbeitnehmer). In such a climate it comes as no surprise that the right-wing party would see art as another possible form of mystification of social conditions.

26. John Beardsley, "Personal Sensibilities in Public Places," *Artforum* 19, no. 10 (June 1981), p. 44.

27. Ibid.

28. Louis Althusser has specified the role of what he calls Ideological State Apparatuses, among which he includes culture, as "the reproduction of the conditions of production." In order for this reproduction to take place, what must be assured is the workers' "subjection to the ruling ideology." Thus one of the functions of the cultural object confronting workers would be that of teaching them how to bear their subjugation. See Louis Althusser, "Ideology and the Ideological State Apparatuses (Notes towards an Investigation)," in *Lenin and Philosophy,* trans. Ben Brewster (New York: Monthly Review Press, 1971), pp. 127–186.

29. Douglas Stalker and Clark Glymour, "The Malignant Object: Thoughts on Public Sculpture," *The Public Interest,* no. 66 (Winter 1982), pp. 3–21. For other neoconservative attacks on public spending for art, see Edward C. Banfield, *The Democratic Muse: Visual Arts and the Public Interest* (New York: Basic Books, 1984); and Samuel Lipman, "Cultural Policy: Whither America, Whither Government?" *The New Criterion* 3, no. 3 (November 1984), pp. 7–15.

30. Beardsley, "Personal Sensibilities," p. 45.

31. On this subject, the central texts are the early writings of Karl Marx on the state and civil society; see especially "On the 'Jewish Question,'" in *Karl Marx: Early Writings,* trans. Rodney Livingstone and Gregor Benton (New York, Vintage Books, 1975), pp. 211–241. See also the reinterpretation of the relation between state and civil society and the importance of consensus in the work of Antonio Gramsci.

32. To anyone who followed the case closely, the public hearing on *Tilted Arc* was a mockery. The hearing was presided over, and the four other panelists were selected by, William J. Diamond, Regional Administrator of the General Services Administration, who had publicly asked for the removal of *Tilted Arc* and who had circulated petitions and solicited testimonies favoring its removal. And although two-thirds of the people testifying at the hearing favored retaining *Tilted Arc* on Federal Plaza, Diamond's panel nevertheless recommended removal to the GSA. For a complete account of the *Tilted Arc* case, including Serra's unsuccessful attempts to reverse the GSA decision in court, see Weyergraf-Serra and Buskirk, *The Destruction of* Tilted Arc.

33. See Weyergraf-Serra and Buskirk, *The Destruction of* Tilted Arc, pp. 26–29.

34. Ibid., p. 28.

35. Ibid., p. 117.

Three

Objects

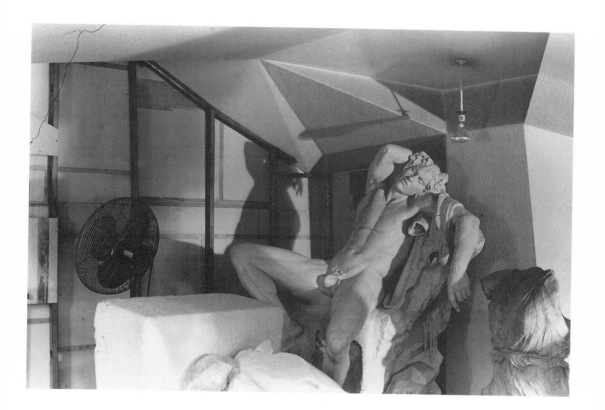

Storage

Queens Museum, Flushing
Meadow—Corona Park, New York, on
loan from the Metropolitan Museum
of Art, restored with funds from the
Chase Manhattan Bank, 1984.

Did you see your parent of the opposite sex naked? A chance occurrence
or was there no effort to avoid being
nude in your presence?

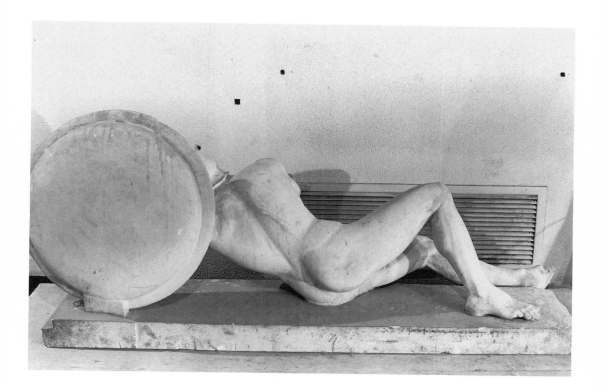

Postmodern History

This Is Not a Museum of Art

Fiction enables us to grasp reality and at the same time that which is veiled by reality.
　　Marcel Broodthaers

One "fictions" history on the basis of a political reality that makes it true; one "fictions" a politics not yet in existence on the basis of a historical truth.
　　Michel Foucault

Contrary to the romantic ideal, the artist is not, like the "perfect" mussel, a "clever thing" that can "avoid society's mold and cast itself in its very own."[1] Thus when Marcel Broodthaers decided, "in mid-career," to become an artist, he offered two explanations. The first and most often quoted appeared as the text of an announcement for his 1964 exhibition at the Galerie Saint-Laurent in Brussels:

I, too, wondered if I couldn't sell something and succeed in life. For quite a while I had been good for nothing. I am forty years old. . . . The idea of inventing something insincere finally crossed my mind, and I set to work at once.[2]

The second was written the following year and published in the Belgian journal *Phantomas:*

In art exhibitions I often mused. . . . Finally I would try to change into an art lover. I would revel in my bad faith. . . . Since I couldn't build a collection of my own, for lack of even the minimum of financial means, I had to find another way of dealing with the bad faith that allowed me to indulge in so many strong emotions. So, said I to myself, I'll be a creator.[3]

While we might suspect "insincerity" and "bad faith" of many "creators" nowadays, such negative qualities are rarely so frankly admitted as the necessary stance of the artist working under the conditions of late capitalism. By adopting these attitudes at the outset, however, Broodthaers was able to proceed as if his work as an artist were all part of a fictional ploy. Though it has often been noted that Broodthaers's curious artistic persona began with an acknowledgment of the commodity status of art, it has passed virtually unnoticed that it also entailed the frustration of being unable "to build a collection." This particular admission of "bad faith" may perhaps explain why Broodthaers would become not only a fictive "creator," but also a creator of "museum fictions." For, "with the canny clairvoyance of the materialist,"[4] he would reveal in these fictions the true historical conditions of the collection as they now exist.

∽

In a cryptic entry in file "H" of his *Passagen-Werk,* Walter Benjamin jotted down the phrase "Animals (birds, ants), children, and old men as collectors."[5] The suggested biologism of this notation, implying the existence of a *Sammeltrieb* (a primal urge to collect), could hardly be more surprising, especially insofar as Benjamin's assorted notes on the collector, and especially his essay on Eduard Fuchs, link collecting to the task of the historical materialist. This positive dimension of collecting is indicated, albeit negatively, in the following, also from file "H":

The *positive* countertype of the collector—who at the same time represents his fulfillment, insofar as he realizes the liberation of things from the bondage of utility—should be described according to these words of Marx: "Private property has made us so stupid and passive that an object becomes *ours* only if we own it, that is, if it exists for us as capital, or if it is *used* by us."[6]

For Benjamin, true collectors, the countertype of collectors as we know them, resist the demands of capital by rendering "useless" the objects they form into a collection; collectors' countertypes are thus able to unravel the secret historical meaning of the things they accumulate:

With collecting it is decisive that the object is released from all its original functions in order to enter into the closest possible relationship with its equivalents. This is the diametric opposite of use, and stands under the curious category of completeness. What is this "completeness"? It is a grandiose attempt to transcend the totally irrational quality of a mere being-there through integration into a new, specifically created historical system—the collection. And for the true collector every single thing in this system becomes an encyclopedia of all knowledge of the age, of the landscape, the industry, the owner from which it derives. The collector's most profound enchantment is to enclose the particular in a magic circle where it petrifies, while the final thrill (the thrill of being acquired) runs through it. Everything remembered and thought, everything conscious, now becomes the socle, the frame, the pedestal, and the seal of his ownership. One should not think that the collector, in particular, would be alienated from the *topos hyper-uranios,* which contains, according to Plato, the eternal Ideas of objects. Admittedly he loses himself. But he has the power to get back on his feet by grasping a straw, and out of the ocean of fog that blurs his mind the object just acquired emerges like an island. Collecting is a form of practical memory and, among the profane manifestations of "proximity," the most convincing one. Therefore, even the minutest act of political commemoration in the commerce in antiques becomes, in a sense, epochal. We are here constructing an alarm clock that awakens the kitsch of the past century into "re-collection."[7]

"Here" refers to the *Passagen-Werk* itself, and thus Benjamin designates his own projected materialist history of nineteenth-century

Paris a collection (indeed it survives for us as nothing more than a collection of fragments, quotations, and notes). A portion of this passage also appears in the autobiographical essay "Unpacking My Library," in which Benjamin had already described himself as a collector. It is also in this earlier essay that he prophesies the demise of this type, his role having been usurped by the *public* collection:

The phenomenon of collecting loses its meaning as it loses its personal owner. Even though public collections may be less objectionable socially and more useful academically than private collections, the objects get their due only in the latter. I do know that time is running out for the type that I am discussing here and have been representing before you a bit *ex officio*. But, as Hegel put it, only when it is dark does the owl of Minerva begin its flight. Only in extinction is the collector comprehended.[8]

If we find this concept of the positive countertype of the collector difficult to grasp, it is not only because the type has become extinct but also because what has arisen in its stead are two distinct, though related, phenomena. The first of these—the contemporary *private* collection, as opposed to Benjamin's *personal* collection—is amassed by those "stupid and passive" collectors whose objects exist for them only insofar as they literally possess and use them. The second is the public collection, the museum. And it is this latter that gives us greatest difficulty in comprehending Benjamin's ideas, a difficulty that he acknowledges when he says that the public collection appears less objectionable socially, more useful academically. Benjamin here alludes to the conventional, undialectical view of the museum as a progressive historical development, a view that is summed up in the title of a book of documents about the birth of public art institutions in the early nineteenth century, *The Triumph of Art for the Public*.[9] We can begin to understand the true meaning of this "triumph"—that is, who *within* "the public" benefited from it— by reading Benjamin's critique of the educational program of the Social Democratic Party at the turn of the century, which "raised the

whole problem of *the popularization of knowledge*. It was not solved,"
according to Benjamin.

And no solution could be approached so long as the object of this educational work was thought of as the *public* rather than as a class. . . . [The
Social Democrats] thought the same knowledge that secured the rule of the
bourgeoisie over the proletariat would enable the proletariat to free itself
from that rule. In reality, knowledge with no outlet in praxis, knowledge
that could teach the proletariat nothing about its situation as a class, was no
danger to its oppressors. This was especially true of knowledge relating to
the humanities. It lagged far behind economics, remaining untouched by
the revolution in economic theory. It sought only to *stimulate,* to *offer variety,* to *arouse interest*. History was shaken up, to relieve monotony; the
result was *cultural history*.[10]

This cultural history, to which Benjamin opposes historical materialism,[11] is precisely what the museum offers. It wrests its objects
from their original historical contexts not as an act of political commemoration but in order to create the illusion of universal knowledge. By displaying the products of particular histories in a reified
historical continuum, the museum fetishizes them, which, as
Benjamin says, "may well increase the burden of the treasures that
are piled up on humanity's back. But it does not give mankind the
strength to shake them off, so as to get its hands on them."[12] Herein
lies the genuine difference between the collection as Benjamin
describes it and the collection as we know it in the museum. The
museum constructs a cultural history by treating its objects indepen-
dently both of the material conditions of their own epoch and of
those of the present. In Benjamin's collection, objects are also
wrested from history, but they are "given their due," re-collected in
accordance with the political perception of the moment. Thus the
difference: "Historicism presents an eternal image of the past, historical materialism a specific and unique engagement with it. . . . The
task of historical materialism is to set to work an engagement with

history original to every new present. It has recourse to a consciousness of the present that shatters the continuum of history."[13]

༄

It is just this consciousness of the present, and the specific and unique engagement with the past determined by such consciousness, that brought about Broodthaers's museum fictions. Broodthaers could no longer perform the task of the historical materialist in the guise of the collector's countertype. Instead he commemorated the loss of this outmoded figure by assuming another guise—the "countertype" of the museum director. Beginning with the Section XIXème Siècle, Broodthaers founded his Musée d'Art Moderne, Département des Aigles, "under pressure of the political perception of its time"[14]—"this invention, a jumble of nothing, shared a character connected to the events of 1968, that is, to a type of political event experienced by every country."[15] The "museum" was inaugurated only a few months after May 1968, when Broodthaers had participated with fellow artists, students, and political activists in an occupation of the Palais des Beaux Arts in Brussels. Acting in solidarity with the political manifestations taking place throughout Europe and the United States,[16] the occupiers declared their takeover of the museum to be a contestation of the control over Belgian culture exerted by its official institutions, as well as a condemnation of a system that could conceive of culture only as another form of capitalist consumption.[17]

But in spite of his participation in a political action with these explicit goals, it is not immediately apparent how Broodthaers intended his fictive museum to "share in their character." At the end of the occupation Broodthaers wrote an open letter addressed "A mes amis" and dated "Palais des Beaux Arts, June 7, 1968"; it began as follows:

Calm and silence. A fundamental gesture has been made here that throws a vivid light on culture and on the ambitions of certain people who aspire to control it one way or another: what this means is that culture is an obedient material.

What is culture? I write. I have taken the floor. I am a negotiator for an hour or two. I say I. I reassume my personal attitude. I fear anonymity. (I would like to control the *meaning/direction* [sens] of culture.)[18]

Recognizing that culture is obedient to those who would exert control over it, Broodthaers also recognizes that he, too, would like to exert such control. Having taken up the profession of artist, as he had self-consciously done only four years earlier, and now participating in the occupation of the museum, Broodthaers wavers between his role as negotiator and the resumption of a personal attitude, a fundamentally duplicitous position. He ironically restates this duplicity in the letter that announces, exactly three months later, the opening of his museum. Whereas the occupiers of the Palais des Beaux Arts had specifically contested the power of the ministers of culture, Broodthaers makes his announcement under their auspices, typing as a heading of his letter: "CABINET DES MINISTRES DE LA CULTURE. Ostende, le 7 sept. 1968,"[19] and signing it "Pour l'un des Ministres, Marcel Broodthaers." The text of the letter reads,

We have the pleasure of announcing to the customers and the curious the opening of the "Département des Aigles" of the Musée d'Art Moderne.

The works are in preparation; their completion will determine the date at which we hope to make poetry and the plastic arts shine hand-in-hand.

We hope that our formula "Disinterestedness plus admiration" will seduce you.[20]

The suggestion that a museum might wish to seduce "customers and the curious" by employing the mock-Kantian formula "disinterestedness plus admiration" is perhaps the most elliptical yet precise critique of institutionalized modernism ever offered. But once again Broodthaers implicates himself in this game of seduction.

One further letter (which, as Benjamin Buchloh has shown, became the basis, with significant alterations, for the "industrial poem" entitled *Museum*), precedes the actual opening of the Musée d'Art Moderne. The first open letter to be datelined from one of the museum's various departments—in this case "DEPARTEMENT DES AIGLES"—it provides another instance of Broodthaers's contradictory position:

I feel solidarity with all approaches that have the goal of objective communication, which presupposes a revolutionary critique of the dishonesty of those extraordinary means that we have at our disposal: the press, radio, black [sic] and color television.

But what can be meant by "objective communication" in a letter that begins

MUSEUM
. . . A rectangular director. A round servant . . .
. . . A triangular cashier. A square guard . . .

and then ends

. . . no people allowed. One plays here everyday until the end of the world.[21]

A week later the Musée d'Art Moderne, Département des Aigles, Section XIXème Siècle, "officially" opened in Broodthaers's house/studio at 30, rue de la Pépinière in Brussels. Despite (or perhaps confirming?) the warning "no people allowed,"[22] some sixty invited art-world personalities attended the event, in which an inaugural address was given by Johannes Cladders, Director of the Städtisches Museum in Mönchengladbach. What was there for these guests to see were empty picture crates borrowed for the occasion from Menkes Continental Transport and stenciled with such typical warning signs as "keep dry," "handle with care," and "fragile";

Marcel Broodthaers, *Musée d'Art Moderne, Département des Aigles, Section XIXème Siècle*, rue de la Pépinière, Brussels, September 27, 1968–September 27, 1969. Broodthaers speaking at the opening with Dr. Johannes Cladders, then director of the Städtisches Museum, Mönchengladbach, standing next to him (photo Ruth Kaiser, courtesy Johannes Cladders).

Bus taking guests from the closing of the Section XIXème in Brussels to the opening of Section XVIIème Siècle, at gallery A 37 90 89 in Antwerp, September 27–October 4, 1969 (photo Ruth Kaiser, courtesy Johannes Cladders).

together with thirty postcards of nineteenth-century French paintings by such "masters" as David, Ingres, Courbet, Meissonnier, and Puvis de Chavannes. A ladder leaned against a wall, numbers on doors appeared to designate rooms as galleries, and the words "musée/museum" were inscribed on the windows, readable from the outside. During the event, slides of prints by Grandville were projected.

Broodthaers described the Section XIXème Siècle in an open letter of two months later:

POEM

I am the director. I don't care. Question? Why do you do it?

POLITICS

The Département des Aigles of the Musée d'Art Moderne, Section XIXème Siècle, was in fact inaugurated on the 27th of September, 1968, in the presence of leading representatives of the public and the military. The speeches were on the subject of the fate of Art (Grandville). The speeches were on the subject of the fate of Art (Ingres). The speeches were on the subject of the relationship between institutional and poetic violence. I cannot and will not discuss the details, the sighs, the high points, and the repetitions of these introductory discussions. I regret it.

INFORMATION

Thanks to the cooperation of a shipping company and of several friends, we have been able to create this department, which includes primarily the following:

1)   crates

2)   postcards   "overvalued"

3)   a continuous projection of images (to be continued)

4)   a devoted staff [23]

Two fundamental aspects of Broodthaers's initial museum installation, both relating directly to other facets of his work, are crucial: its focus on the artwork's institutional framing conditions and its fasci-

nation with the nineteenth century. The first of these is signaled—
quite obviously—by the presence of the means of transport and
installation; by the pretenses of the art opening, including letter of
announcement, invitation, *buffet froid,* and inaugural address; by the
postcards (the museum's cheap reminder of the "overvaluation" of
art that makes it an object of luxury consumption);[24] and by the very
designation of the artist's studio as a museum. Conflating the site of
production with that of reception, Broodthaers reveals their interdependence and calls into question the ideological determination of
their separation: the bourgeois liberal categories *private* and *public.*
Three years after Broodthaers's conversion of his studio to a
museum, Daniel Buren, who attended the opening in the rue de la
Pépinière, wrote,

> The museum and gallery on the one hand and the studio on the other are
> linked to form the foundation of the same edifice and the same system. To
> question one while leaving the other intact accomplishes nothing. Analysis
> of the art system must inevitably be undertaken in terms of the studio as
> the *unique space* of production and the museum as the *unique space* of
> reception.[25]

Such an analysis was initiated, in Broodthaers's case, by fiat,
destroying the uniqueness of each by making them identical. But
unlike Buren, whose polemic against the studio focuses on its twentieth-century manifestations, Broodthaers's analysis leads him to the
preceding century, when the definitive separation of studio and
museum was accomplished and each was accorded its respective role
in the art system.[26]

Broodthaers's return to the past, evidenced by the title of the
museum section, by the paintings reproduced on the postcards, and
by Grandville—this "altogether dated aura of 19th century bourgeois culture that many of his works seem to bring to mind might
easily seduce the viewer into dismissing his works as being
obviously obsolete and not at all concerned with the presuppositions
of contemporary art."[27] On the contrary, however, it is in this very

D e p a r t e m e n t
d e s
A i g l e s

Paris, le 29 novembre 1968.

Chers Amis,

Mes caisses sont vides. Nous sommes au bord du gouffre.
Preuve: Quand je n'y suis pas, il n'y a personne. Alors?
Assumer plus longtemps mes fonctions? Le système des musées
serait-il aussi compromis que celui des galeries? Cependant,
notez que le Département des Aigles est encore indemne bien
que l'on s'efforce à le détruire.
     Chers amis, mes caisses sont superbes; ici un peintre
célèbre, là un sculpteur connu, plus loin une inscription qui
fait prévoir l'avenir de l'Art. Vive l'histoire d'Ingres!
Ce cri résonne au fond de ma conscience. Cri de guerre. Je suis
en péril. Je renonce à vous donner des explications qui
m'exposent à un péril supplémentaire ....

                    P o è m e
Je suis le directeur. Je m'en fous. Question ?
Pourquoi le faites-vous ?
                    P o l i t i q u e
Le département des aigles du musée d'art moderne, section XIXe
siècle, a été effectivement inauguré le 27 septembre 1968 en
présence de personnalités du monde civil et militaire. Les
discours ont eu pour objet le destin de l'Art.(Grandville). Les
discours ont eu pour objet le destin de l'Art.(Ingres). Les
discours ont eu pour objet le rapport entre la violence institu-
tionalisée et la violence poétique.
     Je ne veux, ni ne peux vous exposer les détails, les soupirs,
les étoiles, les calculs de cette discussion inaugurale. Je le
regrette.
                    I n f o r m a t i o n
Grâce au concours d'une firme de transport et de quelques amis,
nous avons pu composer ce département qui comprend en ordre
principal: 1/ des caisses
          2/ des cartes postales   "surévaluées"
          3/ une projection continue d'images   (à suivre)
          4/ un personnel dévoué.

Chers amis, je suis désolé du trop long silence dans lequel je
vous ai laissés depuis mes lettres datées de ....
Je dois, pour l'instant, vous quitter.Vite, un mot d'affection,

                    votre Marcel Broodthaers.

P.S.Mon ordre, ici, dans l'une des villes de Duchamp est peuplé
de poires; on en revient à Grandville.
Correspondance: Musée d'Art Moderne, Département des Aigles,
          30 rue de la Pépinière,Bruxelles 1. Tél.02/12.09.54

Marcel Broodthaers, open letter, Paris,
November 29, 1968.

preoccupation—shared by Walter Benjamin in many of its points of reference (Baudelaire, Offenbach, Grandville; advertising, fashion, kitsch)—that we can most clearly see Broodthaers's consciousness of the present. For it was in the early nineteenth century that the "romantic disposition," to which Broodthaers constantly points as the source of contemporary attitudes about culture, took hold of art and provided it with an always ready alibi for its alienation from social reality. And it was at the same time that the museum arose to institutionalize that alibi. The idealist conception of art, the classificatory systems imposed on it, the construction of a cultural history to contain it—all of these were secured by the museum as it developed during the past century. And this institutional "overvaluation" of art produced a secondary effect, which Benjamin called "the disintegration of culture into commodities"[28] and Broodthaers referred to as "the transformation of art into merchandise."[29] This, as Benjamin wrote and as Broodthaers surely recognized, "was the secret theme of Grandville's art."[30]

The dilemma of contemporary art in the late 1960s—as it attempted to break this double stranglehold of the museum and the marketplace and to become engaged in the political struggles of its time—had its roots in the nineteenth century. Working as an archeologist of the present, Broodthaers would uncover that point of origin in his four-year-long fiction, whose first episode was the Section XIXème Siècle.

ᔄ

Throughout the year that the Section XIXème Siècle remained open, and continuing until the "closing" of the Musée d'Art Moderne at *Documenta 5* in 1972, Broodthaers periodically issued open letters written under his museum's letterhead. (The letterhead varies from the hand-written or rubber-stamped "Département des Aigles" to the typed or typeset "Musée d'Art Moderne, Section Littéraire, Département des Aigles.") These letters compose the fictive museum's Section Littéraire.[31] As if in accord with Benjamin's specification of the task of the historical materialist—"to set to work an

J. J. Grandville, *An Exhibition Gallery*, illustration for the book *Un autre monde*, Paris, 1844.

engagement with history original to every new present"—a central
feature of these letters is the constant reflection upon and revision of
previous activities, works, and statements.[32] Their often comic and
contradictory tone masks a considerably more serious, consistent
(and probably impossible) endeavor: to keep pace with the culture
industry's extraordinary capacity to outmaneuver the individual
producer. But Broodthaers's running commentary is not limited to
his own production; it extends to that of his colleagues. "In the visual arts," he said, "my only possible engagement is with my adversaries."[33] Indeed, working at the moment of conceptual art, a
category into which Broodthaers's work was sometimes shoehorned, the Section Littéraire can be read as a critique of conceptual-
ism's often naive claims to have escaped the dominant mechanisms
of art's institutionalization, dissemination, and commercialization.[34]
Broodthaers counterposes the very designation "literary," again
with its "pejorative," archaic ring, to the supposed innovation of
"art as idea" or "art as language."

ى

The ceremony to mark the closing of the Musée d'Art Moderne's
Section XIXème Siècle was conducted at Broodthaers's Brussels
home. The Section XVIIème Siècle opened immediately thereafter
at A 37 90 80, an alternative space in Antwerp. An invitation to the
event announced that a bus would be provided to take the guests to
Antwerp—"From Brussels to Antwerp is fifty kilometers. Not
enough time to reflect upon this museum. So I thought in parenthe-
ses without words inside."[35] Consisting of objects similar to those of
the museum in the rue de la Pépinière in Brussels, this new section
substituted postcard reproductions of works by Rubens for those by
nineteenth-century painters. It remained open for a week.

Several months later, the nineteenth-century section reappeared
in a different guise (and for only two days) as the Section XIXème
Siècle (bis) in the exhibition *between 4* at the Städtische Kunsthalle in
Düsseldorf. For this "continuation" of the nineteenth-century section Broodthaers selected and installed eight nineteenth-century

paintings borrowed from the Kunstmuseum Düsseldorf, thereby briefly lending the temporary exhibition space the appearance of a museum gallery.[36] Stacking the paintings in two rows of four, Broodthaers's installation recalls nineteenth-century hanging methods, but his arrangement of pictures according to size and shape also suggests a prior museological moment in the eighteenth century, when picture galleries constituted a kind of "décor."[37] Like many of Broodthaers's interventions, the Section XIXème Siècle (bis) is a mere gesture, but its resonances are far-reaching. Much of the present-day flurry of museum activity consists of a similar reordering of fetish-objects, whether permanent collections or loans—reconfigurations that demonstrate only that the museum's construction of cultural history can undergo ever new permutations without disrupting the ideology of historicism. One has only to think, as regards the particular century of Broodthaers's interest, of the new Musée d'Orsay in Paris, a "Section XIXème Siècle" of ultimate proportions. Objects transported across the Seine from the Louvre and the Jeu de Paume and appropriated from the French provinces are now regrouped in a setting of such grandiosity as to nullify political recollection all the more fully.[38]

∽

Broodthaers's fictive museum materialized next as the Section Cinéma at Haus Burgplatz 12 in Düsseldorf. The announcement card stated that, beginning in January 1971, "didactic films" would be shown every Thursday from two to seven P.M. Around the periphery of the basement room that housed the Section Cinéma, Broodthaers displayed a number of disparate objects, labeling each with a stenciled figure number or letter—"fig. 1," "fig. 2," "fig. A,"—as if they were intended as illustrations in an old encyclopedia. The objects thus "didactically" marked included a light bulb, a chair, the September 12 page of a daily calendar, an accordion case, a film splicer. A copy of Georges Sadoul's *L'invention du cinéma* was placed in a trunk with other objects. A carpentered piano case labeled "Les Aigles" stood against a wall bearing the inscriptions "Musée" and

"Museum." Recalling the later reinstallation of these objects in the Mönchengladbach museum under the title *Théorie des figures,* Broodthaers enumerated still others: "a cardboard box, a clock, a mirror, a pipe, also a mask and a smokebomb."[39] In this odd assortment we again see the musty charm of the nineteenth century, the time, indeed, of the "invention of cinema."[40] In addition, we see for the first time among the museum fictions the formation of a *collection.* Because Benjamin's "countertype of the collector" has now become extinct, however, Broodthaers can only conjure up its image with the willful gesture of appending a figure number to each object. "If we are to believe what the inscription says," Broodthaers remarked, "then the object takes on an illustrative character referring to a kind of novel about society."[41] But can we believe it? Or does the Section Cinéma commemorate only that type of collection in which "the object is released from its original functions" so that "every single thing becomes an encyclopedia of all knowledge of the age . . ."?

∽

Broodthaers's most literal embodiment of the confession that he would become a creator in order to compensate for his inability to be a collector is the work entitled *Ma collection,* a "collection" of documents of exhibitions in which the artist had participated, each provided, once again, with a figure number. The work was exhibited at the Wide White Space Gallery in the 1971 Cologne Art Fair. At the same time, "due to bankruptcy," the Musée d'Art Moderne was put up for sale under the aegis of its Section Financière. The offering was made in the form of a special edition of nineteen copies of the art fair catalogue, each wrapped with a book jacket stating, "Musée d'Art Moderne à vendre, 1970 bis 1971, pour cause de faillite." Evidently, though, the museum didn't find a buyer,[42] because its most ambitious manifestation, the Section des Figures, opened the following summer at the Städtische Kunsthalle in Düsseldorf.

∽

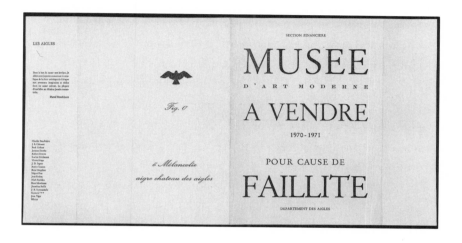

Marcel Broodthaers, Musée d'Art Moderne, Département des Aigles, Section Financière, Kunstmarkt, Cologne, October
5–10, 1971. Announcement for the sale of
the museum in the form of a wrapper for
the Cologne Art Fair catalogue.

The Section des Figures comprised 266 objects representing eagles, borrowed from forty-three "real" museums as well as from private collections including Broodthaers's own, and ranging in date "from the Oligocene to the present." Shown in glass cases and vitrines, hung on walls, or free standing, each object was provided with a label stating in English, French, or German, "This is not a work of art"—"a formula obtained by the contraction of a concept by Duchamp and an antithetical concept by Magritte."[43] Under the heading "Method" in the first of the exhibition's two catalogue volumes, these two concepts—the readymade and what Michel Foucault, in his text "Ceci n'est pas une pipe," called the "broken calligram"—are illustrated with reproductions of Duchamp's *Fountain* and Magritte's *La trahison des images*.[44] Following these, Broodthaers writes,

The public is confronted here with the following art objects: eagles of all kinds, some of which are fraught with weighty symbolic and historical ideas. The character of this confrontation is determined by the negative inscription: "This is not . . . this is not a work of art." This means nothing other than: Public, how blind you are!

Thus, either-or: either information on so-called modern art has played an effective role, in which case the eagle would inevitably become part of a method; or the inscription appears as mere nonsense—that is, it does not correspond to the level of discussion concerning, for example, the validity of the ideas of Duchamp and Magritte—and then the exhibition simply follows the classical principles: the eagle in art, in history, in ethnology, in folklore. . . . [45]

Two possible readings, depending on how efficacious modern art has been: either Broodthaers's museum opposes cultural history, or it is simply another instance of it, taking the eagle as its subject.[46]

The Section des Figures is Broodthaers's most "complete" collection, "a grandiose attempt," indeed, as Benjamin put it, "to transcend the totally irrational quality of a mere being-there through

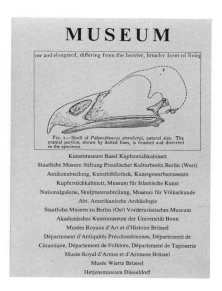

Marcel Broodthaers, covers for two-volume catalogue of Musée d'Art Moderne, Département des Aigles, Section des Figures *(Der Adler vom Oligozän bis heute)*, Städtische Kunsthalle, Düsseldorf, May 16–July 9, 1972.

integration into a new, specifically created historical system. . . ."
And this new system has an "epochal" goal: the nullification of
another. As Duchamp's readymades made clear, the function of the
art museum (and of the artist working within its discursive authority) is to declare, in regard to each of the objects housed there, "This
is a work of art." Broodthaers's labels reverse this proposition
through the application of Magritte's linguistic formula "Ceci n'est
pas une pipe." The museum's "this is a work of art"—apparently
tautological—is exposed as an arbitrary *designation,* a mere
representation.[47]

"The concept of the exhibition," Broodthaers wrote, "is based
on the identity of the eagle as an idea with art as an idea."[48] But the
result of "the eagle as an idea" is in this case such a vast diversity of
objects—from paintings to comic strips, from fossils to typewriters,
from ethnographic objects to product logos—that their juxtaposition can only seem "surreal." When asked, however, if "this sort of
claim to embrace artistic forms as far distant from one another as an
object can be from a traditional painting" did not remind him of
"the encounter of a sewing machine and an umbrella on an operating table," Broodthaers merely remarked upon the museum's system of classification:

A comb, a traditional painting, a sewing machine, an umbrella, a table
may find a place in the museum in different sections, depending upon their
classification. We see sculpture in a separate space, paintings in another,
ceramics and porcelains . . . , stuffed animals. . . . Each space is in turn
compartmentalized, perhaps intended to be a section—snakes, insects, fish,
birds—susceptible to being divided into departments—parrots, gulls,
eagles.[49]

The Section des Figures demonstrates the oddness of the museum's
order of knowledge by presenting us with another, "impossible"
order. In this, Broodthaers's fiction recalls Foucault's archeology,
the initial method he devised to oppose cultural history. *The Order
of Things,* Foucault tells us,

Installation detail of Musée d'Art Moderne,
Département des Aigles, Section des Fi-
gures *(Der Adler vom Oligozän bis heute)*,
Städtische Kunsthalle, Düsseldorf, May 16–
July 9, 1972 (photo Walter Klein).

arose out of a passage in Borges, out of the laughter that shattered, as I read
the passage, all the familiar landmarks of my thought—*our* thought. . . .
This passage quotes a "certain Chinese encyclopedia" in which it is written
that "animals are divided into: (a) belonging to the Emperor, (b)
embalmed, (c) tame, (d) sucking pigs, (e) sirens, (f) fabulous, (g) stray
dogs, (h) included in the present classification, (i) frenzied, (j) innumerable,
(k) drawn with a very fine camelhair brush, (l) *et cetera,* (m) having just
broken the water pitcher, (n) that from a long way off look like flies." In
the wonderment of this taxonomy, the thing we apprehend in one great
leap, the thing that, by means of the fable, is demonstrated as the exotic
charm of another system of thought, is the limitation of our own, the stark
impossibility of thinking *that.*[50]

It is impossible to think *that,* Foucault explains, because Borges
"does away with the *site,* the mute ground upon which it is possible
for entities to be juxtaposed. . . . What has been removed, in short,
is the famous 'operating table.'"[51] The purpose of Foucault's archeology is to show that the site that allows us to juxtapose heterogeneous entities is that of discourse, and that discursive formations
undergo historical mutations of such magnitude as to render them
entirely incompatible with one another. At the same time, Foucault
explains that our own historicizing system of thought, which arose
in the beginning of the nineteenth century, forces knowledge into a
continuous chronological development that effectively conceals the
incompatibility.[52] Our cultural history universalizes—and ultimately
psychologizes—all knowledge by tracing its course in an infinite
regress of origins.[53]

The title Broodthaers gave to the Section des Figures—*Der
Adler vom Oligozän bis heute* ("The Eagle from the Oligocene to the
Present")—can only be a parody of this historicizing enterprise.
Under the heading "Figure 0" in the second volume of the cata-
logue, Broodthaers wrote,

Such notions are dangerous. Sometimes they precipitate a kind of anes-
thesia from which there is no awakening. Profoundly terrified . . . knowing

nothing . . . finally, admiring, without reservation. The sublime idea of art and the sublime idea of the eagle. From the oligocene to the present—this is all very sublime. Why oligocene? The direct relationship between the eagle-fossil, which was found in excavations of the tertiary strata, and the various forms of presentation of the symbol are perhaps weak, if they exist at all. But geology had to enter the sensationalist title so as to imbue it with a false air of scholarship, which accepts the symbol of the eagle without reflection, without even putting it up for discussion.[54]

Within cultural history, categories that arose at particular historical moments—categories such as art—are never questioned; thus art can be seen to have come into existence along with "man himself" and his "creative instinct." Similarly, a fully historical phenomenon such as collecting is also psychologized, understood to be a transhistori-cal, cross-cultural *impulse*.[55] And the museum, reductively under-stood only as the institution that houses a collection, was therefore always simply *there* as the "natural" answer to the collector's "needs." In spite of the fact that the museum is an institution that emerged with the development of modern bourgeois society, cul-tural historians pursue its origins, together with those of the collec-tion, into "time immemorial."

There is no cultural history of the art museum that does not find its own origin in that curious book, understood however as a classic, by Julius von Schlosser, *Die Kunst- und Wunderkammern der Spätrenaissance,* originally published in 1908. The director of the Kunsthistorisches Museum in Vienna—the museum whose very name pays homage to cultural history (and which lent an aquiline suit of armor to the Section des Figures)—Schlosser begins his book with a brief reflection on the universality of his subject:

Whoever endeavors to write a history of collecting from its origins and in all its various ramifications and developments—and this would be an inter-esting subject both for psychology and for cultural history—should perhaps not disdain to descend to the *gazza ladra* and the various and noteworthy

Suit of armor, North German, early six-
teenth century, collection Kunsthistorisches
Museum, Vienna, included in Musée d'Art
Moderne, Département des Aigles, Section
des Figures *(Der Adler vom Oligozän bis
heute)*, Städtische Kunsthalle, Düsseldorf,
May 16–July 9, 1972 (photo courtesy Kunsthistorisches Museum, Vienna).

observations that can be made regarding the *Sammeltrieb* in the animal kingdom.[56]

From the lower depths of the thieving magpie, Schlosser proceeds up the evolutionary ladder to the collections of children and "savages," thence to the fabulous collections of the Incas and Aztecs, of Aladdin and the *Thousand and One Nights,* and finally to the advent of *history:* the treasuries of the Greek temple and the medieval cathedral as museums, the Renaissance antiquities gallery as museum. Only after this litany does Schlosser turn his attention to his actual subject, the *Wunderkammer.* It is this "cabinet of rarities" that he considers the immediate precursor of the Kunsthistorishes Museum, whose "prehistory" in the *Wunderkammer* at Schloss Ambras he has set out to write.

Anyone who has ever read a description of a *Wunderkammer,* or *cabinet des curiosités,* would recognize the folly of locating the origin of the museum there, the utter incompatibility of the *Wunderkammer*'s selection of objects, its system of classification, with our own.[57] This late Renaissance type of collection did not *evolve* into the modern museum. Rather it was *dispersed;* its sole relation to present–day collections is that certain of its "rarities" eventually found their way into our museums (or museum departments) of natural history, of ethnography, of decorative arts, of arms and armor, of history . . . even in some cases our museums of art.

The Section des Figures does not, of course, return to the *Wunderkammer.* But it does recollect the heterogeneous profusion of its objects and the museum's reclassification of them during the nineteenth century. On the front and back covers of both volumes of the Section des Figures catalogue Broodthaers listed the museums from which he borrowed his eagles:

Kunstmuseum Basel Kupferstichkabinett / Staatliche Museen Stiftung Preussischer Kulturbesitz Berlin (West) . . . Museum für Islamische Kunst / Nationalgalerie, Skulpturenabteilung . . . Musée Royal d'Armes et d'Armures Brüssel / Musée Wiertz Brüssel . . . The Ethnography Department of the British Museum London / Imperial War Museum London / Victoria & Albert Museum London . . . Museum of the American Indian Heye Foundation New York / Musée de l'Armée, Hôtel des Invalides, Paris / Musée des Arts Décoratifs Paris . . . Musée d'Art Moderne Département des Aigles Brüssel Düsseldorf.

This is a list that points, in the conjunction of place names and museological classifications, to the *truly* historical dimension of modern "public" collections: their link with power—not only the imperial power that the eagle so consistently signifies but also the power that is constituted through their systems of knowledge. More important, it points to the *relationship* of imperial power to knowledge-power.[58] As recent radical scholarship has consistently shown, ethnocentric, patriarchal "knowledge" has been as essential to imperialist regimes as have been all the invading armies from Napoleon's to those of the present.

∽

While the Section des Figures remained in place, a Section Publicité showing photographs of the Düsseldorf exhibition opened at Documenta, the major international art exhibition held periodically in Kassel. This final appearance of Broodthaers's museum comprised two additional parts as well. The first of these, the Musée d'Art Moderne, Département des Aigles, Section d'Art Moderne, was in place from the opening of Documenta at the end of June until the end of August. In the so-called Abteilung Individuelle Mythologien ("Personal Mythologies Section"),[59] organized by Harald Szeemann, Broodthaers painted a black square on the floor of the Neue Galerie and inscribed within it, in white script and in three languages, "Private Property." The square was protected by stanchions supporting chains on all four sides. The words "musée/museum" were written on the window, readable from outside, just as they had appeared four years earlier in the rue de la Pépinière, but this time they were accompanied by "Fig. 0," legible from inside. There were also the

Interior of the Museum Wormianum,
Copenhagen, from Ole Worm, *Museum
Wormianum*, 1655 (courtesy Smithsonian
Institution).

usual directional signs of the museum: "entrée, sortie, caisse, vestiaire," and so forth, together with "Fig. 1, Fig. 2, Fig. 0. . . ."

At the beginning of September, the fiction changed its name and character. Now called the Musée d'Art Ancienne, Département des Aigles, Galerie du XXème Siècle, the black square was repainted and inscribed in the following manner:

Ecrire Peindre Copier

Figurer

Parler Former Rêver

Echanger

Faire Informer Pouvoir[60]

Taken together, these three final gestures point pessimistically to a new phase in the museum's history, the one we are now experiencing: the conjuncture of exhibitions as a form of public relations, of the ultimate reduction of art to private property, and of the evolution of artistic strategies into those of a pure alignment with power. Broodthaers did not live to see the fulfillment of his darkest predictions in the present takeover of the culture industry by corporate interests and, at the same time, the final eclipse of the commemorative role of the collector as historical materialist. But he did foresee what had become of his own Musée d'Art Moderne:

This museum, founded in 1968 under pressure of the political perception of its time, will now close its doors on the occasion of Documenta. It will therefore have exchanged its heroic and solitary form for one that borders on consecration, thanks to the Kunsthalle in Düsseldorf and to Documenta.

It is only logical that it will now model itself on boredom. Of course this is a romantic point of view, but what can I do about it? Whether we look at St. John the Evangelist or Walt Disney, the symbol of the eagle is always particularly weighty when it concerns the written word. Nevertheless I am writing these lines because I conceive of the romantic disposition as a nostalgia for God.[61]

Notes

My introduction to Broodthaers's work came from Benjamin H. D. Buchloh's essays "Marcel Broodthaers: Allegories of the Avant-Garde," *Artforum* 18, no. 9 (May 1980), pp. 52–59; and "The Museum Fictions of Marcel Broodthaers," in *Museums by Artists* (Toronto: Art Metropole, 1983), pp. 45–56. I also had the opportunity of working with Buchloh on the special issue of *October* on Broodthaers (no. 42, Fall 1987), for which he was guest editor. In addition, he lent me his personal copies of many of the documents I consulted in the preparation of this essay.

Among source materials, apart from Broodthaers's own writings, the masters theses by Dirk Snauwaert ("Marcel Broodthaers. Musée d'Art Moderne, Département des Aigles, Section des Figures. Der Adler vom Oligozän bis heute: Een Analyse," Rijksuniversiteit, Gent, 1985) and Etienne Tilman ("Musée d'Art Moderne, Département des Aigles, de Marcel Broodthaers," Université Libre de Bruxelles, Faculté de Philosophie et Lettres, Brussels, 1983–84) were especially useful in reconstructing various aspects of Broodthaers's museum fictions, none of which I saw firsthand.

1. "This clever thing has avoided society's mold./She's cast herself in her very own./ Other look-alikes share with her the anti-sea./She's perfect" (Marcel Broodthaers, "The Mussel," trans. Michael Compton, in "Selections from *Pense-Bête*," *October*, no. 42 [Fall 1987], p. 27).

2. Marcel Broodthaers, text of exhibition announcement, Galerie Saint-Laurent, Brussels, 1964.

3. Marcel Broodthaers, "Comme du beurre dans un sandwich," *Phantomas*, nos. 51–61 (December 1965), pp. 295–296; quoted in Birgit Pelzer, "Recourse to the Letter," *October*, no. 42 (Fall 1987), p. 163.

4. Benjamin H. D. Buchloh, "Introductory Note," *October*, no. 42 (Fall 1987), p. 5.

5. Walter Benjamin, *Das Passagen-Werk*, vol. 1, (Frankfurt am Main, Suhrkamp, 1982), p. 280.

6. Ibid., p. 277 (italics in original). This statement of Marx is further illuminated by another, which immediately follows it in Benjamin's notes: "The place of all physical and mental senses has been taken by the simple alienation of all these senses by the sense of possession."

7. Ibid., p. 271.

8. Walter Benjamin, "Unpacking My Library" (1931), in *Illuminations,* trans. Harry Zohn (New York: Schocken Books, 1969), p. 67.

9. Elizabeth Gilmore Holt, ed., *The Triumph of Art for the Public* (Garden City, N.Y.: Anchor Books, 1979).

10. Walter Benjamin, "Eduard Fuchs, Collector and Historian" (1937), in *One-Way Street and Other Writings,* trans. Kingsley Shorter (London: New Left Books, 1979), pp. 355–356 (italics in original).

11. Since Engels's 1892 definition of *historical materialism* as "that view of the course of history which seeks the ultimate cause and the great moving power of all important historic events in the economic development of society, in the changes in the modes of production and exchange, in the consequent division of society into distinct classes, and in the struggle of these classes against one another," the concept has been the subject of considerable debate within Marxist theory, especially regarding the notion of a single "ultimate cause." Walter Benjamin's materialist conception of history—elaborated throughout his writings and the subject of his last completed text, "Theses on the Philosophy of History" (in *Illuminations,* pp. 253–264)—is one of the most subtle and complex in all of Marxist thought.

12. Benjamin, "Eduard Fuchs," p. 361.

13. Ibid., p. 352.

14. Marcel Broodthaers, open letter on the occasion of *Documenta 5*, Kassel, June 1972.

15. Marcel Broodthaers, in a conversation with Jürgen Harten and Katharina Schmidt, circulated as a press release on the occasion of the exhibition *Section des Figures: Der Adler vom Oligozän bis heute,* Düsseldorf, Städtische Kunstalle, 1972; quoted in Rainer Borgemeister, "*Section des Figures:* The Eagle from the Oligocene to the Present," *October,* no. 42 (Fall 1987), p. 135.

16. Broodthaers actually specifies—in an open letter datelined Kassel, June 27, 1968 (reprinted in *Museum in Motion?: The Art Museum at Issue,* ed. Karel Blotkamp et al. [The Hague: Government Printing Office, 1979], p. 249), and, with some deletions, in the plastic plaque related to it and entitled *Tirage illimité (le noir et le rouge)*—a number of cities in which the political activities of 1968 took place: "Amsterdam, Prague, Nanterre, Paris, Venice, Brussels, Louvain, Belgrade, Berlin, and Washington." See Benjamin H. D. Buchloh, "Open Letters, Industrial Poems," *October,* no. 42 (Fall 1987), pp. 85–87.

17. See the documents published in facsimile in *Museum in Motion,* p. 248.

18. Marcel Broodthaers, open letter, datelined Palais des Beaux Arts, June 7, 1968, addressed "A mes amis," published in *Museum in Motion,* p. 249 (italics in original).

19. The sea resort Ostend is, as Benjamin Buchloh has written, "the least likely place in Belgium for the offices of the ministers of culture to be found" (Buchloh, "Open Letters, Industrial Poems," p. 91).

20. Marcel Broodthaers, open letter, Ostend, September 7, 1968, published in *Museum in Motion,* p. 249.

21. Marcel Broodthaers, open letter, Düsseldorf, September 19, 1968, published in *Museum in Motion,* p. 250.

22. Because we lack the French revolutionary tradition, *people* does not carry the political connotations of *peuple,* which could also be translated as "the masses, the mul-

titude, the crowd, the lower classes." Benjamin Buchloh notes the difference between the text of the open letter and that of the plastic plaque entitled *Museum,* 1968: "The statement 'people are not admitted'—ringing with connotations of class and politics—is changed in the plaque version into the more grotesque and authoritarian 'Children are not admitted'" (Buchloh, "Open Letters, Industrial Poems," p. 96).

23. Marcel Broodthaers, open letter, Paris, November 29, 1968, addressed "Chers Amis."

24. "Is a picture post card of a painting by Ingres worth a couple million?" (Marcel Broodthaers, quoted in Benjamin H. D. Buchloh, "Formalism and Historicity—Changing Concepts in American and European Art since 1945," in *Europe in the Seventies: Aspects of Recent Art* [Chicago: Art Institute of Chicago, 1977], p. 98).

25. Daniel Buren, "The Function of the Studio," trans. Thomas Repensek, *October,* no. 10 (Fall 1979), p. 51.

26. That this separation was a point contested in the nineteenth century can be seen in Alois Hirt's attempt to make the Berlin Museum a kind of studio, the only remaining clue to which in the museum itself is to be found in Hirt's frieze inscription. See "The Postmodern Museum," this volume.

27. Buchloh, "Formalism and Historicity," p. 98.

28. Benjamin, "Eduard Fuchs," p. 360.

29. Marcel Broodthaers, "To Be *Bien Pensant . . .* or Not to Be. To be Blind," trans. Paul Schmidt, *October,* no. 42 (Fall 1987), p. 35.

30. "The correlative to this [enthronement of the commodity] was the ambivalence between its utopian and its cynical element. Its refinements in the representation of dead objects corresponded to what Marx calls the "theological capers" of the commodity. They took clear shape in the *spécialité:* under Grandville's pencil, a way of designating goods which came into use around this time in the luxury industry transformed the whole of Nature into specialties. He presented the latter in the same spirit in which advertisements—this word too (*réclames*) came into existence at that time—were beginning to present their wares. He ended in madness" (Walter Benjamin, "Paris—the Capital of the Nineteenth Century," in *Charles Baudelaire: A Lyric Poet in the Era of High Capitalism,* trans. Harry Zohn [London: New Left Books, 1973], p. 165). See also file "G," "Ausstellungswesen, Reklame, Grandville," in Benjamin, *Das Passagen-Werk,* pp. 232–268.

31. Because Broodthaers's museum was a fiction, it is sometimes difficult to decide what constitutes one of its "real" sections and what exists merely as a matter of Broodthaers's elliptical pronouncements. Thus we can only say that the Section Littéraire exists insofar as Broodthaers used this rubric on his letterhead from time to time. On the two occasions that Broodthaers himself specified the sections of his museum—on the announcement of the Section Cinéma in 1971 and in the second volume of the catalogue of the Section des Figures in 1972—he lists only the following: Section XIXème Siècle, Brussels, 1968; Section XVIIème Siècle, Antwerp, 1969; Section XIXème Siècle (bis), Düsseldorf, 1970; Section Cinéma,

Düsseldorf, 1971; Section des Figures, Düsseldorf, 1972. In addition to these, however, there were also the Section Financière at the Cologne Art Fair in 1971 and the Section Publicité, the Section d'Art Moderne, and the Musée d'Art Ancien, Galerie du XXème Siècle at *Documenta 5*, Kassel, in 1972. The announcement for the exhibition of Broodthaers's plastic plaques at the Librarie Saint-Germain des Prés in 1968 identified another section in the following manner: "M.U.SE.E .D'.A.R.T./CAB.INE.T D.ES. E.STA.MP.E.S./ Département des Aigles." Broodthaers also mentions a Section Documentaire (for which he thanks Herman Daled) in *Marcel Broodthaers: Catalogue/Catalogus* (Brussels: Palais des Beaux-Arts, 1974), p. 26; and a Section Folklorique appears on the list of museum sections in several posthumously published catalogues.

32. For an in-depth analysis of the open letters, see Pelzer, "Recourse to the Letter."

33. Marcel Broodthaers, "Ten Thousand Francs Reward," trans. Paul Schmidt, *October,* no. 42 (Fall 1987), p. 45. Broodthaers reserved his most pointed political criticism for one colleague in particular—Joseph Beuys. For an analysis of Broodthaers's letter to Beuys—written in the form of a "found" letter from Offenbach to Wagner—regarding the cancellation of Hans Haacke's exhibition at the Guggenheim Museum in 1971, see Stefan Germer, "Haacke, Broodthaers, Beuys," *October,* no. 45 (Summer 1988), pp. 63–75. Broodthaers also made his first announcement of his "museum" in a letter to Beuys of July 14, 1968, in which he wrote, "We announce here the creation of the Musée d'Art Moderne in Brussels. No one believes it."

34. This aspect of Broodthaers's open letters has been extensively argued by Benjamin Buchloh in his various writings on Broodthaers. See especially "Formalism and Historicity" and "Open Letters, Industrial Poems."

35. Marcel Broodthaers, open letter, Antwerp, May 10, 1969, addressed "Chers amis."

36. Because, outside of Germany, the function of the art museum (housing a collection) and that of the art exhibition hall (mounting temporary exhibitions) are generally fulfilled by the same institution, Broodthaers's conversion of the one into the other loses much of its meaning in our context. It should also be noted that the Kunst*halle* is as much a nineteenth-century development as is the Kunst*museum*.

37. A series of installations by Broodthaers created in 1973–74, after the dissolution of his fictional museum, were called Décors.

38. See Patricia Mainardi, "Postmodern History at the Musée d'Orsay," *October,* no. 41 (Summer 1987), pp. 31–52.

39. Broodthaers, "Ten Thousand Francs Reward," p. 43.

40. As Broodthaers said, "I would never have obtained this kind of complexity with technological objects, whose singleness condemns the mind to monomania: minimal art, robot, computer" (ibid.).

41. Ibid.

42. The offering itself, however, did. The nineteen catalogues specially marked by Broodthaers were sold to the art dealer Michael Werner.

43. Broodthaers, "Ten Thousand Francs Reward," p. 47.

44. Marcel Broodthaers, "Methode," in *Der Adler vom Oligozän bis heute*, vol. 1 (Düsseldorf: Städtische Kunsthalle, 1972), pp. 11–15; see also *October,* no. 42 (Fall 1987), pp. 152–153. Under Magritte's name in this section on method, Broodthaers simply writes, "Read the text by M. Foucault 'Ceci n'est pas une pipe.'" See Michel Foucault, "Ceci n'est pas une pipe," trans. Richard Howard, *October,* no. 1 (Spring 1976), pp. 7–21.

45. Marcel Broodthaers, "Adler, Ideologie, Publikum," in *Der Adler vom Oligozän bis heute,* vol. 1, p. 16.

46. Broodthaers gives some sense of how well the lessons of modern art have been learned by printing the comments of visitors to the exhibition in the second volume of the catalogue. See "Die Meinung des Publikums," in ibid., vol. 2, pp. 8–12.

47. For a more complete discussion of Broodthaers's "method," see Borgemeister, "*Section des Figures.*"

48. Marcel Broodthaers, "Section des Figures," in *Der Adler vom Oligozän bis heute,* vol. 2, p. 19. Broodthaers's identification of art and eagle suggests a linguistic substitution to which he never specifically alluded. In French, the phrase "Il n'est pas un aigle" means "he's no genius." We might therefore assume that "Ceci n'est pas un objet d'art," accompanied by the image or object representing an eagle, negates the common association of art with genius. For the most part, Broodthaers's remarks on the eagle link it, however, not with genius but with power. See, for example, his various pronouncements on the eagle in "Section des Figures," pp. 18–19.

49. Broodthaers, "Ten Thousand Francs Reward," p. 46.

50. Michel Foucault, *The Order of Things* (New York: Pantheon, 1970), p. xv.

51. Ibid., p. xvii. ". . . like the umbrella and the sewing machine on the operating table; startling though their propinquity may be, it is nevertheless warranted by that *and,* . . . by that *on* whose solidity provides proof of the possibility of juxtaposition" (ibid., p. xvi).

52. It is precisely this that the historical materialist opposes: "The historical materialist leaves it to others to be drained by the whore called 'Once upon a time' in historicism's bordello. He remains in control of his powers, man enough to blast open the continuum of history" (Benjamin, "Theses on the Philosophy of History," p. 262).

53. See Foucault, "The Retreat and Return of the Origin," in *The Order of Things,* pp. 328–335.

54. Broodthaers, "Section des Figures," p. 18.

55. Thus, for example, "Twenty years' experience as curator and director in American museums has convinced me that the phenomenon of art collecting is too instinctive and too common to be dismissed as mere fashion or the desire for fame. It is a complex and irrepressible expression of the inner individual, a sort of devil of which great personalities are frequently possessed" (Francis Henry Taylor, *The*

Taste of Angels: Art Collecting from Ramses to Napoleon [Boston: Little, Brown & Co., 1948]).

56. Julius von Schlosser, *Die Kunst- und Wunderkammern der Spätrenaissance: Ein Beitrag zur Geschichte des Sammelwesens* (Braunschweig, Germany: Klinkhardt & Biermann, 1978), p. 1.

57. For descriptions of various cabinets of curiosities, see Oliver Impey and Arthur MacGregor, eds., *The Origins of Museums: The Cabinet of Curiosities in Sixteenth- and Seventeenth-Century Europe* (Oxford, Clarendon Press, 1985). The title of this publication—stemming from a symposium held to celebrate the tercentenary of the Ashmolean Museum—is an example of the obliviousness of traditional art historians to questions posed to cultural history by Foucault's archeology.

58. The explicit analysis of power/knowledge is, of course, the direction Foucault's work would take in its "genealogical" phase after *The Archeology of Knowledge*. Broodthaers's Section des Figures anticipates this direction even though he could not have known it, as its first manifestation, *Discipline and Punish,* was published in 1975, three years after the "close" of Broodthaers's museum.

59. We almost have to wonder whether this absurd category was invented specifically in order for Broodthaers to mock it.

60.

Write Paint Copy

Figure

Speak Form Dream

Exchange

Make Inform Power

Pouvoir is also, of course, a verb, meaning "to be able; to have power," but it is the only word in the list that can, in French, also be a noun—hence the ambiguity of the inscription.

61. Marcel Broodthaers, open letter, Kassel, June 1972.

The Art of Exhibition

In the winter of 1880–81, Edward J. Lowell wrote a series of letters to the *New York Times* regarding what he thought was an insufficiently documented aspect of the American Revolution. He began his account with the following paragraph:

The little city of Cassel is one of the most attractive in North Germany to a passing stranger. Its galleries, its parks and gardens, and its great palaces are calculated to excite admiration and surprise. Here Napoleon III. spent the months of his captivity amid scenes which might remind him of the magnificence of Versailles, which, indeed, those who planned the beautiful gardens had wished to imitate. For the grounds were mostly laid out in the last century, when the court of France was the point towards which most princely eyes on the Continent were directed; and no court, perhaps, followed more assiduously or more closely, in outward show at least, in the path of the French court than that of the Landgraves of Hesse-Cassel. The expense of all these buildings and gardens was enormous, but there was generally money in the treasury. Yet the land was a poor land. The three or four hundred thousand inhabitants lived chiefly by the plough, but the Landgraves were in business. It was a profitable trade that they carried on, selling or letting out wares which were much in demand in that century, as in all centuries, for the Landgraves of Hesse-Cassel were dealers in men; thus it came to pass that Landgrave Frederick II. and his subjects played a part in American history, and that "Hessian" became a household word, though not a title of honor, in the United States.[1]

When, one century after this was written, the largest and most prestigious international art exhibition advertises itself with a postcard photograph of the sculptural monument to this same Frederick II, it

Johann Heinrich Tischbein the Elder, *The Inauguration of the Monument to Langrave Friedrich II in Kassel's Friedrichsplatz, August 14, 1783* (photo courtesy Staatliche Kunstsammlungen, Kassel).

is perhaps worthwhile to reflect once more on these historical facts. For erected on the dead and mutilated bodies of thousands of those Hessian mercenaries and of the men they fought against, as well as on the backbreaking labors of those who lived by the plough, is the Museum Fridericianum, always proudly proclaimed as the first museum building in Europe. We would therefore do well to recall the words of Walter Benjamin written just a few months before his suicide on the French border during the grimmest days of the Occupation:

A historical materialist views [cultural treasures] with cautious detachment. For without exception the cultural treasures he surveys have an origin which he cannot contemplate without horror. They owe their existence not only to the efforts of the great minds and talents who have created them, but also to the anonymous toil of their contemporaries. There is no document of civilization which is not at the same time a document of barbarism. And just as such a document is not free of barbarism, barbarism taints also the manner in which it was transmitted from one owner to another. A historical materialist therefore dissociates himself from it as far as possible. He regards it as his task to brush history against the grain.[2]

ဢ

. . . *documenta* 7. Not a bad name, because it suggests an attractive tradition of taste and discrimination. It is no doubt an honorable name. Therefore it may be followed by a subtitle as in those novels of long ago: *In which our heroes after a long and strenuous voyage through sinister valleys and dark forests finally arrive in the English Garden, and at the gate of a splendid palace.*

So wrote Artistic Director Rudi Fuchs in his introduction to the catalogue for the *Documenta* exhibition of 1982.[3] What one actually encountered, however, at the gate of the splendid palace, the Museum Fridericianum, was not heroes at all but rather a junky-looking construction workers' trailer displaying various objects for sale. Whether these objects were works of art or merely souvenirs was not immediately apparent. Among the T-shirts, multiples, and other wares to be found here and at other stands throughout the English garden were sheets of stationery whose upper and lower margins were printed with statements set in small type. At the top of one sheet the following could be read:

If it is not met with respectful seriousness, the work of art will hardly or not at all be able to stand its ground in the environment: the world around it, customs and architecture, politics and cooking—they all have become hard and brutal. In constant noise one can easily miss hearing the soft sounds of Apollo's lyre. Art is gentle and discreet, she aims for depth and passion, clarity and warmth.

On the lower margin of the same sheet the source of this astonishing claim was given: "Excerpts from a letter to the participating artists by the Director of Documenta 7, R. H. Fuchs, edited and published by Louise Lawler."

Not officially invited to participate in *Documenta*, Lawler was not a recipient of the letter from which her stationery quotes. She was, however, represented in the show in this marginal way through a subterfuge. Jenny Holzer, who had been invited, asked Lawler to contribute work to her collaborative venture with Fashion Moda, an alternative gallery situated in the South Bronx. That is to say, Fashion Moda is located in the very heart of an environment that is hard and brutal indeed, one of the most notorious black and Latino ghettos in the United States, and Fashion Moda is there not to stand its ground against the environment but rather to engage with it constructively.

Though Lawler had not received Fuchs's letter, she had been interested to read it, as many of us had, for it had become the focus of art-world gossip about the forthcoming major contemporary art event. With its absurd title—"Documenta 7: A Story"—and its equally absurd opening sentence—"How can I describe the exhibition to you: the exhibition which floats in my mind like a star?"—

this letter revealed Fuchs's fundamentally contradictory objectives. On the one hand he claimed that he would restore to art its precious autonomy, while on the other hand he made no secret of his desire to manipulate the individual works of art in conformity with his inflated self-image as master artist of the exhibition. Whether the participating artists intended it or not, Fuchs would endeavor to ensure that their works would in no way reflect on their environment: the world around them, customs and architecture, politics and cooking.

I, too, had read the letter, circulated in the spring of 1982, and it made me curious to attend a press conference Fuchs was to give at Goethe House in New York as part of the promotional campaign for this costliest of international art exhibitions. I fully expected Fuchs to confirm there the rumors that his exhibition would constitute a return to conventional modes of painting and sculpture, thereby breaking with the earlier *Documentas'* inclusion of experimental work in other mediums such as video and performance, as well as practices that openly criticized institutionalized forms of both production and reception. This, of course, Fuchs did, as he showed slide after slide of paintings and sculptures, mostly in the neoexpressionist style that had recently come to dominate the art market in New York and elsewhere in the Western world. What I had not expected from the press conference, though, was that at least half of the artistic director's presentation would be not about artworks but about work in progress to ready the exhibition spaces for installation. "I feel," he said, "that the time one can show contemporary art in makeshift spaces, converted factories and so on, is over. Art is a noble achievement and it should be handled with dignity and respect. Therefore we have finally built real walls."[4] And it was these walls, together with the lighting design and other details of museological enterprise, that he took great pains to present to his listeners.

In his foreword to *Documenta*'s catalogue, Fuchs succinctly summarized his art of exhibition. "We practice this wonderful craft," he wrote, "we construct an exhibition after having made rooms for this exhibition. In the meantime artists attempt to do their best, as it should be."[5] Everything as it should be: the artistic director builds walls—permanent now, since there will be no return to that time when temporary structures would suffice or even be preferable to meet the unconventional demands of unconventional art practices—and in the meantime the artists apply themselves to the creation of works of art appropriate to this hallowed setting.

No wonder, then, that the status of those objects in the Fashion Moda pavilions remains in question. Louise Lawler's stationery, Jenny Holzer's posters of streetwise provocations, the knickknacks produced by members of Colab, Christy Rupp's T-shirts silk-screened with the image of an attacking rat—whatever else these things may be, they are certainly not appropriate to the sacred precincts of art as reaffirmed by Rudi Fuchs. For these are deliberately marginal practices, works manufactured cheap and sold cheap, quite unlike the majority of paintings and sculptures within the museum buildings, whose real but disguised condition is that of the international market for art, dominated increasingly by corporate speculation. Moreover, the Fashion Moda works intentionally confront, rather than deny, dissemble, or mystify, the social bases of their production and circulation. Take, for example, Christy Rupp's rat image.

Rupp and I live in the same building in lower Manhattan, just a few blocks from City Hall, where the most reactionary mayor in New York's recent history delivers the city over to powerful real estate developers while city services decline and our poorer citizens are further marginalized. The combination of the Reagan administration's cuts in federal programs to aid the poor and New York's cynically manipulated housing shortage has resulted in a reported 30,000 homeless people now living on the streets of the city.[6] The hard and brutal conditions of these people's lives can be imagined by observing the few of them who spend every evening in the alleyway behind our building, where they compete with rats for the garbage

Christy Rupp, *Rat Patrol*, 1979.

left there by McDonald's and Burger King. Mayor Edward I. Koch was publicly embarrassed in the spring of 1979 when the media reported the story of a neighborhood office worker attacked by those rats as she left work. Such an event would certainly have been routine had it happened in one of the city's ghetto districts, but in this case the Department of Health was called in, and their findings were rather sensational: the vacant lot adjoining the alleyway contained thirty-two tons of garbage and was home to an estimated 4,000 rodents.[7] But the health department also found something else, even more difficult to explain to the public. Pasted to the temporary wall barricading the vacant lot from the street were pictures of a huge, sinister, attacking rat, reproductions of a photograph from the health department's own files. And these pictures were not only there but everywhere else in the vicinity where the city's usual accumulations of rotting garbage might indeed attract rats. It was as if a health department guerrilla action had posted advance warnings of the incident that had now taken place. The coincidence of scandalous event and the pictures that seemed to foretell it was an aspect of the story the news media were eager to report, and so they tracked down the guerrilla herself, Christy Rupp. But who was this woman? Interviewed on TV, she clearly knew a considerable amount about the city's rat problems, more even than the bureaucrats from the health department. Why, then, did she call herself an artist? And why did she refer to those ugly pictures as her art? Surely a photograph of a rat borrowed from health department files and mechanically reproduced is not a creation of artistic imagination; it has no claim to universality; it would be unthinkable to see the picture on exhibition in a museum.

But that, of course, is part of its point. Rupp's *Rat Patrol,* as she called her activity, is one of those art practices, now fairly numerous, that makes no concessions to the institutions of exhibition, even deliberately confounds them. As a result, it cannot be understood by most people as art, for only exhibition institutions can, at this historical juncture, fully legitimate any practice as art.

Our understating of this fact has been intensified recently because, since the late 1960s, it has been the subject of much important work by artists themselves. And it is precisely this understanding that Rudi Fuchs sought to suppress through his exhibition strategies and rhetoric at *Documenta 7*. One can only assume that his attempts were fully calculated, since Fuchs, in his capacity as director of the Stedelijk van Abbemusuem in Eindhoven, Holland, had been one of the foremost proponents of art practices that revealed or criticized the conditions imposed on art by its modes of exhibition, or of art that broke with the notion of aesthetic autonomy by directly confronting social reality.

Needless to say, Fuchs was not entirely successful at *Documenta* in imposing his new view of art as merely gentle and discreet, standing its ground against the environment. Because he worked with four other curators, he was forced to include a number of artists who took it as their responsibility to unmask his art of exhibition. Thus at the approach to the Fridericianum one was confronted with various disruptions of the decorum that Fuchs had wanted to assure. I have already mentioned the Fashion Moda stand, which the curator in charge of the American selection, Coosje van Bruggen, had insisted on accepting. Perhaps even more provocative was the work of Daniel Buren. This consisted of pennants of Buren's familiar striped material strung from high poles, which also carried loudspeakers. From these were broadcast fragments of musical compositions, played in chronological order, by composers ranging from Lully through Mozart and Beethoven to Verdi and Scott Joplin. The music was periodically interrupted by recitations of color names in fourteen languages. Buren thereby created at the entrance to the exhibition an atmosphere that critic Benjamin Buchloh described as "appropriate to a fun fair or the grand opening of a gas station."[8] Such an atmosphere was considerably more suitable to the self-promotion of the state of Hesse and the festive gathering of the international art world than Fuchs's wished-for air of reverence would have been. Moreover, Buren simultaneously parodied the

Daniel Buren, *Les Guirlandes*, 1982, at *Documenta 7*, with Johann August Nahl's *Monument to Frederick II* in the foreground (photo Daniel Buren).

Lawrence Weiner, *Many Colored Objects
Placed Side by Side to Form a Row of Many
Colored Objects*, 1982 (photos Daniel Buren).

show's simplistic notion of history (one volume of the catalogue, for example, arranged the participants according to their birth dates) and of nationalism, a category newly revived to foster stronger market competition.

Inside the three museum buildings—the Fridericianum, the Orangerie, and the Neue Galerie—Fuchs willfully distributed works by each artist throughout the galleries so that they would appear in perversely unlikely juxtaposition with works by various other artists. The result was to deny difference, dissemble meaning, and reduce everything to a potpourri of random style, although Fuchs liked to speak of this strategy as effecting dialogue among artists. The real significance of these groupings, however, was more accurately captured in Lawrence Weiner's phrase printed on the Fridericianum's frieze: "Viele farbige Dinge nebeneinder angeordnet bilden eine Reihe vieler farbiger Dinge." Translated into English for the wrapper that bound together the two hefty volumes of the show's catalogue, the statement reads, "Many colored objects placed side by side to form a row of many colored objects."

Within the precincts of the museum buildings it was considerably more difficult to force an awareness of Fuchs's tactics. One work, however, strongly countered Fuchs's program to override art's involvement with significant public issues. This was Hans Haacke's *Oelgemaelde, Hommage à Marcel Broodthaers,* which was relegated to the Neue Galerie rather than given pride of place in the Fridericianum. Haacke's work consisted of a confrontation: on one wall was a meticulously painted oil portrait of President Reagan; on the wall opposite, a gigantic photomural of a peace demonstration. The portrait was surrounded by the museological devices traditionally used to enhance the artwork's aura, to designate the work of art as separate, apart, inhabiting a world unto itself, in conformity with Fuchs's doctrine. Contained within its gold frame, illuminated in its own special glow by a small picture lamp, provided with a discreet wall label, protected by a velvet rope strung between stanchions, the painting was kept, like the *Mona Lisa,* a safe distance from the

admiring viewer. With this parody of museological trappings
Haacke paid tribute to Broodthaers's museum fictions while simultaneously mocking Fuchs's desire to elevate and safeguard his
masterpieces.

From this little shrine of high art a red carpet led underfoot to
the facing wall, where Haacke installed a mural-size photograph
taken in Bonn just one week before the official opening of *Documenta*. The photo was shot at a demonstration, the largest held in
postwar Germany, to protest President Reagan's arrival to lobby
support in the Bundestag for deployment of American cruise and
Pershing 2 missiles on German soil.

In its high degree of specificity, Haacke's work was able to do
what the vast majority of paintings and sculptures in the exhibition
could not. Not only did Haacke insert into this context a reminder
of actual historical conditions, but he also reflected on the terms of
current aesthetic debates. If not for Haacke's work, one would
hardly have known that photography had recently become an
important medium for artists attempting to resist the hegemony of
the traditional fine arts, or that Walter Benjamin's classic essay on
mechanical reproduction had become central to critical theories
of contemporary visual culture. Nor would one have understood
that this debate also encompasses a critique of the museum institution in its function of preserving the auratic status of art that was
Benjamin's main target. All we learn of this from Fuchs is that
"our culture suffers from an illusion of the media," and that this is
something to be overcome by the exhibition enterprise.[9]

But more important than these debates, Haacke's *Oelgemaelde*
suggested to the viewer that the relevant history of the town of
Kassel was closer than the one to which *Documenta*'s artistic director
constantly made reference. Fuchs sought to locate his *Documenta*
within the grand tradition of the eighteenth century, when the aris-
tocrats of Hesse-Kassel built their splendid palace. The official postcard of *Documenta* 7 was a photograph of the neoclassical statue of
the Landgrave Frederick II by Johann August Nahl, which stands in

Hans Haacke, *Oelgemaelde, Hommage à
Marcel Broodthaers*, 1982 (photo courtesy
Hans Haacke).

front of the Museum Fridericianum; in addition, each volume of the catalogue carries on its cover a photograph of one of the allegorical sculptures adorning the pediment of the museum, not surprisingly those representing the old beaux-arts categories of painting and sculpture.

Kassel has, however, as I said, a recent history that is far more urgent. If Fuchs had to build walls within the museum, this was because the original ones had been destroyed by Allied bombings in World War II. Kassel, once at the very center of Germany, was one of Hitler's strategic ammunition depots. But in 1982 the city no longer lay at the center of Germany; rather it lay only a few miles from the border of the other Germany to the east. Haacke's work might thus have evoked for *Documenta*'s visitors not Kassel's glorious eighteenth-century past but its precarious present, at a time when the tensions of the cold war had been dangerously escalated once again. Perhaps it is this hard and brutal fact above all that Fuchs would have had us forget as we were lulled by the soft sounds of Apollo's lyre.

∽

Fuchs's desire to reaffirm the autonomy of art against the incursion of urgent historical events was more thoroughly realized in another international exhibition staged later in 1982, also in Germany. Appropriately titling their show *Zeitgeist,* the organizers, Norman Rosenthal and Christos Joachamides, were much bolder than Fuchs in their denial of the realities of the political climate and in their exclusion of any art that might unsettle the mystificatory tendencies they presented as exemplary of the spirit of the times. Once again the exhibition was mounted in a historic museum building, the Kunstgewerbemuseum in Berlin, now known as the Martin Gropius Building after its architect. Joachamides made reference to this building's history in the closing paragraph of his catalogue introduction:

When Mario Merz came to Berlin a number of months ago and visited the Martin Gropius Building to discuss his contribution to the exhibition, he quite spontaneously remarked, "Che bell Palazzo!" [Here we are again, in front of a splendid palace.] On another occasion, Norman Rosenthal spoke of the tension between the interior and the exterior, between the reality and the memory that the building evokes. Outside, an environment of horror, made up of the German past and present. Inside, the triumph of autonomy, the architectural "Gesamtkunstwerk" which in masterly and sovereign manner banishes reality from the building by creating its own. Even the wounds which reality has inflicted on it are part of the beauty. That is also—ZEITGEIST: the place, *this* place, *these* artists, at *this* moment. For us the question is how does an autonomous work of art relate to the equally autonomous architecture and to the sum of memories which are present today. [10]

How indeed? But first, we might be a bit more specific about what those memories are and what that present reality consisted of. The Martin Gropius Building lay virtually in complete ruin after the war, since it was in direct proximity to the Gestapo headquarters, the SS office building, Ernst Sagebiel's Ministry of Aviation, and Albert Speer's Reichs Chancellery. Defended to the last, this administrative center of Nazi power came under the heaviest bombing and shelling of any area of the city. Throughout the period of reconstruction, the Kunstgewerbemuseum remained a neglected pile of rubble; not until the late 1970s was restoration undertaken. Even now, much of the ornamentation is irreparably damaged. But perhaps even more relevant than these traces of shelling is the fact that one enters the building from the rear, since the former front stands only a few yards from the Berlin Wall. This presumably is the environment of horror to which Rosenthal referred as he mused on the triumph of autonomy of this building and the works of art to be contained within it.

Had Rosenthal and Joachamides invited artists such as Hans Haacke to participate in *Zeitgeist,* their rhetorical questions might

Martin Gropius, Kunstgewerbemuseum,
Berlin, 1877–1881, etching by Lorenz Ritter
(courtesy Landesbildstelle, Berlin).

Postwar ruins of Berlin's Kunstgewerbemuseum (photo courtesy Landesbildstelle,
Berlin).

have received some answers of genuine significance.[11] For it is part of the stated program of Haacke's enterprise, as well as that of other artists employing a similar approach, that the context of the exhibition dictates the nature of the intervention he will make. As Haacke put it, "The context in which a work is exhibited for the first time is a material for me like canvas and paint."[12] This means, of course, that Haacke's work must relinquish its claim to autonomy and universality, as well as its status as an easily marketable commodity. And Rosenthal and Joachamides have shown themselves to be primarily devoted to just these aspects of art. Nevertheless, the idea of commissioning works specifically for the context of *Zeitgeist* did not entirely elude the curators. In order to give an impressive sense of uniformity to the grand atrium space of the museum, they asked eight of the participating artists each to paint especially for the exhibition four paintings with the dimensions of three by four meters. The artists dutifully complied, adjusting the size and format of their products to meet the demands of exhibition, just as a dress designer might alter the shape of a creation to suit the needs of an unusually portly client. The American painter David Salle even took the daring step of foregoing his usual cryptic titles and labeled his tailor-made creations *Zeitgeist Painting Nr. 1, Zeitgeist Painting Nr. 2, Zeitgeist Painting Nr. 3,* and *Zeitgeist Painting Nr. 4.* The prospective collectors would no doubt be very pleased to acquire works thus stamped with the imprimatur of a prestigious international show.

For a description of the *zeitgeistig* artworks, I will rely upon one of the American contributors to the catalogue, the art historian Robert Rosenblum, whose agility in adapting to any new aesthetic fashion makes him especially qualified to speak for this one:

The ivory towers where artists of an earlier decade painstakingly calculated hairbreadth geometries, semiotic theories, and various visual and intellectual purities have been invaded by an international army of new artists who want to shake everything up with their self-consciously bad manners. Everywhere, a sense of liberating eruption can be felt, as if a turbulent world of myths, of memory, of molten, ragged shapes and hues had been released from beneath the repressive restraints of the intellect which reigned over the most potent art of the last decade. The objective territory of formal lucidity, of the impersonal, static surfaces of photographic imagery has been toppled by earthquakes which seem both personal and collective, outbursts of the artists' own fantasies culled, however, from the most public range of experience, whether from mythology, history, or the vast inventory of earlier works of art that constantly assail the contemporary eye and mind in every conceivable place, from magazines and postcards to subway stations and middle-class interiors.

From this Pandora's Box, a never-ending stream of legendary creatures is emerging, populating these new canvases in the most unexpected ways. This attack upon the traditional iconoclasm of abstract art and the empirical assumptions of photographic imagery has aggressively absorbed the wildest range of beings taken from the Bible, from comic strips, from historical legend, from literary pantheons, from classical lore. An anthology of works by artists represented here might include images, for example, not only of Jesus (Fetting), Pegasus (LeBrun), Brünnhilde (Kiefer), Orion (Garouste), Prometheus (Lüpertz), Victor Hugo (Schnabel), and Picasso (Borofsky), but also of Bugs Bunny (Salle), and Lucky Luke (Polke). The result is a visual Tower of Babel that mixes its cultures—high and low, contemporary and prehistoric, classical and Christian, legendary and historical—with an exuberant irreverence that mirrors closely the confusing glut of encyclopedic data that fills our shared visual environment and provides us with the material of dreams and art.[13]

One could spend some time analyzing a text in which ivory towers are invaded by international armies, who then proceed to build, still within the ivory tower, a Tower of Babel; or again, a prose whose vagaries of terminology can slide from "historical legend" to the binary opposition "legendary" versus "historical." It is, in any case, a peculiar view of history that sees one decade as ruled by an intellect that is called repressive and the next as liberated by an eruption of self-consciously bad manners. But this history is, after all, only *art* history, an institutionalized discipline of which Rosenblum is a reigning master. For him, the word *history* might well be replaced with *Zeitgeist,* for he comprehends little more than changes in sensibility and style. Thus, the art-historical shift that is chronicled by the exhibition *Zeitgeist* is merely another predictable swing of the pendulum of style from cool to hot, from abstract to figurative, from Apollonian to Dionysian. (We may note that in this regard Rudi Fuchs confused his terms when he invoked the soft sounds of Apollo's lyre, for at *Documenta,* too, the dominant mode of painting was the bombast of neoexpressionism.)

Rosenblum's history as *Zeitgeist* was corroborated in the exhibition catalogue by his colleague Hilton Kramer, who reduced it finally to a simple matter of changing tastes. Kramer had hit upon this novel idea that new art could be explained as a change in taste when trying to come to grips in his *New York Times* column with the work of Julian Schnabel and Malcolm Morley. Clearly pleased that he had found the solution to the dilemma, he decided to quote himself in his *Zeitgeist* essay:

Nothing is more incalculable in art—or more inevitable—than a genuine change in taste. . . . Although taste seems to operate by a sort of law of compensation, so that the denial of certain qualities in one period almost automatically prepares the ground for their triumphal return later, its timetable can never be accurately predicated. Its roots lie in something deeper and more mysterious than mere fashion. At the heart of every genuine change in taste there is, I suppose, a keen feeling of loss, an existential ache—a sense that something absolutely essential to the life of art has been allowed to fall into a state of unendurable atrophy. It is to the immediate repair of this perceived void that taste at its profoundest level addresses itself.[14]

Kramer goes on to explain that what had been lost from art during the 1960s and the 1970s was poetry and fantasy, the drama of the self, the visionary and the irrational; these had been denied by the orthodoxies of pure, cerebral abstraction. Again, it is a question only of style and sensibility and the subject matter they can generate.

But what is left out of these descriptions of contemporary art? What is, in fact, suppressed? The hidden agenda of this version of recent history is the calculated exclusion of the truly significant developments of the art of the past two decades. By characterizing the art of this period as abstract, geometric, intellective, the real terms of art practice are elided. Where do we read in these texts of the critique of the institutions of power that seek to limit the meaning and function of art to the purely aesthetic? Where is a discussion of the attempted dissolution of the beaux-arts mediums and their replacement with modes of production that could better resist those institutions? Where do we find an analysis of work by feminists and minorities whose marginalization by the art institutions became a significant point of departure for the creation of alternative practices? Where do we find mention of those direct interventions by artists in their local social environments? Where, in short, in these essays can we learn of the political critique that has been a major force in recent art?

The answer is, of course, Nowhere. For Rosenblum and Kramer, for Rosenthal and Joachamides, and for Fuchs, politics is what art must deny. For them, art is gentle and discreet, it is autonomous, and it exists in an ivory tower. Art is, after all, only a matter of taste. To this endeavor, politics is a threat. But what of *their* politics? Is there only an *art* of exhibition? Is there not also a politics of exhibition? Is it not a politics that chooses as the symbol of an exhibition the statue of an eighteenth-century imperial ruler? that invites only one woman to participate in an exhibition of forty-three artists?[15] Can we not recognize a politics that would limit a discussion of repression and liberation to matters of style? It is not, assuredly, a politics that wants to confine art to a pure realm of the aesthetic?

Hilton Kramer's conversion to the aesthetics of neoexpressionism occurred at about the same time that he underwent another, somewhat more concrete, conversion. After sixteen years as an art critic for the *New York Times,* arguably the most influential newspaper in America, Kramer resigned his position to found his own magazine. Generously financed by major right-wing foundations,[16] Kramer's *New Criterion* became, as soon as it appeared, the principal intellectual organ of the Reagan administration's cultural policies. Under the guise of a return to established moral values and critical standards, these policies in fact include a defunding and further marginalization of all cultural activities seen as critical of the conservative political agenda and a gradual dismantling of government support for the arts and humanities, to be replaced by monies from the "private sector." This latter term, a favorite of the present U.S. government, is best translated as corporate self-interest, which has already begun to tighten its grip on all aspects of American cultural activity, from television programming to art exhibitions. Kramer's efforts in this regard are well served by his publisher, Samuel Lipman, who sits on President Reagan's National Council on the Arts, the body that oversees the activities of the National Endowment for the Arts. The effectiveness of Kramer's new magazine may be discerned from the fact that within several months of the publication of an article in the *New Criterion* condemning the National Endowment's fellowships for art critics, the chairman of the endowment announced their cancellation.[17]

It is in this context that we must see Kramer's claim of a high-minded neutrality on aesthetic issues, his abhorrence of the politicization of art. In an article in the *New Criterion* entitled "Turning Back the Clock: Art and Politics in 1984," Kramer vehemently attacked a number of recent exhibitions that dealt with the issue of art and politics. His argument was that any attempt to see the workings of ideology within the aesthetic is a totalitarian, even Stalinist, position, which leads inevitably to an acquiescence in tyranny. But what is tyranny if not that form of government that seeks to silence all criticism of or opposition to its policies? And what is the aesthetic production most acceptable to tyranny if not that which either directly affirms the status quo or contents itself with solipsistic exercises in so-called self-expression? Kramer's own acquiescence in the tyrannical suppression of opposition is most evident in his essay's implicit call for the defunding of those exhibition venues showing political art, which he reminds his readers time and again are recipients of public financial support, or in his questioning the suitability for academic positions of those politically committed art critics who acted as curators for the shows. But these McCarthyite insinuations are hidden behind a veil of supposedly disinterested concern for the maintenance of aesthetic standards. In Kramer's estimation, it is virtually inconceivable that political art could be of high aesthetic quality; but what is worse, such art appears intentionally to negate aesthetic discourse altogether. To prove his point, Kramer singled out Hans Haacke's contribution to an exhibition at the CUNY Graduate Center Mall, organized under the auspices of Artists Call against U.S. Intervention in Central America. Here is his discussion of Haacke's work:

In the show . . . we were shown, among much else, a huge, square, unpainted box constructed of wood and standing approximately eight feet high. On its upper side there were some small openings and further down some words stencilled in large letters. A parody of the Minimalist sculpture of Donald Judd, perhaps? Not at all. This was a solemn statement, and the words told us why: "Isolation Box As Used by U.S. Troops at Point Salines Prison Camp in Grenada." The creator of this inspired work was Hans Haacke, who was also represented in the "Art and Social Conscience" exhibition [this exhibition, also a target of Kramer's attack, was held at the Edith C. Blum Art Institute at Bard College] by a photographic lightbox poster attacking President Reagan [*The Safety Net,* 1982]. Such works are not only devoid of any discernible artistic quality, they are pretty much devoid of any discernible artistic existence. They cannot be experienced as art, and they are not intended to be. Yet where else but in an art exhibition would they be shown? Their purpose in being entered into the art context, however, is not only to score propaganda points but to undermine the very

Hans Haacke, *U.S. Isolation Box, Grenada,*
1983, 1984 (photo courtesy Hans Haacke).

idea of art as a realm of aesthetic discourse. President Reagan and his policies may be the immediate object of attack, but the more fundamental one is the idea of art itself.[18]

But whose idea of art? Whose realm of aesthetic discourse? Whose artistic quality? Kramer speaks as if these were all decided matters, and that everyone would therefore agree that Haacke's work can be nothing other than propaganda, or, as was suggested in a *Wall Street Journal* editorial, pornography.[19] It seems to have escaped Kramer's attention that Haacke used the historically sanctioned aesthetic strategy of appropriation in order to create a work of rigorous factual specificity. Haacke's *Isolation Box, Grenada* is a precise reconstruction of those used by the U.S. army only a few months earlier in blatant disregard of the Geneva Convention. As he read the description in the *New York Times* of the prison cells built expressly for the brutal humiliation of Grenadian and Cuban hostages,[20] Haacke did not fail to note their resemblance to the "minimalist sculpture of Donald Judd," and thus to recognize the possibility of appropriating that sculptural aesthetic for a work of contemporary political significance. But apparently for Kramer it is an acquiescence in tyranny to reclaim an aesthetic position for the purpose of questioning a government that disregards international law to invade a tiny sovereign state, that mistakenly bombs a mental asylum and kills scores of innocent people, and that exercises total press censorship throughout the invasion.

∽

Hilton Kramer's failure to recognize the historical avant-garde strategy in Haacke's *Isolation Box, Grenada* is not governed simply by his desire to forestall the hard political questions that Haacke's work raises. Kramer's purpose is more sweeping: to suppress any discussion of the links between the artistic avant-garde and radical politics, and thus to claim for modern art a continuous, unproblematic aesthetic history that is entirely severed from episodes of political engagement. The lengths to which Kramer will go to fulfill this purpose can be determined by reading, in the same "Art and Politics" essay, his attack on one of the curators of the New Museum's *Art & Ideology* exhibition, the main target of Kramer's rage:

Benjamin H. D. Buchloh, . . . who teaches art history at the State University of New York at Westbury, defends the propaganda materials he has selected for this exhibition by, among other things, attacking the late Alfred H. Barr, Jr., for his alleged failure to comprehend "the radical change that [modern] artists and theoreticians introduced into the history of aesthetic theory and production in the twentieth century." What this means, apparently, is that Alfred H. Barr would never have accepted Professor Buchloh's Marxist analysis of the history of modern art, which appears to be based on Louis Althusser's *Lenin and Philosophy.* (Is this really what is taught as modern art history at SUNY Westbury? Alas, one can believe it.)[21]

I will not dwell upon, but will simply call attention to, the parenthetical remark, should anyone doubt that Kramer's tactics include red-baiting. More important in our context is the deliberate falsification achieved by the word *modern,* which Kramer placed in brackets. To accuse Alfred Barr of failing to comprehend *modern* artists and theoreticians is something that even the most extremist critics of Barr's position would be hesitant to do, and it is not at all what Buchloh did. Here is a fuller portion of the passage from which Kramer quoted:

When one of the founding fathers of American Modernism and the first director of the institution that taught the American Neo-avant-garde arrived in the Soviet Union in 1927 on a survey journey to take stock of international avant-garde activities for their possible import into the United States, he saw himself confronted with a situation of seemingly unmanageable conflicts. One the one hand, there was the extraordinary productivity of the modernist avant-garde in the Soviet Union (extraordinary by the numbers of its constituency, men and women, its modes of production, ranging from Malevich's late Suprematist work through the laboratory period of the Constructivists to the LEF Group and the Productivist Program, from Agit Prop theater productions to avant-garde film production for mass audiences). On the other hand, there was the obvious general awareness among the artists and cultural producers, critics and theorists that they were participating in a final transformation of the modernist aesthetic, which would irretrievably and irrevocably alter the conditions of production and reception as they had been inherited from bourgeois society and its institutions (from Kant's aesthetics and the modernist practices that had originated in them). Moreover, there was the growing fear that the process of that successful transformation might be aborted by the emergence of totalitarian repression from within the very system that had generated the foundations for a new socialist collective culture. Last of all and crucial, there was Alfred Barr's own disposition of interests and motivations of action within that situation: searching for the most advanced modernist avant-garde in a moment and place where that social group was just about to dismantle itself and its specialized activities in order to assume the new role and function in the newly defined collective process of social production of culture.

The reasons why Alfred Barr, one of the first "modern" art historians, then just about to discover and establish the modern avant-garde in the United States, was determined (in the literal sense) to fail in comprehending the radical change that those artists and theoreticians introduced into the history of aesthetic theory and production in the twentieth century, are obviously too complex to be dealt with in this context. . . . [22]

Although Buchloh devoted a lengthy paragraph to detailing the special historical circumstances of *those* artists and theoreticians that Barr failed to comprehend fully (again, as Buchloh says, for historically specific, or determined, reasons), Kramer substituted the general term *modern* for Buchloh's *those*—those productivists who were at that moment in the late 1920s on the brink of dissolving the autonomous modernist mediums in favor of collective social production.

I have quoted Buchloh's essay at length not only to demonstrate the insidious, falsifying tactics of Hilton Kramer's criticism but also because it is of particular pertinence to the contemporary art of exhibition. For it is precisely the desire to dissemble the history of disruptions of the modernist aesthetic development that constitutes the present program of the museum that Alfred Barr helped to found. It was Buchloh's point that the Museum of Modern Art had presented a history of modern art to the American public, and more particularly to the artists within that public, that never fully articulated the historical avant-garde position. For that position included the development of cultural practices that would critically reveal the constricting institutionalization of art within modern bourgeois society. At the same time, those practices were intended to function socially outside that institutionalized system. At MOMA, however, both in its earlier period and still more today, the works of the Soviet avant-garde, of Duchamp, and of the German dada artists have been tamed. They are presented, insofar as is possible, as if they were conventional masterpieces of fine art. The radical implications of this work have been distorted by the institution so as not to allow interferences with its portrayal of modern art as a steady development of abstract and abstracting styles.

Although it is perfectly clear that the current installation of MOMA's collections is intended to present not merely individual objects of modern art but rather a narrative *history* of those objects—"These collections tell the story of modern art," proclaims a recent MOMA press release—it is also clear that the justification for the false construction of that history is connoisseurship; MOMA's primary responsibility, as its directors apparently see it, is to provide the public with a direct experience of great works of art unburdened by the weight of history. This rationale is, in fact, spelled out in the new museum installation at the entrance to the Alfred H. Barr Jr. Galleries. On the dedicatory plaque, Barr is quoted as once having defined his task as "the conscientious, continuous, resolute distinction of quality from mediocrity."[23] To determine just how this con-

Installation of Soviet avant-garde works at
the Museum of Modern Art, New York,
1984 (photo Louise Lawler).

noisseurship principle is exercised in the interest of a biased history would require a detailed analysis of, among other things, the relative weight and density given to particular artists and movements—of the prominence accorded Picasso and Matisse, for example, as opposed to, say, Duchamp and Malevich; of the special care taken with the installation of cubism as against that of the Soviet avant-garde, now relegated to a cluttered stairwell; of the decisions to exhibit certain works owned by the museum while others are banished to storage.

There is, however, a less complex but far more effective means by which MOMA imposes a partisan view of the objects in its possession. This is the rigid division of modern art practices into separate departments within the institution. By distributing the work of the avant-garde to various departments—Painting and Sculpture, Drawings, Prints and Illustrated Books, Architecture and Design, Photography, and Film—that is, by stringently enforcing what appears to be a natural parceling of objects according to medium, MOMA automatically constructs a formalist history of modernism.[24] Because of this simple and seemingly neutral fact, the museum goer can have no sense of the significance of, to give just one example, Rodchenko's abandonment of painting in favor of photography. Rodchenko saw painting as a vestige of an outmoded culture and photography as possibly instrumental for the creation of a new one—the very situation that Alfred Barr witnessed during the trip to the Soviet Union to which Buchloh referred—but this history cannot be articulated because of the consignment of Rodchenko's various works to different fiefdoms within the museum. As it is, one experiences Rodchenko merely as an artist who worked in more than one medium, which is to say, as a versatile artist, like many "great" artists. Seen within the Department of Photography, Rodchenko might seem to be an artist who increased the formal possibilities of photography, but he cannot be understood as one who saw photography as having a far greater potential for social praxis than painting, if for no other reason than that photography readily lent itself to a wider system of distribution. Mounted and framed as individual auratic works of art, Rodchenko's photographs cannot even convey this most simple historical fact. Such a misinterpretation of modernism and of avant-garde interventions within modernism, inherent in the very structure of MOMA, was to have particular consequences for postwar American art—the point of Buchloh's discussion of this issue in his essay for the *Art & Ideology* show—and we are now experiencing those consequences in their fuller contradictions in the contemporary art of exhibition, a point to which I shall return.

Hilton Kramer's summary dismissal of Buchloh's analysis of Barr's encounter with the Soviet avant-garde, effected simply by labeling the analysis Althusserian,[25] can be more fully understood when placed alongside his own characterization of this crucial episode, which transpired just before the founding of the museum in 1929. In a special issue of the *New Criterion* devoted entirely to an essay on the renovated museum, Kramer is again careful to separate aesthetics from politics:

[Barr] had been to Germany and Russia in the Twenties, and had been deeply impressed with the art—and with the ideas governing the art—which he studied there. These ideas were radical in more than an aesthetic sense—although they were certainly that. They were radical, or at least were thought to be at the time, in their social implications as well. At the Bauhaus in Germany and in the councils of the Russia Avant-garde in the early years of the revolution, the very conception of what art was or should be was altered under the influence of a powerful utopian ideology. As a result, the boundary separating fine art from industrial art was, if not completely abandoned by everyone concerned, at least very much questioned and undermined. Henceforth, from this radical perspective, there were to be no aesthetic hierarchies. A poster might be equal to a painting, a factory or a housing project as much to be esteemed as a great work of sculpture.

It is my impression that at no time in his life was Barr very much interested in politics. It was not, in any case, the political implications of this development that drew him to it. What deeply interested him were its aesthetic implications, and therefore, under his influence, what governed the museum's outlook from its earliest days was a vision that attempted to effect a kind of grand synthesis of modernist aesthetics and the technology of industrialism.[26]

Whether or not Kramer fairly appraises Barr's political interests, he attributes to him an understanding of the aesthetics of the avant-garde that fully deradicalizes them, though Kramer persists in using the term *radical*.[27] It is by no means the case that the early avant-garde was simply interested in giving to "architecture, industrial design, photography, and film a kind of parity with painting, sculpture and the graphic arts," to elevate work in other mediums "to the realm of fine art."[28] On the contrary, the true radicalism of the early avant-garde was its abandonment of the very notion of fine art in the interests of social production, which meant, for one thing, destroying easel painting as a form. The original avant-garde program did not consist of an aesthetic with social implications; it consisted of a politicized aesthetic, a socialist art.[29]

Kramer is, however, quite correct in his discussion of the historical results of the deradicalization of the avant-garde: "The aesthetic that originated at the Bauhaus and other avant-garde groups has been stripped of its social ideology and turned into the reigning taste of the cultural marketplace." Indeed, the works of the avant-garde, severed from their political setting and presented as fine art, could serve as examples for product design and advertising. As if to illustrate this process of transforming agitprop into advertising,[30] the entrance to MOMA's design galleries displays posters by members of the Soviet avant-garde juxtaposed with advertisements directly or indirectly influenced by them. Underneath Rodchenko's poster for the Theater of the Revolution is an ad for Martini designed by Alexei Brodovich, a Russian emigrant who had clearly absorbed his design lessons early and directly. On the opposite wall Gustav Klucis and Sergei Senkin's agitprop "Let Us Carry Out the Plan of

Entrance foyer of Architecture and Design
Galleries, Museum of Modern Art, New
York, 1984 (photos Louise Lawler).

the Great Work" and El Lissitsky's "USSR Russische Ausstellung" announcement are hung next to a recent advertisement for Campari. To this deliberate blurring of important distinctions in meaning, Kramer of course nods his approval, noting that in this regard MOMA has fulfilled its mission. But now that modernism has been fully assimilated into consumer culture, when we enter the current design department, "well, we suddenly find ourselves in something that looks vaguely reminiscent of Bloomingdale's furniture department," and so "it becomes more and more difficult to believe such an installation is necessary."[31] Mission accomplished, then, MOMA has come full circle. It can now get back to the business of art as it had been prior to Barr's "radical notion" of a broadened definition of aesthetic endeavor. "Today," Kramer concludes, "it is only as an institution specializing in high art that the new MOMA can claim to have a great and necessary purpose."[32]

In this, the official neoconservative view of the current purposes of the museum, it is one of the consequences of the distortion of the historical avant-garde that the museum should abandon altogether its task of presenting any practices that do not conform to the traditional view of fine art, to return, that is, to the prerogatives of painting and sculpture. And indeed, the inaugural exhibition at the reopened Museum of Modern Art, entitled *An International Survey of Recent Painting and Sculpture,* did just that. Specifically citing *Documenta 7* and *Zeitgeist* as precedents for the show, Kynaston McShine, the curator responsible for the selection, claimed to have looked at "everything, everywhere," because "it was important to have work from a lot of different places and to introduce a large public to a great deal of current activity. I wanted it to be an international cross-section of what is going on."[33] To limit "what is going on" to painting and sculpture, however, is to dissemble willfully the actual facts of artistic practice at this historical juncture. To look at "everything everywhere" and to see only painting and sculpture is to be blind—blind to every significant endeavor to continue the work of the avant-garde. The scandal of the international survey—

quite apart from its haphazard inclusion of just about any trivial product of today's market culture and its chaotic, bargain-basement installation—is its refusal to take account of the wide variety of practices that question and propose an alternative to the hegemony of painting and sculpture. And the scandal is made all the more complete when one remembers that it was also McShine who organized MOMA's last major international exhibition of contemporary art, the *Information* show of 1970, a broad survey of conceptual art and related developments. Like Rudi Fuchs, then, McShine cannot claim ignorance of the work of the late 1960s that makes a return to painting and sculpture so historically problematic. Even within the absurd terms of McShine's stated principle of selection—that only those artists whose reputations were established after 1975 would be considered[34]—we are given no reason whatsoever for the exclusion of all those artists whose work continues and deepens the tendencies shown in *Information*. The short introduction to the catalogue, unsigned but presumably written by McShine, slides around the problem with the following statement:

The exhibition does not encompass mediums other than painting and sculpture. However one cannot help but register the current tendency of painters and sculptors to cross the border into other disciplines such as photography, film, video and even architecture. While these "crossovers" have become expected in recent years, less familiar to a general audience is the attraction to music and performance. Represented here are artists active not only in painting and sculpture but also in performance art. Inevitably, some of their theatrical concerns present themselves in their work, most often in a narrative or autobiographical form.[35]

Such a paragraph, in its deliberate weakness and vagueness, is designed to tell us nothing at all about the opposition to conventional painting and sculpture that persists in certain segments of the art world. By his choice of the term *crossover,* McShine once again resorts to the myth of artistic versatility to demean the significance of genuinely alternative and socially engaged art production. That the reactionary tradition represented in the international survey might be placed in jeopardy, shown to be historically bankrupt, by such production is completely ignored by McShine.

It is interesting in this regard to recall the interview given to *Artforum* ten years earlier by William Rubin, director of MOMA's Department of Painting and Sculpture. There Rubin stated what was at the time a fairly common view of contemporary aesthetic developments. New art practices such as conceptual art and earthworks, Rubin surmised, might signal the end of modernism, which was just possibly a circumscribed historical concept, one that Rubin linked to easel painting, private collecting, and the museum. The new art practices, Rubin suggested, "want another environment (or should want it) and, perhaps, another public."[36]

Though Rubin hestitates to endorse the view he presents, he seems to have had a remarkably clear understanding of the actual facts of art history of the 1960s and early 1970s. It is therefore all the more astonishing that the museum department headed by Rubin should mount an exhibition that unquestionably attempts to negate that understanding. What do Rubin and McShine believe transpired in the intervening decade? Were the endeavors that Rubin saw as having possibly created a rupture with modernism only "passing phenomena," as he suggested the coming years might tell? Judging not only from McShine's survey but also from the installation of that part of the permanent collection comprising the art of the 1960s and the 1970s, the answer must be affirmative, for there is no evidence of the "postmodern" art of which Rubin speaks. With the exception of a few works of minimal sculpture, there is no trace of the art of that period that led even Rubin to wonder if modern art, traditionally defined, had come to an end.

Yet anyone who has witnessed the art events of the past decade might come to a very different conclusion. On the one hand, there has been an intensification of the critique of art's institutionalization, a deepening of the rupture with modernism. On the other hand, there has been a concerted effort to suppress this fact and to reestablish the traditional fine art categories by all conservative forces of society, from cultural bureaucracies to museum institutions, from corporate boardrooms to the marketplace for art. And this has been accomplished with the complicity of a new breed of entrepreneurial artists, utterly cynical in their disregard of both recent art history and present political reality. These newly heralded "geniuses" work for a parvenu class of collectors who want art with an ensured resale value, which will at the same time fulfill their desire for mildly pornographic titillation, romantic cliché, easy reference to past "masterpieces," and good decor. The objects on view to celebrate the reopening of MOMA were made, with very few exceptions, to cater to this taste, to rest easily over the sofa in a Trump Tower living room or to languish in a bank vault while prices escalate. No wonder then that McShine ended his catalogue introduction with the very special hope "to encourage everyone to be in favor of the art of our time." Given what he has presented as the art of our time, his currying of our favor could hardly be at odds with that of the sponsors of the exhibition, the AT&T Corporation, who mounted an advertising campaign to coincide with the show. "Some of the masterpieces of tomorrow are on exhibit today," reads the ad's banner headline, under which appears a reproduction of one of Robert Longo's glorifications of corporate style, now in MOMA's permanent collection. That corporate interests are in perfect accord with the art presented in MOMA's inaugural show is a point underscored in the catalogue preface written by the museum's director, whose long paragraph of praise and thanks to AT&T contains the following statement: "AT&T clearly recognizes that experiment and innovation, so highly prized in business and industry, must be equally valued and supported in the arts."[37]

Experiment and innovation are prized in business and industry, of course, because they result in expanding consumer markets and higher profits. That this is also the motive of the works presented in *An International Survey of Recent Painting and Sculpture* is hardly less obvious. But in case the thousands of visitors who flocked to the newly reopened museum failed to grasp this fact, MOMA confronted them with a still more persuasive demonstration of the corporate idea of art, something that Hilton Kramer referred to as "the most audacious *coup de théâtre* anyone has ever attempted at MOMA."[38] Our first glimpse of this was in a full-page photograph that appeared in the *New York Times Magazine* above the caption "While celebrating its permanent collection of masterworks from the modernist period, the museum will continue to exhibit the new." The "new" in question, the *coup de théâtre*, was shown being installed in the dramatic two-story space over the escalator leading to the design galleries; the "new" is a helicopter. Here is how a museum press release described the new acquisition:

An ubiquitous contemporary artifact, the Bell 47D helicopter was acquired several months ago by the [Architecture and Design] Department, and will be suspended above visitors as they enter the fourth floor galleries. Utilitarian in appearance—it is the helicopter equivalent of the jeep—the model 47 went into production in 1947 and set an industry record by remaining in production for the next three decades. As an example of industrial mass production, it is, according to Department Director Arthur Drexler, "a peculiarly memorable object."

Just how memorable a helicopter may be was well illustrated in January 1984 at New York's Museo del Barrio, in an exhibition presented in conjunction with Artists Call against U.S. Intervention in Central America. The show contained some fifty drawings by Salvadoran and Guatemalan refugee children living across the borders in Honduras and Nicaragua, and virtually every one of the drawings depicted this "ubiquitous contemporary artifact," ubiquitous indeed, since it is and has been the most essential instrument of counterinsurgency warfare since the Korean War. Even Francis Ford Coppola did not fail to understand the sinister symbolic value of this "memorable object" in his highly mythologized portrayal of Americans in

Entrance foyer of Architecture and Design
Galleries, Museum of Modern Art, 1984
(photo courtesy The Museum of Modern
Art, New York).

Vietnam. But symbols aside, the hard facts are that Bell helicopters are manufactured by the Fort Worth corporation Textron, a major U.S. defense contractor, which supplies the Bell and Huey model helicopters used against the civilian populations of El Salvador, Honduras, Nicaragua, and Gautemala.[39] But because the contemporary art of exhibition has taught us to distinguish between the political and the aesthetic, a *New York Times* editorial entitled "Marvelous MOMA" was able to say of MOMA's proud new object:

A helicopter, suspended from the ceiling, hovers over an escalator in the Museum of Modern Art. . . . The chopper is bright green, bug-eyed and beautiful. We know that it is beautiful because MOMA showed us the way to look at the 20th Century."[40]

Notes

1.   Edward J. Lowell, *The Hessians* (Port Washington, N.Y.: Kennikat Press, 1965), pp. 1–2.

2.   Walter Benjamin, "Theses on the Philosophy of History," in *Illuminations,* trans. Harry Zohn (New York: Schocken Books, 1969), pp. 256–257.

3.   Rudi Fuchs, "Introduction," in *Documenta 7,* vol. 1 (Kassel, 1982), p. xv.

4.   Quoted in Coosje van Bruggen, "In the Mist Things Appear Larger," in *Documenta 7,* vol. 2, p. ix.

5.   Rudi Fuchs, "Foreword," in *Documenta 7,* vol. 2, p. vii.

6.   The U.S. Department of Housing and Urban Development reported on May 1, 1984, that there were an estimated 28,000–30,000 homeless people in New York City. A spokesman for the Community of Creative Nonviolence, a private non-profit group that works with the homeless, said, however, that the official government statistics were "utterly ridiculous" and that the Reagan administration was vastly underestimating the scope of the problem for political reasons. Estimates of the number of homeless nationwide by nongovernment antipoverty groups are often ten times the government figures of 250,000–300,000. See Robert Pear, "Homeless in U.S. Put at 250,000, Far Less Than Previous Estimates," *New York Times,* May 2, 1984, p. A1.

7.   See Andy Soltis and Chris Oliver, "Super Rats: They Never Say Die," *New York Post,* May 12, 1979, p. 6, in which an official of the Health Department's Pest Control Bureau is reported as saying, "You go into the South Bronx and this happens on an ongoing basis. It was highlighted here because of the woman who was bitten."

8.   Benjamin H.D. Buchloh, "Documenta 7: A Dictionary of Received Ideas," *October,* no. 22 (Fall 1982), p. 112.

9.   Fuchs, "Foreword," p. vii.

10. Christos Joachamides, "Achilles and Hector before the Walls of Troy," in *Zeitgeist* (New York: Braziller, 1983), p. 10.

11. This essay was written prior to Haacke's work for the Neue Gesellschaft für Bildende Kunst in West Berlin, a work that fully confirmed my speculation. *Broadness and Diversity of the Ludwig Brigade* (1984) does indeed use as its starting point the proximity of the Berlin Wall to the place of the exhibition, the Künslterhaus Bethanien. And it therefore takes as its subject German-German relations, relations which were then much in the news because of the postponement, under Soviet pressure, of Eric Honecker's proposed visit to Bonn (see *October,* no. 30 [Fall 1984], pp. 9–16).

Here is one more example of the way in which Rosenthal and Joachamides might have received real answers to their question: In the 1983 *Art & Ideology* exhibition at the New Museum of Contemporary Art in New York, Allan Sekula showed *Sketch for a Geography Lesson,* a work consisting of photographs and accompanying text that, again, took the effects of the renewal of cold war tensions in Germany as its subject, although in a manner quite different from Haacke's *Oelgemaelde.*

12. Quoted in Jeanne Siegel, "Leon Golub/Hans Haacke: What Makes Art Political?" *Arts Magazine* 58, no. 8 (April 1984), p. 111.

13. Robert Rosenblum, "Thoughts on the Origins of 'Zeitgeist,'" in *Zeitgeist,* pp. 11–12.

14. Hilton Kramer, "Signs of Passion," in *Zeitgeist,*
     p. 17. It is interesting that Kramer here speaks of changes in art as *compensatory* for a sense of loss inherent in a previous style, for it is precisely that sense of loss and its periodic *intensification* that Leo Steinberg proposed, in his "Contemporary Art and the Plight of Its Public" (in *Other Criteria* [New York: Oxford University Press, 1972]), as the very condition of innovation within modernism. It was with this contrast between, on the one hand, Steinberg's understanding of modernism and, on the other hand, Kramer's resentment of it that Annette Michelson began her review of Hilton Kramer's *The Age of Avant-Garde;* see Michelson, "Contemporary Art and the Plight of the Public: A View from the New York Hilton," *Artforum* 13, no. 1 (September 1974), pp. 68–70.

15. These are the figures for the *Zeitgeist* exhibition. *A New Spirit in Painting,* an earlier show organized in London by Rosenthal and Joachamides, together with Nicholas Serota, contained work by thirty-eight artists, not one of whom was a woman.

16. For details of *The New Criterion*'s financing, see Hans Haacke, "U.S. Isolation Box, Grenada, 1983," in *Hans Haacke: Unfinished Business,* ed. Brian Wallis (Cambridge, Mass.: The MIT Press, 1986), pp. 258–259.

17. See Hilton Kramer, "Criticism Endowed: Reflections on a Debacle," *New Criterion* 2, no. 3 (November 1983), pp. 1–5. Kramer's argument consisted of an accusation of conflict of interest, wherein "at the core of the program there was certainly a nucleus of friends and professional colleagues who were assiduous in looking after each other's interests" (p. 3). This is Kramer's characterization of what is otherwise known as the peer-panel system of judging, in which members of the profession are asked to judge the work of their fellow critics. Needless to say, the result will be a certain degree of overlap among grantees and jurors over a period of years. It

seems highly likely, however, that Kramer's real opposition to the critics' fellowships stems from his perception that "a great many of them went as a matter of course to people who were opposed to just about every policy of the United States government except one that put money in their own pockets or the pockets of their friends and political associates" (p. 4).

Frank Hodsell, Chairman of the National Endowment for the Arts, disavowed the influence of Kramer's article on the decision to cancel the fellowships. He did admit, though, that "doubts expressed by the National Council on the Arts" were a deciding factor, and it is said that Samuel Lipman personally provided each member of the council with a copy of Kramer's article. See Grace Glueck, "Endowment Suspends Grants for Art Critics," *New York Times,* April 5, 1984, p. C16.

18. Hilton Kramer, "Turning Back the Clock: Art and Politics in 1984," *New Criterion* 2, no. 8 (April 1984), p. 71.

19. "To our knowledge the CCNY [sic] exhibition has not been reviewed yet by a prominent New York art critic. Perhaps critics have noticed that a few blocks down 42nd Street one can see what's maybe America's greatest collection of obscenity and pornography, and that in this respect, the CCNY artists' interpretation of what the U.S. did in Grenada is in proper company" ("Artists for Old Grenada," *Wall Street Journal,* February 21, 1984, p. 32). For a reply to the editorial by Hans Haacke and Thomas Woodruff, see "Letters," *Wall Street Journal,* March 13, 1984.

20. See David Shribman, "U.S. Conducts Grenada Camp for Questioning," *New York Times,* November 14, 1983, pp. A1, A7. The passages describing the isolation boxes read as follows: "Beyond the control gate and barbed wire, and between two clusters of tents, are the most prominent features of the camp, two rows of newly constructed wooden chambers, each measuring about eight feet by eight feet. . . . Besides [the interrogation booths], however, were 10 isolation booths, each with four small windows and a number of ventilation holes with a radius of half an inch. Prisoners must enter these booths by crawling through a hatch that extends from the floor of the booths to about knee level."

21. Kramer, "Turning Back the Clock," p. 71.

22. Benjamin H.D. Buchloh, "Since Realism There Was . . . (On the Current Conditions of Factographic Art)," in *Art & Ideology* (New York: the Museum of Contemporary Art, 1984), pp. 5–6. A slightly different version of this same discussion appears in Buchloh's essay "From Faktura to Factography," *October,* no. 30 (Fall 1984), pp. 83–119. There Buchloh develops much further the precise circumstances to which Barr was witness on his journey to the Soviet Union, as well as later developments.

23. Hilton Kramer quotes Barr's connoisseurship approvingly in "MOMA Reopened: The Museum of Modern Art in the Postmodern Era," *New Criterion* special issue (Summer 1984), p. 14. Indeed, his entire critique of the new MOMA installations and opening exhibitions is based on what he sees as a failure of the current

museum officials to exercise connoisseurship as fully and wisely as did Barr. For
example, he condemns *An International Survey of Recent Painting and Sculpture* as
"the most incredible mess the museum has ever given us," owing to the fact that
"of anything resembling connoisseurship or critical acumen there is not a trace"
(p. 41).

24. The problems created by MOMA's separate departments are made explicit in a
1973 *Artforum* interview with members of PASTA MOMA (The Professional and
Administrative Staff Association of the Museum of Modern Art), who were on
strike at the time: ". . . the last place where the growing interrelationship in the
arts can have any foot in the door whatsoever is The Museum of Modern Art. If
you were running a museum in Timbuctoo you would have a better chance of
doing that.

"*What is the obstacle in New York?*

"The departments are operated as fiefdoms by the department heads. The interrelationship is ignored despite the fact that these disciplines were established under
one roof because [Alfred] Barr saw relationships between the arts, and that they
could enhance each other. In actual fact the place functions as a group of jealous
individual museums, who obstruct each other. . . . Should the department of
Painting and Sculpture accept a film or a photograph? Of course, it turns out that
the Film and Photography Departments wouldn't accept the works by painters and
sculptors anyway, because they consider their esthetic approach different. Conse-
quently we never accomplish anything, whereas you'll find museums in Europe
are busy collecting good works regardless of their medium. I remember two years
ago this came up, many conversations about reorganization of the Museum, to try
to break down the departmental structure, this very kind of thing. We were framing, and I quote, a 'demand letter' two years ago. One of the things talked about
was this need to make it a much more flexible institution. That's one thing that we
have failed in" ("Strike at the Modern," *Artforum* 12, no. 4 [December 1973],
p. 47).

25. Buchloh's discussion of this very specific moment in the history of modern art
does not, in fact, refer to Althusser's *Lenin and Philosophy*, but his discussion of the
contemporary politicized work of Allan Sekula and Fred Lonidier does. He notes,
"If Althusser's argument is correct that the aesthetic constitutes itself only inside
the ideological, what then is the nature of the practice of those artists who, as we
are suggesting, are in fact trying to develop practice that is operative outside and
inside the ideological apparatus? The first argument that will of course be levelled
against this type of work is that it simply cannot be '*art*'. . ." (Buchloh, "Since
Realism There Was," p. 8). This "first argument" is precisely the one Kramer used
against Hans Haacke and the other political artists he attacked.

26. Kramer, "MOMA Reopened," p. 42.

27. Kramer's version of Barr's encounter with the Soviet avant-garde is virtually identical to Buchloh's, even to the point of noting that Barr severed the art from the
politics that motivated the art. The difference, of course, is that Buchloh shows
that this separation resulted precisely in Barr's failure to comprehend "the radical

change that those artists and theoreticians introduced," whereas Kramer simply repeats Barr's failure.

28. Kramer, "MOMA Reopened," p. 42.

29. For a detailed discussion of this question, see Buchloh, "From Faktura to Factography."

30. This process is, in fact, one of *re*-transformation, since agit-prop had originally transformed advertising techniques for political purposes. See Buchloh, "From Faktura to Factography," pp. 96–104.

31. Kramer, "MOMA Reopened," pp. 43–44.

32. Ibid, p. 44.

33. Quoted in Michael Brenson, "A Living Artists Show at the Modern Museum," *New York Times,* April 21, 1984, p. 11.

34. Ibid. Even this stated criterion is entirely belied by the exhibition of some thirty artists whose reputations were well established by the mid-1970s; five of the artists in the show are listed in the catalogue documentation as having had one-person exhibitions at MOMA before 1977.

    An International Survey of Recent Painting and Sculpture, like *Zeitgeist,* failed to take note of the achievements of women artists. Of 165 artists, only 14 were women. A protest demonstration staged by the Women's Caucus for Art failed to elicit any public response from museum officials. This must be seen in contrast to the various demonstrations of the early 1970s against unfair museum policies, when, at the very least, MOMA was responsive enough to enter into public dialogue over the grievances. But of course, if women were very poorly represented in MOMA's reopening show, it is largely because women are centrally involved in alternative practices. To have admitted them would have been to acknowledge that traditional painting and sculpture are not the most important, and certainly not the only, forms of current art practice.

35. "Introduction," in *An International Survey of Recent Painting and Sculpture* (New York: Museum of Modern Art, 1984), p. 12. That this introductory essay is both unsigned and only two pages long makes one wonder just how seriously contemporary art is being considered at MOMA. McShine was quoted in the *Times* as saying, "The show is a sign of hope. It is a sign that contemporary art is being taken seriously as it should be, a sign that the museum will restore the balance between contemporary art and art history that is part of what makes the place unique" (quoted in Brenson, "A Living Artists Show," p. 11). But if this is the case, why does the curator of the show feel no obligation to provide a critical discussion of the artists chosen and the issues addressed in the contemporary art exhibition? In contrast, the first *historical* show to open at the museum, *Primitivism in Twentieth Century Art,* is accompanied by a two-volume catalogue containing nineteen lengthy essays by fifteen scholars and critics. Perhaps the answer is to be found in the final paragraph of the introduction to the international survey: "Those who see this exhibition will, one trusts, understand that art is about looking and not about reading and listening."

36.   William Rubin, in Lawrence Alloway and John Coplans, "Talking with William Rubin: 'The Museum Concept is Not Infinitely Expandable,'" *Artforum* 13, no. 2 (October 1974), p. 52; see also "The End of Painting," this volume. In this interview, Rubin attempts to defend the museum against the charge that it has become unresponsive to contemporary art. He insists that this art simply has no place in a museum, which he sees essentially as a temple for high art. This, of course, puts him in perfect accord with Kramer's position. What is never acknowledged, however, is that ignoring those forms of art that exceed the museum—whether the work of the historical avant-garde or that of the present—will necessarily give a distorted view of history.

37.   Richard E. Oldenburg, "Preface," in *An International Survey of Recent Painting and Sculpture,* p. 9.

38.   Kramer, "MOMA Reopened," p. 43.

39.   In September 1984, the *New York Times* reported that the U.S. government was planning to double the number of combat helicopters in the Salvadoran force by the end of the year: "In the last few weeks, 10 new Hueys have been sent to El Salvador and 10 to 15 more are expected by the end of the year. . . . Under that schedule, the Salvadoran fleet will have increased to 40 from 24 within six months" (James LeMoyne, "U.S. Is Bolstering Salvador Copters: Plans to Double Fleet by End of Year to Let Latins Use New Tactic on Rebels," *New York Times,* September 19, 1984, p. A1). The article went on to say that "such helicopter attacks were the mainstay of American operations in Vietnam. If the Salvadoran Army masters the tactic, it will have made a considerable advance from the often militarily inept force that has been unable to contain rebel offensives in the last two years."

    Reporting for the *Nation* in October, Scott Wallace described the effects of American helicopters on the people of El Salvador: "Although U.S. officials deny that the helicopter-borne assault teams will be used to terrorize civilians who back the guerrillas, government forces are already rehearsing the tactic. On August 30, around the time the shipment of Hueys arrived, army units launched helicopter assaults on the townships of Las Vueltas and San José Las Flores in rebel-controlled zones of Chalatenango province.

    "Journalists who arrived on the scene ten days later were told by local peasants that at least thirty-seven women, children and old people had been killed in the operation. According to the villagers, helicopters bearing Salvadoran troops, led by the U.S.-trained Atlactl Battalion, stalked a group of several hundred peasants who were escorted by a small force of armed guerrillas. The peasants described their bewilderment and terror as they saw the helicopters land troops on hilltops all around them, cutting them off. When the soldiers closed in, some people panicked and plunged into the rapidly flowing Gualsinga River, where several drowned. Others were cut down by machine-gun fire or taken prisoner" (Scott Wallace, "Hueys in El Salvador: Preparing for a Stepped-Up War?" *Nation,* October 20, 1984, p. 337).

40.   "Marvelous MOMA," *New York Times,* May 13, 1984, section 4, p. 22.

The Postmodern Museum

Knowing full well that postmodern architecture is loaded with historicist gimmicks, sly references, visual puns, I will nevertheless contend that I am the brunt of one of its recent jokes. The one I have in mind was contrived by James Stirling for his celebrated Neue Staatsgalerie in Stuttgart. Stirling's erudite wit is in this case figured in a detail of the museum's slick new front wall where it decomposes into ruin—a winking nod, I will immodestly claim, at my essay "On the Museum's Ruins." I know that this is a reference, as well, to the historical tradition of building picturesque ruins; that it also unmasks a pretense to monumentality by partially revealing, behind the museum's imposing facade, a parking garage; and that it proudly flies in the face of modernism's axiomatic truth to materials by showing that the great travertine and sandstone blocks are really only veneer, that the only "real" stones are those lying on the ground. This wry conceit might even be the postmodern architect's parody of recent artworks that consist of nothing other than large blocks arrayed on the ground, very often in front of museums— Ulrich Ruckriem's *Granite (Normandy),* resting alongside Mies van der Rohe's Neue Nationalgalerie in Berlin, for example, or Richard Serra's *Berlin Block for Charlie Chaplin,* subtly wedged into the plaza of the same museum. But I will still pretend to be paranoid enough to see Stirling here thumbing his nose at my contention that postmodernism is founded on the collapse of the museum's discursive system. If the museum is an institution whose time is up, Stirling seems to ask mockingly, then why would I be building a new addition to the Staatsgalerie? And why is it that, as we enter the era of postmodernism, we are witnessing the largest growth in museum construction since the nineteenth century?

James Stirling, Michael Wilford, and Associates, Neue Staatsgalerie, Stuttgart, 1977–
1982, detail of front facade at street level
(photo Louise Lawler).

Something of the scope of this new expansion could be seen in an exhibition staged in 1985 by one of Frankfurt's new museums, the Deutsches Architekturmuseum designed by Oswald Mathias Ungers, in celebration of the opening of yet another of Frankfurt's new museums, the Museum für Kunsthandwerk designed by Richard Meier. The exhibition showed photographs and plans of those two buildings plus fifteen more of Germany's new museums, including Stirling's Neue Staatsgalerie. By the time the exhibition was shown in Berlin in the new Bauhaus-Archiv, Berlin's own new arts and crafts museum had opened. But the latter was one of fifteen or more other new German museums not shown because they were still under construction at the time the exhibition was organized.

The Frankfurt show hinted at another aspect of the resurgence as well: its symbiotic relationship with a renewal of the kind of art production that rests so comfortably within these new museums. This it did by publishing in the show's catalogue an essay entitled "Art and Architecture," written by the neoexpressionist painter Markus Lüpertz. The triumphant reaction that these developments spell is proudly proclaimed by Lüpertz:

In the past years, in the Seventies to be precise, we experienced the politically engaged architect, who threw himself into the class struggle, behaved like a "leftie," questioned himself and his role, and attempted to undermine the firm idea of architecture as something solid, built, permanent. . . .

It is typical of this period that there was no artistic art (only a few, as always, carried on the tradition) and the official opinion was that we could do without art, without genius, without an elite, without master builders.

This cul-de-sac, this political impasse—for art always fails when politics takes a hand—is now to be opened up by Old Mother ART. . . . As usual, art has to fill in when other, highly praised approaches, political, social approaches, fail.

But Art is alive, there are elitist artists, and artists of genius, artists who are removed from necessity, beyond the senses, who can even do without the walls on which their pictures hang. . . . [1]

Richard Serra, *Berlin Block for Charlie
Chaplin*, 1977 (photo Reinnard Friedrich).

Ulrich Ruckriem, *Granite (Normandy)*, 1985
(photo Thomas Marquard).

In this final sentence Lüpertz's rhetoric becomes disingenuous, for he knows that his pictures are conceived for and utterly dependent on the museum's walls, that, rejecting the critical dimension of art practices of the recent past, he is only too happy to supply museums with his pictures. Indeed, when I visited Stirling's Neue Staatsgalerie, I saw a somewhat compressed selection of its modern and contemporary collection reinstalled in the temporary exhibition galleries, in which a progression of works by these "elitist geniuses" made a perfectly smooth transition from the paintings of Jackson Pollock, Mark Rothko, and Barnett Newman to those of Georg Baselitz, Anselm Kiefer, and Lüpertz himself. The art of the 1960s and 1970s, the period of social and political approaches, as Lüpertz characterized it, had been made to disappear from this progression, just as the exhibition installed somewhat later in the main galleries of the Neue Staatsgalerie—the *German Art in the 20th Century* exhibition, organized for the Royal Academy in London under the sponsorship of the Kohl and Thatcher governments[2]—just as this exhibition excluded such problematic aesthetic approaches as those of John Heartfield, of Hanne Darboven and Bernd and Hilla Becher, and of Ulrich Ruckriem, Lothar Baumgarten, and Hans Haacke. *German Art in the 20th Century* was an exhibition that claimed for modern German art a very particular national—even nationalist— tradition, the tradition of expressionism. It set the stage, through a series of exclusions, falsifications, and underrepresentations, particularly of the art of Weimar and that of the 1960s and 1970s, for the triumph of expressionism, now supposedly represented by an artist such as Lüpertz.[3]

In the culture at large, it is this development that has come to be associated with the term *postmodernism*—the development that repudiates the politicized, materialist practices of the 1960s and 1970s, "rediscovers" national or historical lineages, and returns us to an uninterrupted continuum of museum art. The resurgence of art that comfortably fits within the museum's space, both physical and discursive, the return of easel painting and bronze-cast sculpture, the renewal of an architecture of master builders—it is this that is now popularly known as postmodernism.

If I choose to feel paranoid, then, in front of Stirling's little joke, it is because his version of postmodernism—or Lüpertz's—stands in diametric opposition to the version I proposed when I wrote the essay "On the Museum's Ruins." Whereas their version depends on the eclipse of politicized practices, mine had depended on paying attention to them. For me, postmodernist art *was* those practices, practices such as Daniel Buren's and Marcel Broodthaers's, Richard Serra's and Hans Haacke's, Cindy Sherman's, Sherrie Levine's, and Louise Lawler's. Employing various strategies, these artists have worked to reveal the social and material conditions of art's production and reception—those conditions that it has been the museum's function to dissemble. One could add to these artists a list of others who have turned to modes of production that are altogether incompatible with the museum's space, that seek new audiences, that attempt to construct a social praxis outside the museum's precincts. In short, "my" postmodernism subjected the reigning idealism of mainstream modernism to a materialist critique and thereby showed the museum—founded on the presuppositions of idealism—to be an outmoded institution, no longer having an easy relationship to innovative contemporary art.

My encounter with these art practices suggested to me a complementary project, one that could provide historical depth to a theorization of postmodernism that proceeded from an analysis of the role of the museum in determining the production and reception of art in the culture of modernism. Although it had become a common perception that the museum—and more particularly the museum's imaginary as formulated by André Malraux—had been formative for the very way we are able to think about art, no one had undertaken to explore the institution's history in detail. We needed, it seemed to me, an archeology of the museum on the model of Foucault's analyses of the asylum, the clinic, and the prison. For the museum seemed to be equally a space of exclusions and confinements.

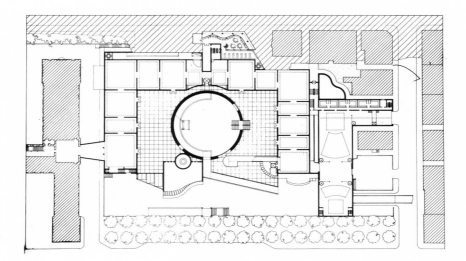

James Stirling, Michael Wilford, and Associates, Neue Staatsgalerie, Stuttgart, 1977–
1982, plan of the gallery level (courtesy
James Stirling, Michael Wilford, and
Associates).

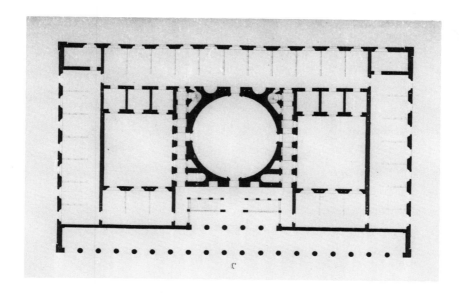

Karl Friedrich Schinkel, Altes Museum,
Berlin, 1823–1830, plan of the picture galleries, from Schinkel's *Sammlung Architektonishcer Entwürfe*, 1841–1843 (courtesy New
York Public Library).

In 1986 I essayed a contribution to such a project by investigating the paradigmatic early art museum, Karl Friedrich Schinkel's museum in Berlin. It is therefore especially interesting to me that James Stirling deliberately based his addition to the Staatsgalerie in Stuttgart on Schinkel's plan: the building that has been called a breakthrough for postmodernism has returned to the building that can be said to embody most perfectly the idea of the museum at its founding moment.

Since Hegel plays a central role in the Berlin Museum and Marx has suggested how we might construe that role, I want to summon them here: "Hegel remarks somewhere," writes Marx in the often-quoted opening sentences of the *Eighteenth Brumaire*, "that all the facts and personages of great importance in world history occur, as it were, twice. He forgot to add: the first time as tragedy, the second as farce."[4] In the historical drama of the art museum as I have written it, my tragic actor is Alois Hirt, whereas the actor in the farce I have already introduced here. His name is Markus Lüpertz, and I'll give him the first lines:

The classical museum is built like this: four walls, light coming in from above, two doors, one for those coming in, the other for those going out. All these *new* museums are often beautiful, noteworthy buildings, but, like all art, hostile to "other" types of art. They do not give simple, innocent pictures, simple, innocent sculptures a chance. . . .

Architecture should possess the greatness to present itself in such a way that art is possible within it, that art is not driven away by architecture's own claim to be art, and without—even worse—art's being exploited by architecture as "decoration."[5]

Now, Lüpertz is indeed an "innocent" painter, and he is therefore most certainly innocent of the fact that he has uttered, some 160 years later, the very criticism that Alois Hirt made of Schinkel's Berlin Museum. But in this earlier drama Hirt is far from the only actor. He is preceded in my narrative by Carl Friedrich von Rumohr.

৶

It is perhaps not generally known within the discipline of art history that von Rumohr, whose *Italienische Forschungen* is the founding work of modern art-historical research,[6] was also the author of a book on the art of cooking, three years before that of Brillat-Savarin. Learning that the title of the former's book is *Geist der Kochkunst*[7] and having tasted German cuisine, we might be tempted to think of this as another example, though rather more trivial, of the disproportion between philosophical speculation and material reality in early nineteenth-century Germany. The Germans, we might say with Marx, have only *thought* what the French have *done*.[8]

But this would be to take at face value von Rumohr's application of the word *Geist* to wurst and saurkraut, and also to miss the point of comparison between this title and that of the essay on aesthetics with which von Rumohr begins the *Italian Researches*. The latter essay is called "Haushalt der Kunst,"[9] and its hominess is polemically intended. Its target is Hegel. Just as von Rumohr pointedly chooses the big word *Geist* for his cookbook, so here he derides Hegel for what he calls "the little word 'idea,' of which the meaning, tottering between the sensuous and the mental, provides opportunity for all kinds of wild assertion, in which all manner of indeterminacy and vagueness is accommodated."[10] In the course of his immensely popular lectures on the aesthetic, Hegel would summarily dispense with von Rumohr's crude criticism,[11] and he would do so by awarding to von Rumohr's method of art-historical scholarship its own prosaic place as the provider of concrete detail to be subsumed within philosophical speculation.[12] In this respect he treated von Rumohr and von Rumohr's archenemy, the dilettante scholar Alois Hirt, with absolute parity.

Although it was Hirt who had first proposed to the king of Prussia, as early as 1797, that he build a museum to house his art collections,[13] and although Hirt would continue to be a central figure in the debates about the character of the institution until its opening in 1830, von Rumohr is generally attributed greater influence over the museum's final form.[14] Never a member of the museum commission in Berlin, von Rumohr's only direct museological task was performed in Italy, where he was sent to acquire paintings to fill in gaps in a collection that was intended to represent a complete history of art.[15] But as teacher, adviser, and confidant of many of the artists, scholars, and bureaucrats responsible for the museum, von Rumohr is said to have acted as éminence grise. I want to claim that role instead, however, for the man who gave a new significance to the color gray, the man whose most often quoted lines are the following: "When philosophy paints its gray in gray, a form of life has grown old, and this gray in gray cannot rejuvenate it, only understand it. The owl of Minerva takes flight when dusk is falling."[16] That man is, of course, Hegel.

In 1817, Karl von Altenstein was appointed Prussia's first minister of culture, and as such he became the highest authority responsible to the king for the new museum. During his very first week in office, he summoned Hegel to Berlin to take up the chair in philosophy vacated by the death of Fichte. Hegel would not disappoint the so-called philosopher-bureaucrat's expectations:[17] within two years he would publish his *Philosophy of Right,* the apologia for the status quo of the Prussian state and the text in which the lines about philosophy's gray in gray appeared. Hegel's circle of friends in Berlin came to include Alois Hirt, who taught the history of architecture at the university, and Karl Friedrich Schinkel, chief architect to the crown and builder of the museum. During the years 1823–1829, the very period of the museum's construction, Hegel delivered his lectures on aesthetics. But earlier portions of the lectures had been developed in Heidelberg, where one of Hegel's students was the young Gustav Friedrich Waagen. During their time there both men traveled to Stuttgart to see the Boisserée brothers' famous art collection, at that time the most important holdings of northern painting. This encounter was partially responsible for the subject of Waagen's first book, a monograph on Jan and Hubert van Eyck published in

1822.[18] On the strength of his scholarship in this completely new field of art history, Waagen was invited to Berlin to participate in the planning of the painting gallery and eventually to become its first director.[19]

No sooner had the museum opened than Waagen had to turn his attention to an unpleasant task, the defense of himself and his mentor von Rumohr from an attack by Hirt in a review of the third volume of von Rumohr's *Italian Researches*.[20] Using as his forum the prestigious *Jahrbücher für wissenschaftliche Kritik,* on whose editorial board Hegel presided until his death that year, Hirt took the opportunity of the review to vent his rage against the establishment of an institution that ran counter to his very conception of a museum. Although much of the polemic in Hirt's essay and Waagen's book-length reply is on the petty level of who knows his Raphael best,[21] this constitutes only the final episode in a long series of disputes between Hirt and the museum commission regarding what kind of institution the museum would be.[22] In all of these, Hirt got his way only once, and then only by default. Hirt provided the inscription for the museum's frieze, and before anyone had the time to object, the scaffolding that would have expedited a change had been pulled down.[23] And so, even today, standing in what has been renamed Marx-Engels-Platz, we read, in Latin, "Friedrich Wilhelm III founded this museum for the study of antique objects of all kinds and the fine arts."[24]

It is a measure of how seriously the Berlin Museum was deliberated in its every detail that there are no less than six memoranda about the inscription, after it was a fait accompli, and that the king ordered the philological class of the academy of sciences to render an opinion on the matter.[25] In a confidential memo to Cabinet Advisor von Albrecht, a member of the museum commission, Alexander von Humboldt wrote that the philology professor Böckh had informed Hirt that every word of his proposed inscription would have to be changed, and he was therefore horrified, on his return from a summer spent in Göttigen, to see emblazoned across the museum that very same inscription, considered, he said, ridiculous by all of Germany.[26] A portion of that ridicule involves the inscription's ungrammatical Latin,[27] but the substantial objections are to the names Hirt employed, the name *museum,* the names of the objects it would house, and the naming of the institution's purpose.

Two alternative inscriptions were proposed, one by the romantic poet Ludwig Tieck and one by the philological class, signed by Friedrich Schleiermacher. Tieck's proposal, composed in German with echoes of Latin phraseology, would rename the institution a "monument of peace for works of fine art."[28] Schleiermacher would call it a "treasury for sculpture and painting distinguished by their age and their art."[29] Both dispense with naming the institution's purpose, and this elision returns us to their rejection of the term *museum.* It is difficult now to comprehend the opposition to Hirt's choice of *museum,* both because during the thirty years of its planning it was always referred to as such and because the Berlin Museum came to be considered the most perfect embodiment of the museum concept in the nineteenth century. Why, we wonder, would anyone object to the name *museum* for the paradigmatic early art museum? Why would *monument* or *treasury* have been preferable?

The answer lies in the word *studio,* which Hirt chose to designate the museum's purpose. For when Hirt used the word *museum* and the others balked, they all had in mind the same thing, the so-called original museum of Ptolemy of Alexandria, which was indeed a place of study.[30] A residence for scholars, containing a library and collections of artifacts, the museum of antiquity was, as one of the memoranda about the inscription stated, "a kind of academy."[31] It was this identification of museum with academy that those concerned with the new institution wanted to foreclose, except, of course, Hirt.

When Tieck proposed *monument of peace* instead of *museum,* the peace he meant was that established at the Congress of Vienna, and it would therefore be adequately signified by the display of Prussian artworks returned from Paris to Berlin after the defeat of Napoleon. At that moment, in 1815, the idea of a museum took on the force of necessity for the first time in Berlin. During the wars against Napoleon the looted Prussian collections came to symbolize the national heritage rather than merely the lost property of the king, and thus Friedrich Wilhelm III bowed to the demand to make his art accessible to the public.[32] This "triumph of art for the public" is a historical development rarely interrogated by art historians, who generally think of themselves as its direct beneficiaries. Art and the public have come to be accepted as stable, rather than historically constructed, ideological categories. But when the public is understood as universal, as unfractured by class divisions, it is Hegel's idealist conception of the state and civil society, rather than Marx's critique of that conception, that is perpetuated.[33] And when art is thought to be naturally lodged in the museum, an institution of the state, it is an idealist rather than a materialist aesthetic that is served. Who is given access? what kind of access? and access precisely to what? are questions in need of asking. At the founding moment of the museum these were far from decided matters. The problem of naming the institution and specifying its purpose as a studio, a place of praxis, is only a detail that may serve to indicate the overall complexity of the issues at stake.

The initial plans for the Berlin Museum called for building a new wing on the academy of sciences to house a study collection for artists and scholars.[34] In this form the museum would have put artworks to a practical purpose, placing heterogeneous collections of objects—antique sculpture, fragments, coins, gems, plaster casts, modern paintings—at the disposal of drawing classes, scholarly investigators, and so-called *Kunstfreunde*. Such a museum would indeed have been a studio. But Schinkel, who had been commissioned to plan the extension of the academy, had a radically different idea for a museum, as was already apparent from his youthful fantasy on the subject sketched probably under the tutelege of Friedrich Gilly in 1800.[35]

In the winter of 1822 Wilhelm von Humboldt accompanied the Prussian king to Italy, where he hoped to impress upon him the symbolic significance of a great art museum for Berlin at a time when it aspired to the status of Athens on the Spree.[36] Upon the king's return, Schinkel presented him, unexpectedly, with elaborately drawn plans and detailed cost analyses for an entirely new museum, separate from the academy, to be built directly across from the schloss on the Lustgarten. The project involved much more than a new museum. Schinkel proposed a complete renewal of the very heart of Berlin, diverting the river Spree, improving shipping facilities, and rebuilding the loading docks and warehouse at the north end of what would later become the Museumsinsel.[37] The centerpiece of the plan was the starkly imposing neoclassical art museum.

The museum commission was immediately won over by Schinkel's new conception,[38] Alois Hirt's being the only dissenting voice. In his minority report attached to the commission's approval,[39] Hirt confessed that he preferred the museum in the academy. If, however, the museum should stand alone in the Lustgarten, then a great many alterations would be required. Ennumerating these changes, Hirt proceeded to oppose, one by one, every major feature of Schinkel's museum—the two-story colonnade of the south facade, raising the building on a high foundation with a grand entrance staircase, the two-story rotunda at the museum's center, and the freestanding columns of the main floor, where the sculpture was to be installed. Hirt suggested alternatives to each of these architectural elements and insisted that the museum's reduction to two simple divisions, a floor for sculpture and one for painting, would have to be reorganized to accommodate at least five departments. These would contain, in addition to painting and sculpture, plaster casts and the collections of objects formerly classed as the Antikenkabinet and Kunstkammer. In Schinkel's scheme these latter had either been banished altogether, as in the case of the casts, or relegated to small rooms in the basement, as in the case of coins, fragments, inscriptions, and so forth.[40]

Karl Friedrich Schinkel, Altes Museum,
Berlin, 1823–1830, perspective view, from
Schinkel's *Sammlung Architektonishcer
Entwürfe*, 1841–1843 (courtesy New York
Public Library).

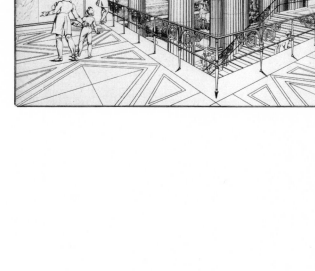

Karl Friedrich Schinkel, Altes Museum,
Berlin, 1823–1830, view of the gallery
from the main staircase, from Schinkel's
Sammlung Architektonishcer Entwürfe, 1841–
1843 (courtesy New York Public Library).

Karl Friedrich Schinkel, Altes Museum,
Berlin, 1823–1830, perspective view of the
rotunda, from Schinkel's *Sammlung Architektonishcer Entwürfe*, 1841–1843 (courtesy
New York Public Library).

Schinkel refuted Hirt's criticisms point for point and at length,[41] but the central argument is contained in a single sentence. "Such a plan," he wrote, "is a totality whose parts work so precisely together that nothing essential can be altered without throwing the ensemble into disarray." This final phrase, not precisely translatable, reads in German, "ohne aus der Gestalt eine Missgestalt zu machen."[42] Schinkel used this notion of his museum as an inviolable gestalt to argue against any objection Hirt might raise, even as it pertained to selections of paintings or the configurations of paintings on a particular wall. No change, it seems, was so minor as not to threaten the ensemble. Faced with such intractability, Hirt made one final appeal to the king, pleading that, after all, "the art objects are not there for the museum; rather the museum is built for the objects."[43] Schinkel, he argued, had subordinated the art to the architecture rather than putting the architecture at the service of art. This flew in the face of the first principle of Hirt's architectural teaching, the principle of *Zweckmässigkeit,* or what we might call functionalism.[44] Scorning what he characterized as Hirt's "trivial" notion of function or purpose, Schinkel regarded his argument as bogged down in that primitive rationalism in which contradictions are understood to be irresolvable.[45] The question for Schinkel was not what he labeled the "pure" purpose of the museum—the housing of works of art—not whether art or architecture was to be privileged, but how the antithesis could be transcended in a higher unity. Approaching the problem of the relation of art and architecture dialectically, Schinkel's museum was itself to constitute the Hegelian *Aufhebung,* or sublation, in which, as Schinkel wrote, "the destiny of art is that representation of its objects which makes apparent as many relationships as possible."[46]

A concrete example of Schinkel's attention to Hegel's aesthetics is the part of the museum that Hirt most detested, the rotunda at the museum's center. Recall that Schleiermacher wanted to designate the contents of the museum as "sculpture and painting distinguished by their age and their art." He went on to explain that this determined a twofold purpose for the museum, "on the one hand to exhibit works that are outstanding in and of themselves, and on the other hand to exhibit works that are important for a history of art."[47] Schleiermacher here alludes to the central question for idealist aesthetics, the conflict between normative beauty and the forward march of history. Hirt's attachment to the classical norm in art was inseparable from his hopes for the present. His insistence on the museum as a studio was determined by his desire for the museum to foster the rejuvenation of art through the study of classical antiquity. But for the philosophy of history such a desire could only be false nostalgia, a denial of the present's realization of historical progress.[48] It is true of antique sculpture, said Hegel, that "nothing can be or become more beautiful."[49] Classical art represents the perfect adequation of sensuous appearance and the Idea. But history has a higher goal than beautiful appearance, and so romantic art—which is to say modern, Christian art—necessarily supersedes classical art. "When romantic art takes the Christian unity of the divine and human for its content," Hegel wrote in the *Aesthetics,* "it abandons altogether the ideal of reciprocal adequacy of content and form attained by classical art. And in its efforts to free itself from the immediately sensuous as such, in order to express a content that is *not* inseparable from sensuous representation, romantic art becomes indeed the self-transcendence of art itself."[50]

Schinkel would preserve the world of classical perfection in his rotunda, designed to be the visitor's first encounter with the museum. "The sight of this beautiful and exhalted space," he wrote, "must create the mood for and make one susceptible to the pleasure and judgment that the building holds in store throughout."[51] Or, as he and Waagen stated even more succinctly in a later memorandum, "First delight, then instruct."[52] This "sanctuary," as Schinkel called it, would contain the prize works of monumental classical sculpture, chosen irrespective of historical sequence, mounted on high pedestals between huge columns, bathed in a dim light from high above. The spectators' mood thus prepared, they were ready for their march through the history of man's striving for Absolute Spirit. Far from finding on their way any indications of the material conditions of art that von Rumohr hoped to restore through his work in the archives of Italy,[53] the museum goers would find only Schinkel's gestalt, in which all relationships among objects were carefully fixed.

Perhaps we can now see why all of Germany thought Hirt's inscription ridiculous, for Schinkel's museum was no studio. It represented not the possibility of art's rejuvenation but the irrevocability of art's end. "The spirit of our world today," says Hegel in the introduction to the *Aesthetics,* "appears as beyond the stage at which art is the supreme mode of our knowledge of the Absolute. The peculiar nature of artistic production and of works of art no longer fulfills our highest need. We have got beyond venerating works of art as divine and worshipping them. The impression they make on us needs a higher touchstone and a different test. Thought and reflection have spread their wings above fine art."[54] It is again the owl of Minerva of which Hegel speaks, and Schinkel's rotunda, bathing the greatest works of classical antiquity in its twilight, prepares the spectator for the contemplation of art, which, as Hegel continues, "has lost for us genuine truth and life, and has rather been transferred into our *ideas* instead of maintaining its earlier necessity in reality. . . . Art invites us to intellectual consideration, and that not for the purpose of creating art again, but for knowing philosophically what art is."[55] It is upon this wresting of art from its necessity in reality that idealist aesthetics and the ideal museum are founded; and it is against the power of their legacy that we must still struggle for a materialist aesthetics and a materialist art.

∽

I originally presented the foregoing discussion of the Altes Museum in a session of the College Art Association chaired by Linda Nochlin and entitled "The Political Unconscious in Nineteenth-Century Art."[56] Acting as respondent for the session was Fredric Jameson, after whose book *The Political Unconscious* the session was named, and whose numerous essays on postmodernism have come to occupy a privileged position in theoretical debate on the subject. Jameson seems to have been especially struck by the rhetorical flourish with which my presentation ended, and so he rejoined,

I have to confess that I have always been uncomfortable with this kind of opposition between materialism and idealism, considered as it were as suprahistorical positions or eternal forces and tendencies and temptations. . . . I'm inclined to wonder, for instance, if "idealism" is always a reactionary position, or whether under certain circumstances—read in a precise historical context as an ideological move, with a certain determinate social and class content—it may not also have had progressive if not revolutionary consequences. . . . I guess what I'm tempted to wonder . . . about this opposition between materialism and idealism that has become a piece of unexamined Left doxa since the sixties and since Maoism is whether it is not itself just a little bit "idealistic."[57]

If in raising this objection Jameson intends to imply that the museum was, in its early history, a progressive institution, then my answer would be that it was only as progressive as the consolidation of bourgeois hegemony itself, insofar as the museum is one of those institutions that works to guarantee that hegemony within the cultural sphere. Once materialized within the museum, idealist aesthetics could be expected to neutralize the possiblity of art as revolutionary praxis or resistance. The effective removal of art from its direct engagement in social life, the creation of an "autonomous" realm for art, became the museum's mission, and it was against this that radical forms of modernist theory and practice were directed. The critique of autonomy and of its institutionalization that Peter Bürger claims for the historical avant-garde[58]—and which we must also claim for certain contemporary art practices—is thus equivalent to what I intended to signal with the phrase "a materialist aesthetics and a materialist art."[59]

Now that we stand at this end of the museum's history, it becomes clearer than ever how reactionary a position idealism has become, for the resurgence of idealism in farcical guise is so often apparent in what has come to be called postmodernism. And it may be Jameson's overdeveloped suspicion of the opposition between materialism and idealism—together with his ignorance of the genuine differences in contemporary aesthetic practices that informed the distinction that I specified with that opposition—that produces the blind spots in his own theory of postmodernism.

Jameson has elaborated that theory in a series of essays, the most complete of which appeared in *New Left Review* under the title "Postmodernism, or the Cultural Logic of Late Capitalism."[60] I do not dispute the importance of this essay's overarching ambition: to provide a theory of contemporary culture that can encompass its vast array of heterogeneous aspects by positioning them within the structure of late capitalism. It is only in Jameson's inattention to detail, the odd choices on which he focuses his analysis, that one at first feels a certain hesitation. But more serious shortcomings have also been noted. Jameson's stated goal is to describe what he calls the cultural dominant and the terms of its periodization. For this he depends on Ernest Mandel's discussion of the third phase of capitalist growth, or late capitalism. As Mike Davis pointed out in the most materially specific of the immediate replies to the essay, however, Jameson appears to resurrect the most disreputable of idealist Marxist concepts—that of a base/superstructure model of economic determinism—and, in addition, to skew Mandel's own periodization:

For Jameson it is crucial to demonstrate that the sixties are a point of rupture in the history of capitalism and culture, and to establish a 'constitutive' relationship between postmodernism, new technology . . . and multinational capitalism. Mandel's *Late Capitalism* (first published in 1972), however, declares in its opening sentence that its central purpose is to understand 'the long *postwar* wave of rapid growth.' All of his subsequent writings make clear that Mandel regards the real break, the definite ending of the long wave, to be the 'second slump' of 1974–75. . . . The difference between Jameson's and Mandel's schemes is crucial: was late Capitalism born circa 1945 or 1960? Are the Sixties the opening of a new epoch, or merely the superheated summit of the postwar boom? Where does the Slump fit into an accounting of contemporary cultural trends?[61]

A rudimentary attempt to answer Davis's questions provides us with a description and periodization of recent history somewhat different from Jameson's. Without wishing to revise and thus to retain a determinist model, it is nevertheless possible to see a relation between the liberal tolerance for radicalized art practices in the 1960s and Davis's "superheated summit of the postwar boom," as well as between the marginalization of those practices, their concealment by reactionary ones, and the "second slump of 1974–75." This revised periodization does not make cultural practices themselves reflections of economic and political conditions, but rather the relative value placed on those practices, their availability, reflects those conditions. The current revalorization of formerly discredited moments within modernism, such as between-the-wars "realism"; the suppression or misrepresentation of other, radical moments, such as the work of the Soviet avant-garde; the current claims of originality for practices that have been with us all along; the increasing marginalization of the current work of resistance—all of these phenomena can be comprehended within the terms of Davis's—in fact, Mandel's—model.

Jameson is, as one of his critics pointed out, "relentlessly Hegelian."[62] This is manifest, in part, in the sweep of his totalizing scheme, the inherent dangers of which Jameson is aware:

The more powerful the vision of some increasingly total system or logic . . . the more powerless the reader comes to feel. . . . I have felt, however, that it was only in light of some conception of a dominant cultural logic or hegemonic norm that genuine difference could be measured and assessed. . . . This has been at any rate the political spirit in which the following analysis was devised: to project some conception of a new systematic cultural norm and its reproduction, in order to reflect more adequately on the most effective forms of any radical cultural politics today.[63]

There is little question of the persuasiveness with which Jameson has carried out his project. He has, indeed, provided the backdrop against which cultural criticism can be mobilized. The problem, however, is that through his inattention to specific oppositional practices, both historical and contemporary, Jameson has reproduced the very effacement of history that he posits as a condition of postmodernism. Repeating Hegel's famous lines about philosophy's gray in gray, Jameson writes, "Dialectical interpretation is always retrospective, always tells the necessity of an event, why it *had* to happen the way it did; and to do that, the event must already have happened, the story must have come to an end."[64] Positioned within the heterogeneity of postmodernism, Jameson finds its unity in what it has displaced: modernism itself, now fully canonized and institutionalized. But he does not recognize this as a *forged* unity, forged precisely through the elimination of threatening disruptions. Sheared of its resistances and criticality, modernism appears to Jameson as it does to the institutions: a modernism predicated upon an "imperative of stylistic innovation,"[65] a modernism of centered bourgeois subjects, of *auteurs*:[66]

The great modernisms were . . . predicated on the invention of a personal, private style, as unmistakable as your fingerprint, as incomparable as your own body. But this means that a modernist aesthetic is in some way organically linked to the conception of a unique self and private identity, a unique personality and individuality, which can be expected to generate its own unique vision of the world and to forge its own unique, unmistakable style.[67]

We cannot fail to recognize in this emphasis on autonomous individuality the current idealist reconstruction of modernism; Jameson's modernism is, in fact, a variant of expressionism, and it is significant in this regard that his exemplars are van Gogh, Munch, and abstract expressionism. No room for Heartfield here either.[68] Jameson's version of modernism is all too commensurate with that of the postmodern museum.

∽

"Four walls, light coming in from above, two doors, one for those coming in, the other for those going out"—James Stirling did, in fact, provide Markus Lüpertz with the postmodern museum he wished for. In spite of the fact that Stirling's museum was commissioned for a collection of modern and contemporary art, he decided to reproduce the plan of Schinkel's museum. Evidently nothing in the practices of the art of the past 150 years suggested to Stirling that the sequence of nineteenth-century picture galleries might have to be reconsidered. For, whatever the differences between Schinkel's and Stirling's museums, and they are of course legion, those parts of the museums built for the installation of works of art are virtually identical. Indeed, in another of his clever historical jokes, Stirling continued the numbering of the galleries that open one onto another *en filade* from those of the old Staatsgalerie to which the permanent collection galleries of the new building attach. The idea of art as an uninterrupted historical continuum that can be laid out in a suite of connected rooms is never for a moment interrupted. Whatever disruptions of art as thus conceived and institutionalized there have been, current, postmodern museology will not register them as such. And the same holds for architecture itself. As one paean to Stirling has it,

It is difficult to find another building that conveys, with such perfection, a linguistic coherence and faithfulness to the syntax of the most radical *avant garde* of the Modern Movement, and this despite the use of various historical quotations. These quotations—Neo-Classical, Baroque, Corbusian, Constructivist or Loosian—have another important programmatic value:

James Stirling, Michael Wilford, and Associates, Neue Staatsgalerie, Stuttgart, 1977–
1982, permanent collection galleries (photo
Richard Bryant).

they demonstrate how eclecticism can use recent traditions, and thus, how the Modern Movement can be included in the continuum of history.[69]

I want to conclude with a consideration of the rotunda at the museum's center, for this element above all forces the comparison to Schinkel's museum. Given the very different treatment of this space in the hands of Stirling, its inaccessibility from the museum's exhibition rooms, its parodic treatment of classical sculpture, it would be hard to imagine this rotunda—or courtyard, since this one is open to the sky—as Schinkel imagined his, that is, as a sanctuary. Yet the spirit of idealism, albeit once again in farcical guise, is not so easily banished. Here is how one critic has written of Stirling's rotunda:

[The] episodes of architectural parody, brilliant as they are, rapidly recede into the background when, in awe, we call to the fore the powerful, earthy sounds which seem to emanate from the marble chords composing the circular courtyard. The ramp can be perceived as *crescendo,* the wall openings as *basso continuo* and the open sky as a chorus. But they cannot, by themselves, explain the powerful telluric sound which pervades this chamber as if it were coming from a gigantic mountain horn. This courtyard is one of Stirling's most memorable creations to date. To walk inside is to enter a magical domain where architecture is condensed to its essentials: the courtyard is a processional stage set where the spirit of architecture promenades its hieratic presence.

Not unlike Cameron—who draped a most princely garment on provincial St. Petersburg's imperial dreams—it has again taken a British architect—the greatest since Luytens—to sing with a marble voice the legitimate cravings of the German soul for a secular chamber where to celebrate a Te Deum in quiet grandeur. In this courtyard dwell together the spirits of Biedermeier and Schinkel; if ever a present-day culture were to declare that its longings have found permanent embodiment, Germany would have to point to this courtyard. It is a reformulation of the recurring archetype of

James Stirling, Michael Wilford, and Associates, Neue Staatsgalerie, Stuttgart, 1977–
1982, courtyard (photos Richard Bryant).

the Pantheon, but with a roof made of transient clouds. By providing a monumental frame for ineffable rituals, this courtyard stands as a metaphor for the spirit of the building, and so doing, raises it to the exalted level of memorable architecture.[70]

Although it would be unfair to hold Stirling accountable for the irresponsible nonsense written by his apologists, when we once again hear talk of the cravings of the German soul we must be aware that idealism is rearing its ugliest head. And in this context we should recall that the American critic Donald Kuspit has written similarly of the new German painters, including Markus Lüpertz, claiming that, because "art still has a redemptive power of transformation over history," these painters "can signal a new German freedom."

The new German painters perform an extraordinary service for the German people. They lay to rest the ghost . . . of German style, culture, and history, so that the people can be authentically new. They are collectively given the mythical opportunity to create a fresh identity. . . . They can be freed of a past identity by artistically reliving it.[71]

Anyone familiar with the rhetoric of the German Right will recognize here the cultural equivalent of the Christian Democratic government's project of "normalization." Helmut Kohl and Franz Josef Strauss also wish to "perform an extraordinary service for the German people" in a "redemptive transformation of history," carried out, for example, through such means as the symbolic reconciliation of victims and perpetrators of Nazi terror in the simultaneous ceremonies at Bitburg and Bergen-Belsen in May 1985. Among the immediate consequences of the "new German freedom"—a freedom to forget recent history—is the resurgence of xenophobia, expressed now not only against Jews but against a whole new population of *Gastarbeiter* and political refugees.

In a central text for any discussion of idealism and materialism, Marx provided the succinct rejoinder to ideas of freedom achieved through "redemption": "It is only possible," he wrote, "to achieve real liberation in the real world by employing real means. . . . 'Liberation' is an historical and not a mental act, and it is brought about by historical conditions. . . ."[72]

A less pernicious discussion of the rotunda of the Neue Staatsgalerie has suggested that its achievement is the reconciliation of classicism with modernism, insofar as Stirling has reinterpreted Schinkel's rotunda through the spatial planning of Le Corbusier. Stirling's rotunda is not the central focus of his museum, at least insofar as a museum is conceived as a space for art; it is, rather, a fissure in the museum's plan. One can ascend a ramp in front of the museum, enter the space of the rotunda, circle around one side of it, and exit on the street above without ever having entered the museum proper, whereas to enter the space from inside the museum, one must weave one's way to it as if to the center of a labyrinth. At no point does the rotunda give directly onto the art galleries.[73] Stirling's own erudite manner of signaling his reconciliation of the classical and the modern is given in a drawing of the rotunda. Employing a rendering style borrowed not from Le Corbusier but from Mies van der Rohe, Stirling montaged photographs of neoclassical sculptures onto a working drawing. The allusion brings to mind, in the present context, a trivial little essay by Philip Johnson entitled "Schinkel and Mies,"[74] in which the most facile of formalist comparisons are drawn. A "postmodernist" *avant la lettre*, Johnson was always careful to detach modernism from its material history and social project, and one cannot but wonder whether his love for Schinkel developed simultaneously and in concert with his admiration for the most vicious and fraudulent idealists of all, the National Socialists. The Nazis must, after all, be credited with being the first to build a new version of Schinkel's Altes Museum, the Haus der Deutschen Kunst by Paul Ludwig Troost.

Philip Johnson played a decisive role in the construction of the history of modern architecture as a history of master builders; he plays an equally decisive role in the reconstruction of that history in the service of postmodernist historicism. It may therefore be worth reflecting upon Johnson's "repressed" past in the context of the present discussion of these two constructions. On the scene in Germany when the Nazis came to power, Johnson's sole concern appears to have been whether or not his mentor Mies would retain his position of prominence in the fascist state, with whose general principles Johnson apparently felt no scruple:

It would be false to speak of the architectural situation in national socialist Germany. The new state is faced with such tremendous problems of reorganization that a program of art and architecture has not been worked out. Only a few points are certain. First, *Die Neue Sachlichkeit* [by which Johnson seems to have meant the Bauhaus] is over. Houses that look like hospitals and factories are taboo. But also, the row houses which have become almost the distinguishing feature of German cities are doomed. They all look too much alike, stifling individualism. Second, architecture will be monumental. That is, instead of bathhouses, Siedlungen, employment offices and the like, there will be official railroad stations, memorial museums, monuments. The present regime is more intent on leaving a mark of its greatness than in providing sanitary equipment for workers.

To Johnson, Mies was the man for the job:

Mies has always kept out of politics and has always taken his stand against functionalism. No one can accuse Mies' houses of looking like factories. Two factors especially make Mies' acceptance as the new architect possible. First Mies is respected by the conservatives. Even the Kampfbund für Deutsche Kultur has nothing against him. Secondly Mies has just won (with four others) a competition for the new building of the Reichsbank. The Jury were older architects and representatives of the bank. If (and it may be a long if) Mies should build this building it would clinch his position.

Karl Friedrich Schinkel, Altes Museum,
Berlin, 1823–1830 (photo c. 1910, courtesy
Landesbildstelle, Berlin).

Paul Ludwig Troost, Das Haus der
Deutschen Kunst, Munich, 1937 (photo by
Jaeger & Goergen for the Nazi publication
Architektur und Bauplastik der Gegenwart,
1938, by Werner Rittich).

A good modern Reichsbank would satisfy the new craving for monumentality, but above all it would prove to the German intellectuals and to foreign countries that the new Germany is not bent on destroying all the splendid modern arts which have been built up in recent years.[75]

The moral revulsion provoked by reading Johnson is not, to my mind, incommensurate with a *political* stand against the reactionary postmodernism that he has come to represent. For that moral revulsion comes from a determination to know the meaning of history. It is on this point that I am troubled by Fredric Jameson's insistence, in his essays on postmodernism, on opposing political analysis to what he calls "older left habits of formulating politico-moralizing judgments, whereby the principle activity of the left critic is conceived as just this 'deciding' whether works are progressive or reactionary, contestatory and oppositional or a replication of the system and a reinforcement of its formal ideologies."[76] Jameson is surely right to insist on a dialectical reading of postmodernism, one that can account for both its progressive and its reactionary features. But unless we also insist on a thoroughgoing attention, in the formulation of our theories, to both historical and contemporary practices that can properly be called materialist—in the clear sense given to the term by Marx—we risk contributing to the idealist conception of history and the consequent marginalization of resistance that the "other" postmodernism—that of the postmodern museum—portends.

Notes

1. Markus Lüpertz, "Art and Architecture," in *New Museum Buildings in the Federal Republic of Germany* (Frankfurt am Main, 1985), pp. 31, 33 (translation modified).

2. Facing the title page of the exhibition's catalogue is a list of the exhibition's corporate sponsors, all of them German-based companies, followed by the following notice: "The exhibition has received generous financial assistance from the Government of the Federal Republic of Germany through the Federal Ministry of Foreign Affairs. The Royal Academy of Arts is also grateful to Her Majesty's Government for its help in agreeing to indemnify the exhibition under the National Heritage Act 1980." See *German Art in the 20th Century,* ed. Christos M. Joachimides, Norman Rosenthal, and Wieland Schmied (London and Munich, 1985).

3. The exhibition's subtitle, *Painting and Sculpture 1905–1985,* indicates one of the justifications, hardly unique to this show, for its exclusions of more overtly political practices or for that matter any practices that would problematize the show's expressionist thesis: Heartfield's work is, of course, photomontage, not painting or sculpture, and although the exhibition included a very few examples of photomontage by Hannah Höch and Raoul Hausmann, German dada was deceptively represented in the exhibition by the paintings of Max Ernst and by uncharacteristic painterly works by Kurt Schwitters. In conjunction with the London exhibition, a colloquium was organized to address the exhibition and its catalogue. The proceedings appear in *The Divided Heritage: Themes and Problems in German Modernism,* ed. Irit Rogoff (Cambridge, England: Cambridge University Press, 1991); see especially Rosalyn Deutsche, "Representing Berlin: Urban Ideology and Aesthetic Practice," pp. 309–340.

4. Karl Marx, *The 18th Brumaire of Louis Bonaparte* (New York: International Publishers, 1963), p. 15.

5. Lüpertz, "Art and Architecture," p. 32.

6. Carl Friedrich von Rumohr, *Italienische Forschungen,* 3 vols. (Berlin and Stettin, 1827–1831). See also the later edition, edited and with an introduction, entitled "Carl Friedrich von Rumohr als Begründer der neueren Kunstforschung," by Julius Schlosser (Frankfurt am Main, 1920).

7. Carl Friedrich von Rumohr, *Geist der Kochkunst* (Leipzig, 1822; reprinted Frankfurt am Main, 1978).

8. "Only Germany could develop the speculative philosophy of law, this abstract and high-flown *thought* of the modern state, the reality of which remains part of another world (even if this other world is only the other side of the Rhine). Con-

versely, the *German* conception of the modern state, which abstracts from *real man,* was only possible because and in so far as the modern state itself abstracts from *real man* or satisfies the whole in a purely imaginary way. The Germans have *thought* in politics what other nations have *done*" (Karl Marx, "Critique of Hegel's Philosophy of Right. Introduction" [1843–44], in *Karl Marx: Early Writings,* trans. Rodney Livingstone and Gregor Benton [New York: Vintage Books, 1975], p. 250, italics in original).

9.   Over half of the first volume of the original edition of *Italienische Forschungen* is devoted to two essays on aesthetic theory: "Haushalt der Kunst," pp. 1–133, and "Verhältnis der Kunst zur Schönheit," pp. 134–154.

10. Von Rumohr, *Italienische Forschungen,* p. 13; cited and translated in Michael Podro, *The Critical Historians of Art* (New Haven: Yale University Press, 1982), p. 28.

11. "However often use is made of the word 'Idea' in theories of art, still vice versa extremely excellent connoisseurs of art have shown themselves particularly hostile to this expression. The latest and most interesting example of this is the polemic of von Rumohr in his *Italienische Forschungen.* It starts from the practical interest in art and never touches at all on what we call the Idea. For von Rumohr, unacquainted with what recent philosophy calls 'Idea', confuses the Idea with an indeterminate idea and the abstract characterless ideal of familiar theories and schools of art—an ideal the very opposite of natural forms, completely delineated and determinate in their truth; and he contrasts these forms, to their advantage, with the Idea and the abstract ideal which the artist is supposed to construct for himself out of his own resources. To produce works of art according to these abstractions is of course wrong—and just as unsatisfactory as when a thinker thinks in vague ideas and in his thinking does not get beyond a purely vague subject-matter. But from such a reproof what *we* mean by the word 'Idea' is in every respect free, for the Idea is completely concrete in itself, a totality of characteristics, and beautiful only as immediately one with the objectivity adequate to itself" (G. W. F. Hegel, *Aesthetics: Lectures on Fine Art,* vol. 1, trans. T. M. Knox [Oxford: The Clarendon Press, 1975], p. 107).

12. Hegel differentiates two modes of knowledge of art, empirical scholarship and abstract theory, the latter having become outmoded: "Only the scholarship of the history of art has retained its abiding value. . . . Its task and vocation consists in the aesthetic appreciation of individual works of art and in a knowledge of the historical circumstances which condition the work of art externally. . . . This mode of treating the subject does not aim at theorizing in the strict sense, although it may indeed often concern itself with abstract principles and categories, and may fall into them unintentionally, but if anyone does not let this hinder him but keeps before his eyes only those concrete presentations, it does provide a philosophy of art with tangible examples and authentications, into the historical particular details of which philosophy cannot enter" (ibid., p. 21). It is because for Hegel the Idea is present in the concrete particular that he both rejects the concept of the abstract universal ideal and places such importance on empirical scholarship, such as von Rumohr's researches. His discussion of Italian painting depends heavily on von

Rumohr. See especially *Aesthetics,* vol. 2, pp. 875ff.

13. See Paul Seidel, "Zur Vorgeschichte der Berliner Museen; der erste Plan von 1797," *Jahrbuch der Preussischen Kunstsammlungen* 49 (1928), supplement 1, pp. 55–64.

14. See, for example, the introduction by Friedrich Stock to "Rumohr's Briefe an Bunsen: Über Erwerbungen für das Berliner Museum," *Jahrbuch der Preussischen Kunstsammlungen* 46 (1925), supplement, pp. 1–76. Before choosing Wilhelm von Humboldt to head the museum commission in 1829, Friedrich Wilhelm III had considered von Rumohr for the position; see R. Schöne, "Die Gründung und Organisation der Königlichen Museen," in *Zur Geschichte der Königlichen Museen in Berlin: Festschrift zur Feier ihres fünfzigjährigen Bestehens am 3. August 1880* (Berlin, 1880), pp. 31–58.

15. For von Rumohr's own account of his role, see his *Drey Reisen nach Italien* (Leipzig, 1832), pp. 258–302. Among the many exceptional aspects of the Berlin Museum was this intention, instigated by the professional art historians among its founders (this, too, is exceptional, most early museums having been founded by artists and/or state bureaucrats), to represent a complete history of art. To that end, the Prussian royal collections were enriched by the acquisition of two major private collections, the Giustiniani in 1815 and the Solly in 1821, as well as von Rumohr's individual purchases. In the final selection for the Berlin Museum for its opening installation in 1830, 677 paintings came from the Solly collection, 73 from the Giustiniani, 346 from the king's various residences, and 111 were new acquisitions made expressly for the museum. The Prussian royal collections thus composed less than a third of the total pictures.

16. G. W. F. Hegel, *Philosophy of Right,* trans. T. M. Knox (London: Oxford University Press, 1967), p. 13.

17. It was Sulpiz Boisserée who dubbed Altenstein "der philosophierende Minister." Altenstein's post was, precisely, Minister für Geistliche- , Unterrichts- , und Medizinangelegenheiten.

18. Gustav Friedrich Waagen, *Über Hubert und Johann van Eyck* (Breslau, 1823).

19. See Alfred Woltmann, "Gustav Friedrich Waagen, eine biographische Skizze," in Gustav Friedrich Waagen, *Kleine Schriften* (Stuttgart, 1875), pp. 1–52.

20. Alois Hirt, "Italienische Forschungen von C. F. von Rumohr. Dritter Theil," *Jahrbücher für wissenschaftliche Kritik* (Berlin), nos. 112–114 (December 1831), pp. 891–911.

21. Gustav Friedrich Waagen, *Der Herr Hofrath Hirt als Forscher über die neuere Malerei in Erwiderung seiner Recension des dritten Theils der italiensichen Forschungen des Herrn C. F. von Rumohr* (Berlin and Stettin, 1832). Hirt answered Waagen's book with his own: Alois Hirt, *Herr Dr. Waagen und Herr von Rumohr als Kunstkenner* (Berlin, 1832).

22. Hirt had been an original member of the museum commission, but after a series of conflicts, especially those surrounding the Schinkel plan of 1823, he was ultimately removed from the commission in April 1826; his replacement was Waagen.

23. See Paul Ortwin Rave, *Karl Friedrich Schinkel. Berlin, erster Teil: Bauten für die*

Kunst, Kirchen, Denkmalpflege (Lebenswerk) (Berlin, 1941), p. 55. See also Beat Wyss, "Klassizismus und Geschichtsphilosophie im Konflikt. Aloys Hirt und Hegel," in *Kunsterfahrung und Kulturpolitik im Berlin Hegels, Hegel Studien,* ed. Otto Pöggeler and Annemarie Gethmann-Siefert, supplement 22 (Bonn, 1983), p. 117. My argument owns a special debt to Wyss's article, as well as to aspects of this volume as a whole. This special issue of *Hegel Studien* collects the papers presented at a symposium held in Berlin in 1981 in conjunction with the exhibtion *Hegel in Berlin,* organized by the Staatsbibliothek Preussischer Kulturbesitz in conjunction with the Hegel-Archiv der Ruhr Universität Bochum and the Goethe-Museum Düsseldorf on the occasion of the 150th anniversary of Hegel's death.

24. "FRIDERICVS GVILELMVS III STVDIO ANTIQVITATIS OMNIGENAE ET ARTIVM LIBERALIVM MVSEVM CONSTITVIT MDCCCXXIII." My English version is a translation of Hirt's own German rendering of what he intended by the Latin: "Friedrich Wilhelm III. stiftete das Museum für das Studium alterthümlicher Gegenstände jeder Gattung und der freien Künste" ("Bericht des Hofraths Hirt vom 21. December 1827 an Seine Majestät den König, über die Inschrift auf dem Königlichen Museum in Berlin," in *Aus Schinkels Nachlass. Reisetagebücher, Briefe und Aphorismen,* vol. 3, ed. Alfred von Wolzogen [Berlin, 1863], p. 277).

25. The documents pertaining to the inscription appear in Wolzogen, *Aus Schinkels Nachlass,* vol. 3, pp. 271–283.

26. Ibid., pp. 275–276.

27. "As one now reads it, one naturally connects the genitives *antiquitatis omnegenae et liberalium artium* with *studio,* and one is very surprised later to encounter *museum.* One is unsure whether the former genitives belong to it or to *studio* or should be divided between the two, or if, as appears to be intended, *studio* should be dependent upon *museum.* . . . Moreover, if *antiquitatis* is here supposed to mean the antique alone, then *omnigenae* cannot follow it. If one is to understand by this term, instead, antique objects, then one must employ the plural *antiquitates,* the singular *antiquitas* being incorrect" ("Gutachten des Staatsraths Süvern über die Inschrift am Museum vom 15. October 1827," in Wolzogen, *Aus Schinkels Nachlass,* vol. 3, p. 273).

28. "Friedrich Wilhelm III., denen Werken Bildender Kuenste, ein Denkmal des Friedens, erbauet im Jahre 1829" ("Gutachten Ludwig Tiecks über die Inschrift," in Wolzogen, *Aus Schinkels Nachlass,* vol. 3, p. 274).

29. "Fridericus Guilelmus III. Rex signis. tabulisque arte. vetustate. eximiis. collocandis thesaurum exstruxit. A. MDCCCXXVIII" ("Gutachten der historisch-philologishen Klasse der Academie vom 21. December 1827 wegen der Inschrift am Museum," in Wolzogen, *Aus Schinkels Nachlass,* vol. 3, p. 282).

30. "The word *museum* designated, among the ancients, an establishment where scholars of different fields lived together at leisure and in common communication to cultivate the sciences. Such an institute was that of Ptolemy of Alexandria, the model of today's learned societies and academies. Along with the king's residence and a great library there was an extensive apartment building for the learned soci-

ety's members, a large assembly hall, colonades and gardens" ("Bericht des Hofrath Hirt," in Wolzogen, *Aus Schinkels Nachlass*, vol. 3, p. 277).

31.   "During all of antiquity only those places that were dedicated to science and the study of science were designated by this term, never places defined as depositories for archeological and art objects. The oldest and greatest public institution that bears this name, that of Alexandria, was a unique establishment in which a specified number of scholars lived, maintained at public expense. They lived there undisturbed, pursuing the sciences with the support of a great library—thus, a kind of academy" ("Gutachten des Staatsraths Süvern," in Wolzogen, *Aus Schinkels Nachlass*, vol. 3, p. 272).

32.   See Wyss, "Klassizismus und Geschichtsphilosophie," p. 116.

33.   See Karl Marx, "Critique of Hegel's Philosophy of Right," pp. 243–257, and "On the Jewish Question," in *Karl Marx: Early Writings,* pp. 211–241.

34.   See Rave, *Karl Friedrich Schinkel,* p. 14.

35.   See ibid., p. 13.

36.   See Paul Ortwin Rave, "Schinkels Museum in Berlin oder die klassische Idee des Museums," *Museumskunde* (Berlin) 29, no. 1 (1960), p. 8.

37.   For a detailed description of the plans and costs, see "Schinkels Bericht an Seine Majestät den König vom 8. Januar 1823" and "Erläuterungen zu dem beifolgenden Projekte in fünf Blatt Zeichnungen für den Bau eines neuen Museums am Lustgarten," in Wolzogen, *Aus Schinkels Nachlass*, vol. 3, pp. 217–232.

38.   See "Konferenz-Protokoll der Museums-Bau-Commission, vom 4. Februar 1823," in Wolzogen, *Aus Schinkels Nachlass*, vol. 3, pp. 235–240.

39.   "Gutachten des Hofraths Hirt, vom 4. Februar 1823, über den neuen Entwurf des Königlichen Museums in dem Lustgarten; als Beilage zu dem Protokoll der heutigen Verhandlung der Commission," in Wolzogen, *Aus Schinkels Nachlass*, vol. 3., pp. 241–243.

40.   For a discussion of the debate over the inclusion of plaster casts in the museum, see G. Platz-Horster, "Zur Geschichte der Berliner Gipssammlung," in *Berlin und die Antike* (exhibition catalogue) (Berlin, 1979). The fact that the Antikenkabinet and Kunstkammer played no central role in the formation of the collections of the Berlin Museum belies the often-stated notion that the art museum as we know it evolved out of earlier types of collections, such as *cabinets des curiosités* and *Wunderkammern*. For the standard discussion of earlier institutions of collecting understood as prototypes of modern museums, see Julius Schlosser, *Die Kunst- und Wunderkammern der Spätrenaissance. Ein Beitrag zur Geschichte des Sammelwesens* (Leipzig, 1908). For a description of the formation and contents of the Berlin *Kunstkammer,* see Christian Theuerkauff, "The Brandenburg *Kunstkammer* in Berlin," in *The Origins of Museums: The Cabinet of Curiosities in Sixteenth- and Seventeenth-Century Europe,* ed. Oliver Impey and Arthur MacGregor (Oxford: The Clarendon Press, 1985), pp. 110–114.

41.   See "Schinkels Votum vom 5. Februar 1823 zu dem Gutachten des Hofraths Hirt," in Wolzogen, *Aus Schinkels Nachlass*, vol. 3, pp. 244–249.

42.   Ibid., p. 244.

43. "Hirts Bericht an den König vom 15. Mai 1824," in Wolzogen, *Aus Schinkels Nachlass*, vol. 3, p. 253.

44. For Hirt's architectural theories, see Alois Hirt, *Die Baukunst nach den Grundsätzen der Alten,* 3 vols. (Berlin, 1809).

45. For a discussion of the Schinkel-Hirt debate over functionalism, see Hans Kauffmann, "Zweckbau und Monument: Zu Friedrich Schinkels Museum am Berliner Lustgarten," in *Eine Freundesgabe der Wissenschaft für Ernst Hellmut Vits,* ed. Gerhard Hess (Frankfurt am Main, 1963), pp. 135–166.

46. Karl Friedrich Schinkel, "Aphorismin," in Wolzogen, *Aus Schinkels Nachlass*, vol. 2, p. 207, cited in Kauffmann, "Zweckbau und Monument," p. 138.

47. "Gutachten der historishe-philolgischen Klasse," in Wolzogen, *Aus Schinkels Nachlass*, vol. 3, p. 283.

48. See Wyss, "Klassizismus und Geschichtsphilosophie," pp. 126-127.

49. Hegel, *Aesthetics,* vol. 1, p. 517; cited in Wyss, "Klassizismus und Geschichtsphilosophie," p. 126.

50. *Hegel on the Arts* (an abridgement of the *Aesthetics*), trans. Henry Paolucci (New York: Frederick Ungar, 1979), pp. 37–38.

51. "Schinkels Votum vom 5. Februar 1823," in Wolzogen, *Aus Schinkels Nachlass*, vol. 3, p. 244.

52. "Schinkel und Waagen über die Aufgaben der Berliner Galerie" (1828), in Friedrich Stock, "Urkunden zur Vorgeschichte des Berliner Museums," *Jahrbuch der Preussischen Kunstsammlungen* 51 (1930), p. 206.

53. In fact, though both Waagen and von Rumohr worked to restore the work of art to its historical specificity, their theories of art, steeped as they were in German idealism, contradicted their aims. See Heinrich Dilly, *Kunstgeschichte als Institution: Studien zur Geschichte einer Disziplin* (Frankfurt am Main: Suhrkamp, 1979).

54. Hegel, *Aesthetics,* vol. 1, p. 10.

55. Ibid., p. 11.

56. The papers of the session appear in *The Art Journal* 46, no. 4 (Winter 1987).

57. Fredric Jameson, typescript, 1986; Jameson's remarks were not published in *The Art Journal*.

58. Peter Bürger, *Theory of the Avant-Garde,* trans. Michael Shaw (Minneapolis: University of Minnesota Press, 1984).

59. In fact, Jameson's objections to my simple opposition between idealism and materialism are rooted in his conception of the role of materialism in what he calls dialectical historiography, which is the term he uses to describe the project of Manfredo Tafuri, but which I think he also intends as the guiding principle of his own work on postmodernism. In his essay on Tafuri, there is a passage similar to his criticism of my paper: "Now the slogan of 'materialism' has again become a very popular euphemism for Marxism: I have my own reasons for objecting to this particular ideological fashion on the left today: facile and dishonest as a kind of popular-front solution to the very real tensions between Marxism and feminism, the slogan also seems to me extraordinarily misleading as a synonym for 'historical materialism' itself, since the very concept of 'materialism' is a bourgeois Enlightenment (later positivist) concept, and fatally conveys the impression of a

'determinism by the body' rather than, as in genuine dialectical Marxism, a 'determinism by the mode of production'" (Fredric Jameson, "Architecture and the Critique of Ideology," in *Architecture Criticism Ideology*, ed. Joan Ockman, [Princeton: Princeton Architectural Press, 1985], p. 60). Jameson's sense that a certain form of idealism might have progressive, even revolutionary consequences is taken from his reading of Gramsci's notion of counterhegemony, in which only the "idea" of alternative conditions can be kept alive under capitalist hegemony.

60. Fredric Jameson, "Postmodernism, or The Cultural Logic of Late Capitalism," *New Left Review,* no. 146 (July-August 1984), pp. 53–92. An earlier version of this essay is "Postmodernism and Consumer Society," in *The Anti-Aesthetic: Essays on Postmodern Culture,* ed. Hal Foster (Port Townsend, Wash.: Bay Press, 1983), pp. 111–125. See also his "Hans Haacke and the Cultural Logic of Postmodernism," in *Hans Haacke: Unfinished Business,* ed. Brian Wallis (Cambridge, Mass.: The MIT Press, 1986), pp. 38–51.

61. Mike Davis, "Urban Renaissance and the Spirit of Postmodernism," *New Left Review,* no. 151 (May-June 1985), pp. 107–108.

62. Dan Latimer, "Jameson and Post-Modernism," *New Left Review,* no. 148 (November-December 1984), p. 127.

63. Jameson, "Cultural Logic," p. 57.

64. Jameson, "Architecture and the Critique of Ideology," p. 59.

65. Jameson, "Cultural Logic," p. 54.

66. Ibid., p. 53. See also Jameson, "Architecture and the Critique of Ideology," p. 75.

67. Jameson, "Postmodernism and Consumer Society," p. 114.

68. Berlin dada represents one of the most thoroughly politicized moments in modernist aesthetic practice; Heartfield drew from that practice its most radical conclusions by positioning his work squarely within the struggle against fascism. It is therefore crucial that leftist cultural critics not dismiss dada as "trivial irreverence." See Jameson, "Hans Haacke," p. 38.

69. Oriol Bohigas, "Turning Point," *The Architectural Review* 176, no. 1054 (December 1984), p. 36.

70. Emilio Ambasz, "Popular Pantheon," *The Architectural Review* 176, no. 1054 (December 1984), p. 35.

71. Donald Kuspit, "Flak from the 'Radicals': The American Case against Current German Painting," in *New Art from Germany* (St. Louis: The Saint Louis Art Museum, 1983), p. 46.

72. Karl Marx and Frederick Engels, *The German Ideology* (New York: International Publishers, 1970), p. 61.

73. See Alan Colquhoun, "Democratic Monument," *The Architectural Review* 176, no. 1054 (December 1984), pp. 19–22.

74. Philip Johnson, "Schinkel and Mies," in *Program* (Columbia School of Architecture, Spring 1962), pp. 14–34.

75. Philip Johnson, "Architecture in The Third Reich," *Hound and Horn,* no. 7 (October–December 1933), pp. 137, 139.

76. Jameson, "Hans Haacke," p. 39.

Matisse, Morocco, Pencil on Paper

Sargent, 1990

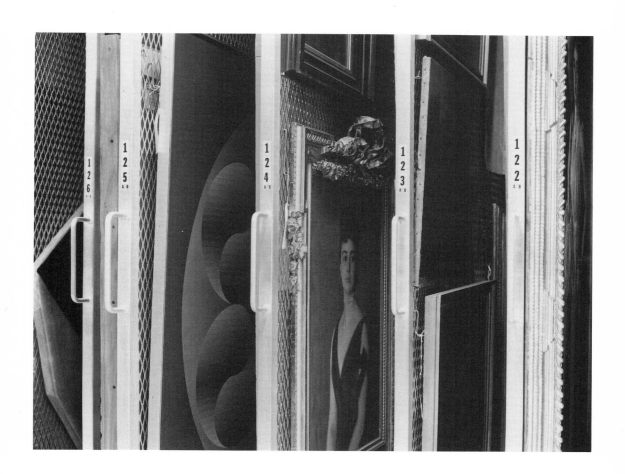

Museo del Teatro

Credits

Versions of these essays have appeared previously:

"On the Museum's Ruins." *October*, no. 13 (Summer 1980).

"The Museum's Old, the Library's New Subject." *Parachute*, no. 22 (Spring 1981).

"The End of Painting." *October*, no. 16 (Spring 1981).

"The Photographic Activity of Postmodernism." *October*, no. 15 (Winter 1980).

"Appropriating Appropriation." In *Image Scavengers: Photography* (Philadelphia: Institute of Contemporary Art, University of Pennsylvania, 1982).

"Redefining Site Specificity." In *Richard Serra: Sculpture* (New York: Museum of Modern Art, 1986).

"This Is Not a Museum of Art." In *Marcel Broodthaers* (Minneapolis: Walker Art Center, 1989).

"The Art of Exhibition." *October*, no. 30 (Fall 1984).

"The Postmodern Museum." *Parachute*, no. 46 (March, April, May 1987).

Index